Sex, Suffrage and the Stage

Leslie Hill

Sex, Suffrage and the Stage

First-Wave Feminism in British Theatre

 palgrave

First published 2018 by
PALGRAVE

Palgrave in the UK is an imprint of Macmillan Publishers Limited,
registered in England, company number 785998, of 4 Crinan Street,
London, N1 9XW.

Palgrave® and Macmillan® are registered trademarks in the United States,
the United Kingdom, Europe and other countries.

ISBN 978–1–137–50922–2 hardback
ISBN 978–1–137–50921–5 paperback

This book is printed on paper suitable for recycling and made from fully
managed and sustained forest sources. Logging, pulping and manufacturing
processes are expected to conform to the environmental regulations of the
country of origin.

A catalogue record for this book is available from the British Library.

A catalog record for this book is available from the Library of Congress.

This book is dedicated to feminist theatre makers past, present and future especially Helen Paris

CONTENTS

LIST OF FIGURES

The author and publishers wish to thank the following for permission to use copyright material:

Cover: Elizabeth Robins as title role in *Hedda Gabler*, 1891, reproduced from The Fales Collection by permission of Independent Age (independentage.org).

Abbreviations

Collections

BL   British Library

HRC   Harry Ransom Center at University of Texas at Austin

LCP   Lord Chamberlain's Plays, an archive in the BL

Individual works

Archer, William

TW93   *The Theatrical 'World' for 1893*. 1894. New York: Benjamin Blom, 1969.

TW94   *The Theatrical 'World' of 1894*. 1895. New York: Benjamin Blom, 1971.

TW97   *The Theatrical 'World' of 1897*. London: Walter Scott, 1897.

ODN   *The Old Drama and the New: An Essay in Re-valuation*. New York: Dodd, Mead & Co., 1923

Ellis, Havelock

SPSII   *Studies in the Psychology of the Sex, Volume II Sexual Inversion*. 1897. Philadelphia: F.A. Davis, 1906.

SPSIII *Studies in the Psychology of Sex, Volume III Analysis of the Sexual Impulse; Love and Pain; The Sexual Impulse in Women*. 1903. New York: Random House, 1936.

SPSVI   *Studies in the Psychology of Sex, Volume VI Sex in Relation to Society*. 1910. Philadelphia: F.A. Davis, 1921.

Hamilton, Cicely

MT   Hamilton, Cicely. *Marriage as a Trade*. London: Chapman and Hall, Ltd, 1909.

Robins, Elizabeth

WS   *Way Stations*. New York: Hodder and Stoughton, 1913.

ACKNOWLEDGEMENTS

Thanks to Lis Austin, Simon Bayly, Sarah Gorman, Adrian Heathfield, Joe Kelleher, Susanne Greenhalgh, Glen Odom, Emily Orley, Jennifer Parker-Starbuck, Susan Painter, Giulia Palladini, Elleanor Roberts, P.A. Skantze, Ioana Szeman, Graham White, Lee White, Fiona Wilke and all my new colleagues at the University of Roehampton London for welcoming me into the Department of Drama, Theatre and Performance. It's wonderful to be back in London working in such a vibrant community of artists and scholars.

Thanks also to many colleagues and students at Stanford University where I undertook much of the work on this project while serving as an associate professor in the Department of Theater and Performance Studies. I am deeply grateful to the Clayman Institute for Gender Research for making me a fellow in the 2014–15 academic year, a fellowship which helped enormously in funding some of the archival research. Thanks to Shelley J. Correll, Andrea Davies, Lori Nishiura Mackenzie, Wendy Skidmore and all at Clayman. I am also grateful to Harry Elam and the Office of the Vice Provost for Undergraduate Education at Stanford for supporting this research through a Faculty Grant for Undergraduate Research which enabled the marvellous Simone Hudson to work with me as an intern over the summer of 2015. Thanks to grad students Rebecca Chaleff, Áine Tyrrell and Angrette McCloskey who worked with me as RAs over the course of this project and extra special thanks to the brilliant Jessi Piggott who made excellent suggestions on two different drafts of the manuscript. Thanks to Lindsey Mantoan and Rebecca Ormiston, and to my talented colleagues, particularly Cherrie Moraga, Jisha Menon and Jennifer DeVere Brody, who each gave feedback on a draft chapter. Thanks to Patrice O'Dwyer and Janet Pineda for helping me with travel and receipts for research trips. Thanks to inspiring young feminist theatre-making students like Madelaine Bixler, Lillian Bornstein, Gianna Clark and Davis Leonard and to my Acting for Activists classes for their brilliant and hopeful performance interventions – you give me faith that the future is in good hands.

Grateful thanks to the staff of the following research libraries – the British Library Rare Books and Music Reading Room and Manuscripts Reading Room, the Fales Library Special Collections at NYU (especially Emily King), the Harry Ransom Center at UT Austin, the V&A Theatre and Performance Archives, the Museum of London and Green Library at Stanford. Thanks to Independent Age for permission to reproduce images from the Elizabeth Robins collection in the Fales. Thanks to Susannah Mayor at Smallhythe Place for moving the death mask of Henry Irving to get to the unpublished manuscript of Jess Dorynne's *The Surprise of His Life*.

Thanks to Nicola Cattini at Palgrave Macmillan for steering this work through publication. Many thanks to the anonymous readers whose comments and suggestions I agreed with and aimed to implement, to the benefit of the manuscript. Huge thank yous to brilliant copy-editors Cathy Tingle and Helen Sharpe for your unflagging attention to detail and many helpful suggestions. I'd also like to remember, with fondness and gratitude, the delightful Penny Simmons, who was the razor-sharp copy-editor of my last two books with Palgrave, but who has since passed away and is sadly missed.

Humble thanks to the many superb feminist theatre historians whose work this book draws on, including but not limited to: Jacky Bratton, Susan Carlson, Gay Gibson Cima, Katherine Cockin, Tracy C. Davis, Elin Diamond, Ellen Donkin, Christine Dymkowski, Sos Eltis, Penny Farfan, Linda Fitzsimmons, J. Ellen Gainor, Maggie B. Gale, Joanne E. Gates, Viv Gardner, Julie Holledge, Angela V. John, Katie N. Johnson, Joel H. Kaplan, Sally Ledger, Mary Luckhurst, Jane Marcus, Jan McDonald, Katherine Newey, Kerry Powell, Kirsten Shepherd-Barr, Margaret D. Stetz, Sheila Stowell and Catherine Wiley.

Thanks to the glorious Sarah Hosking of the Hosking Houses Trust for her generous mission to provide women writers (including me) with residencies in Church Cottage. Finally, thanks to dear friends Ali McArdle, Ross Lyons, Jen Harvie, Debbie Kilbride, Jane Sillars, Tom Arah, Caroline

Bevan, Margaret Stevenson, Philippa Barr, Emmy Minton and Claudia Barton and to my family, Virginia and Paul Resta, Jerry and Barbara Hill, Tony and Juliette Paris and Christine and Mike Paris-Johnstone for all their encouragement and support with this project. Most of all thanks to my incredible partner Helen Paris who has patiently read and commented on multiple drafts and put up with fallen women, New Women, spinsters, unwed mothers and suffragettes all over the dining table for many months.

PS Thanks to Caroline Criado-Perez who launched a campaign for a statue of a woman in Parliament Square and to Mayor of London, Sadiq Khan, who backed her campaign, calling himself 'a proud feminist'. The statue of Millicent Garrett Fawcett by Gillian Wearing will be unveiled to coincide with the centenary celebrations of women's suffrage in the UK in 2018.

INTRODUCTION

On a June afternoon in 1889 Elizabeth Robins, a young American actress newly arrived in London to seek her fame and fortune, was part of a small audience for the British premiere of a play called *A Doll's House* by a little-known author. She was there not for Henrik Ibsen, the Norwegian playwright who would later be known as the 'Father of Realism', but rather because the friend of a friend was playing the lead. Looking back on the performance that was to change British theatre and her own life so profoundly, Robins noted 'There was not a hint in the pokey, dingy theatre, in the sparse, rather dingy audience, that we were on the threshold of an event that was to change lives and literatures' (1928, pp. 9–10). Robins watched in fascination as Nora (Janet Achurch) walked out of her doll's house and shut the door behind her. Despite the humble scale of the production, the play triggered an avalanche of commentary in British newspapers. Subscribers to the widely held Victorian 'separate spheres' ideology that bourgeois women's lives should be defined by their roles as wives and mothers were stunned and outraged by a plot that ended with a woman leaving her husband and children. The progressive critic William Archer described the chain of reactions to the play as 'moral epilepsy', and observed: 'If we may measure fame by mileage of newspaper comment, Henrik Ibsen has for the past month been the most famous man in the English literary world.'[1] In Britain Ibsen, 'Ibsenism' and 'Ibsenite' became synonymous with feminism and ideas of the 'New Woman', a woman determined by self-interest rather than family obligation.

Elizabeth Robins would go on to become one of the most influential feminists of her generation, but in 1889 while male critics raged over Nora's radical choice to leave her family, what struck Robins as the most extraordinary aspect of *A Doll's House* wasn't the gender politics of the plot, but rather the realistic staging and acting of the production. As a seasoned actress who had appeared in over 300 melodramatic ingénue roles in her late teens and early twenties in America,[2] Robins immediately recognized this Ibsen production as a powerful new kind of theatre, remarking that the 'unstagey effect' made it 'less like a play than a personal meeting – with people and issues that seized us and held us, and wouldn't let us go' (1928, p. 10). The production, she reflected, 'with its little-known actors and its poverty-struck setting, was not only the most thrilling, it was the most satisfyingly done modern play I had ever seen' (pp. 12–13). For Robins, who subsequently linked her acting career closely to his works, Ibsen ushered in Modernism, naturalistic acting and explorations of female subjectivity. Looking back on her career years later in *Ibsen & the Actress*,[3] Robins admitted that initially her commitment, like that of other actresses, was to art rather than feminism.

> If we had been thinking politically, concerning ourselves about the emancipation of women, we would not have given the Ibsen plays the particular kind of wholehearted, enchanted devotion we did give. We were actresses – actresses who wouldn't for a kingdom be anything else. We got over that ...
>
> (1928, p. 31)

Robins's trajectory from an actress wanting to play great parts on the stage to a committed feminist writer seeking greater roles for women in the world at large is a microcosm of the story of first-wave feminism in British theatre. Initially, her engagement with realism yielded new models of confronting social limitations and cultivating female agency beyond melodrama's passive reliance on male rescue. Later, a more critical reflection on bourgeois power structures led Robins to break with Ibsen's focus on a Nietzschean individualism[4] in favour of more collective, grass-roots models of action coalescing around the suffrage movement. We will return to Robins briefly at the start of each chapter as a specific personal example of how one woman, a pioneer of both theatre and feminism, strove to balance the demands of artistic innovation, political progress and personal life during these groundbreaking and tempestuous years.

THE NEW DRAMA AND THE WOMAN QUESTION

In the wake of Ibsen, British artists and intellectuals eagerly contributed to the rise of a new movement, often referred to as the 'New Drama', which rejected Victorian spectacle and fast-paced episodic melodrama for the realistic staging of social problem plays, often published before they were performed. These new plays frequently focused on 'the woman question', a late nineteenth-century preoccupation with changing notions of women's roles in society. This new generation of playwrights depicted heroines as more complex, nuanced characters than the easily recognizable 'types' (whores, wives and widows) of their melodramatic predecessors. This book surveys the interwoven history of first-wave feminism and modern British theatre over a 25-year period from the London premiere of *A Doll's House* in 1889 to the outbreak of World War I in 1914. Focusing on representations of women both on stage and off during this prolific and revolutionary era in British theatre, I aim to offer a gateway overview of some of the principal ways in which writers, producers, directors and actors engaged with and influenced first-wave feminist ideas and how feminist agendas (implicit and explicit) in turn shaped the development of modern theatre.

In surveying this collection of plays and this generation of theatre makers, I highlight some of the connections between theatre texts and their writers, realizers and audiences. Exploring networks of shared memories, associations and knowledge – webs of interpersonal and cultural connections Jacky Bratton has called intertheatrical[5] – helps illuminate some of the ways in which common motifs influenced individual experiences of writing, interpreting and reading female characters in this era. Specifically, I attend to connections between theatre and politics, reading plays in relation to events in the streets, in parliament and in prisons during the feminist campaigns that became increasingly militant from 1905 to 1914. Frequent conflicts between feminism and medical science are also central to these stories. The notion of an expanded cultural field, developed by Pierre Bourdieu and others, is also useful for positioning both theatre makers and their audiences as enmeshed within a shared world of ideological and material systems of power and oppression. The clashing reactionary and progressive politics of the *fin de siècle* all feature prominently in this story, in which anxieties over gender and sexual agency are inseparable from notions of race and Empire.

I treat this 25-year period as one theatrical 'generation' in terms of its understanding of theatrical conventions and innovations, literary associations, experiences and memories of current events, and interpersonal connections between people in overlapping social circles. From a sample group of 32 of the theatre artists[6] discussed in this book, the mean year of birth is 1865, making this generation's average age a youthful 24 years old when *A Doll's House* premiered in 1889 and a middle-aged 49 years old at the outbreak of WWI. Throughout the book I use the term 'late Victorian' for the latter years of the nineteenth century and I adopt the common practice of using the term 'Edwardian' to denote the years from the turn of the century to WWI (though the reign of Edward VII only lasted from 1901 to 1910). This theatrical generation witnessed and contributed to a major shift in dramatic representations of women from melodramatic stock characters to the psychologically complex heroines of realism. They expanded on and troubled the familiar Victorian types of the 'angel in the house' as well as her foil the 'fallen woman', and introduced controversial new models of womanhood including the educated 'New Women', independent working women, defiant unwed mothers and militant suffragettes. All of these theatrical representations contributed to shaping emerging ideas of 'the modern woman' in the twentieth century.

The chapters in this book chart theatrical representations of women from tragic 'fallen women' who suffer or die for their sins to New Women (frequently comedic) who are mocked as 'unsexed', to more complex and nuanced interrogations of female characters and feminist issues during the height of the suffrage campaign. The first two chapters focus on late-Victorian plays about 'fallen women' and 'New Women', overlapping but not interchangeable female character types linked by their 'unfeminine' assertions of personal agency. Women in plays from the 1890s are primarily framed by individual, romantic concerns – their transgressions are the products of misguided love, moral weakness, selfish desires or an inflated sense of (masculine) entitlement. Their punishments – suicide and banishment – are likewise personally borne and sometimes self-inflicted. Chapters 3, 4 and 5 concentrate on early twentieth-century plays, looking at ways in which Edwardian dramatists critiqued and re-imagined women's roles as single women (spinsters), wives, students, workers, mothers and political activists. In these plays, women's suffering is framed as sexual exploitation within larger socio-economic models, presenting women as victims of systematic oppression, while still trying to represent possibilities for active individual female agency – a tension that often proved challenging for playwrights to negotiate. Though the suffrage movement, the most prominent of the early feminist movements, is situated at the end of the book, I treat it as a concourse between different ongoing feminist campaigns and the theatre rather than as an end point. Suffragists valorized individual struggle within the context of many larger interconnected political issues. The phrase 'the personal is political' is strongly associated with second-wave feminism, but the concept was also a major guiding force in first-wave feminism and paired well with the emergence of theatrical realism which, unlike the plot-driven world of melodrama, grappled with wider social problems through a tight focus on the psychology of individual characters. Throughout the chapters I have aimed for a middle course between narrative and analytic modes to make the book accessible to student readers without prior knowledge of this theatrical era or the different branches of first-wave feminism.

First-Wave Feminism

First-wave British feminists, though many of them were middle class and most of them were white, drew from and contributed to a long line of collateral benefit in human rights activism reaching back into the past and forward into the future far beyond the middle-class drawing rooms of Victorian ladies. British women's key roles in the Abolitionist movement in the late eighteenth and early nineteenth centuries[7] served to politicize women and develop their critiques around systems of oppression, analyses which they later turned on the institution of marriage, contract and property laws, the inequities of the sexual double standard, and the systematic suppression of women's education and employment. In speaking out against the physical violence, sexual abuse and unpaid labour inflicted on slaves in the colonies, British women began to draw parallels with their own position under British law including the inability to own property (if they were married), a lack of custody over their own children (exclusive to fathers if married) and a disenfranchisement from representation in government. Women developed these critiques of power and oppression during the ascent of the British Empire, the largest empire in history in which upper- and middle-class white British men ruled over roughly a quarter of the mostly non-white population of the globe. In reframing men as their legal and political masters rather than simply in familial terms as their husbands and sons, women were identifying with colonial oppression and challenging the legitimacy of imperial power. Reading these histories from the other side of second-wave feminism, Women of Colour feminism and third-wave feminism requires some delicacy on our part in not rejecting or flattening the historically specific coalitions and projects of this era. In terms of the critical question of who they are speaking for, women in the years covered by this study have moved from speaking for the rights of colonial slaves abroad to speaking on behalf of themselves and other women at home.

In Britain first-wave feminism evolved slowly from the early 1830s, in the wake of the abolition of slavery in the colonies in 1833, to the 1850s when it became more coordinated through the efforts of the Langham Place Group,[8] to the formalization of the women's suffrage campaign in 1866. By the turn of the century 'the woman question' was a mainstream topic of debate and women's movements were a national political force, supported by cross-class coalitions, though still led largely from the middle class. First-wave feminists fought major battles for equal contract and property laws, for education reform, for expanded employment opportunities and for the right to vote. They also challenged the legal and cultural manifestations of the sexual double standard through reform campaigns targeted at legislation on prostitution and sexually transmitted diseases. First-wave feminism laid the foundations for second-wave feminism's campaigns on reproductive rights, notions of consent and sexual freedoms. Many first- (and second-[9]) wave feminists who started with broader political aims intersecting with class and race ultimately chose gender loyalty as a triage strategy in the hopes of gaining political power in order to make their voices heard on a range of issues. Even within the women's movement, focus areas were often tactically compartmentalized for efficacy and women who led reform campaigns on one feminist issue sometimes declined to publicly advocate for others, as noted by suffrage organizer Ray Strachey in her memoir *The Cause:*

> It was obvious, of course, to all the suffragists that the education move-
> ment and the medical women's movement were all part of the same thing.
> But each of these reforms was separate, and all were battling against
> prejudice and obstruction; and it seemed rather dangerous to let the
> general public see what a close connection there was between them all.
>   (1928, pp. 44–45)

Education reformer Emily Davies also remarked on the strategy of feminist compartmentalizing, defending her tactic of steering clear of suffrage politics (which she supported privately) with the justification, 'The scoffers don't see how much is involved in improved education, but they are wide awake about the Franchise' (quoted in Stephen, 1927, p. 109). After suffrage was attained, some feminists, like Elizabeth Robins, turned their efforts specifically to issues of racial injustice,[10] indicating that though activists often worked on human rights campaigns one at a time, they carried a more complex range of concerns than their partitioned efforts necessarily reveal at first glance.

First-wave feminists weren't simply seeking special rights and privileges for middle-class ladies; they were openly challenging the legitimacy of British law and the right of British men to govern the voiceless. This was a threat not only to gender norms, but to the white heteropatriarchal rule of the governors of the Empire. By delegitimizing their rule over women and children, first-wave feminists destabilized notions of paternal white fathers benignly ruling over the 'children' of their imperial colonies.[11] Mohandas Gandhi, who visited London in 1906, was profoundly moved by the civil disobedience of suffragettes and their willingness to serve prison sentences and hunger strike. Gandhi went on to lead the overturn of British rule on the Indian subcontinent, which in turn inspired Martin Luther King's techniques for non-violent social change in America, which in turn inspired the Anti-Apartheid Movement in South Africa and the Arab Spring. LGBTQ activists also trace a direct lineage to first-wave feminism. As Rebecca Solnit observes, in reference to this ongoing chain of human rights activism, 'We are carried along by the heroines and heroes who came before and opened the doors of possibility and imagination' (Solnit, 2017). Thirty years before the first British women won the right to vote,[12] the Scottish novelist Mona Caird, who had already been working on the suffrage campaign for ten years, wrote, 'Every good thing that we enjoy today was once the dream of a "crazy enthusiast" mad enough to believe in the power of ideas' (1888, p. 197). Though their battles aren't our battles, and their world isn't our world, their victories help to make our victories possible.

In the chapters that follow, class critique is much more prevalent than any other type of intersectional critique both in feminist political writing and in the plays examined. Some critiques of heteronormativity are found in the feminist writings and plays covered, especially in Chapters 2, 3 and 4. Direct racial critique is conspicuous by its absence, except in relation to the blatantly racist agenda of the eugenics movement and the derogatory medicalized narratives of race and female sexuality discussed in Chapter 4. Though feminists used arguments developed in the anti-slavery campaign to critique British marriage as bondage and compare British wives to property, in terms of their legal status they did not write specifically about how the legal reforms they fought for might impact British women of colour differently than white women; demographically, this is an issue many were blind to since the immigrant population at this time was primarily Irish and Eastern European Jewish.[13] It would take two to three more generations before second-wave feminists would complete the circle between gender, class and racial oppression, from the anti-slavery campaigns to first-wave feminism to the labour movement into intersectional second-wave feminist work led by women of colour.

Unlike the American suffrage movement, in which women like Sojourner Truth, Mary Church Terrell and Ida B. Wells[14] played prominent roles, few women of colour had a high-profile presence in the British campaign.[15] A notable exception was Princess Sophia Duleep Singh,[16] prominent largely because her title was royal and her godmother was Queen Victoria, underscoring the emphasis on class over race in the British suffrage movement.[17] It is important to note that 'white' in this era includes many subgroups which were classed as degenerate or atavistic based on a range of determinates: by geographic origin or nationality, such as the Irish; by religion or culture such as Jews; by sexual orientation or activity such as homosexuals or women who were sexually active outside marriage; or by circumstance, trade or mental and physical health, such as the unemployed, prostitutes, alcoholics or mental patients. Many of the playwrights of this era belong to these subgroups.[18]

Mid-Victorian anthropologists divided races by common languages and cultures as well as by geographical origin or physical characteristics, conflating race and culture[19] and giving race a much broader meaning than it usually has today. Significantly for the highly stratified Victorians and Edwardians, the porous nature of the term 'race' at this time allowed it to encompass class distinctions. When feminist authors speak of the experiences of British women we can usually infer they are speaking of the white majority, but it does not always follow that they are thinking in terms of ethnicity; most often when they differentiate between individual women's experiences, they are thinking in terms of class. For the majority of upper- and middle-class social reformers, the working class *was* another race. Many first-wave feminists were specific about the potential cross-class benefits of feminism because they had personal experience of the power structures of British class and gender. In the late nineteenth century it was estimated that at least twenty thousand salaried and half-a-million voluntary women from the upper- and middle-class West End of London worked among the poor of the East End (Walkowitz, 1992, pp. 53–54). As well as organized charity work, upper- and middle-class female social reformers sometimes went 'slumming' to experience conditions first-hand and report back with recommendations.[20] While women in the anti-slavery movement campaigned on behalf of people they had never met in places they had never been to, Victorian and Edwardian feminists had frequent contact with working-class women through their philanthropic activities. Unfortunately, their well-intentioned but sometimes patronizing charity work often served to heighten rather than break down class divisions.

THE PROJECT

The selection of texts covered in this book is not comprehensive. Neither are the plays included here representative of literary or theatrical success; rather, I have selected plays that, considered together, provide a mosaic of key feminist issues and representations of women on stage in this era. Some of the dramatists' works, like Oscar Wilde's fallen woman plays, were popular in their day and remain well known today; other works like Clotilde Graves's comedies achieved great box office success, but are largely forgotten now; George Bernard Shaw's early problem plays were banned by the censor so their commercial runs skipped a generation, making them more familiar today than they were to contemporary audiences. Other works like Jess Dorynne's *The Surprise of His Life* were fringe productions then, and are archival relics now. Though I aim to give female dramatists at least an equal voice across the chapters, many of the more widely accessible works from this era are by male authors. Many of the works by female playwrights like Janet Achurch, Florence Bell, Constance Fletcher and Dorothy Leighton are still only available in archives, but happily more and more of them are being published in anthologies like Maggie B. Gale and Gilli Bush-Bailey's collection *Plays and Performance Texts by Women 1880–1930* (2012), Tracy C. Davis's *The Broadview Anthology of Nineteenth-Century British Performance* (2012) and the suffrage play anthologies of Dale Spender and Carole Hayman (1985), Susan Croft (2009) and Naomi Paxton (2013). Many more 'lost' or neglected plays by women will, I hope and trust, become more widely available to readers in the years to come and this book is part of that project.

I've spent most of my career to date as a theatre maker, not a theatre historian. A belief in the theatre's unique capability to bring groups of people together in the same time and space to interrogate power and to imagine things as they might be is what drives me as a theatre maker as well as what has inspired me to work on this historical project. Feminism, which is repeatedly pronounced 'post', dead, irrelevant and/or failed, continues to accomplish important victories all over the world as it is shaped by new women, men, trans and non-binary activists who take up its work in myriad different ways in coalition with many different groups and causes. As we mark the centenaries of voting rights for women in countries around the world, the most fitting tribute we can give suffragists is to remember that the vote was always envisioned as a means, not an end, to claim the power to radically reshape our world. I offer this book as a recitation of milestones and a call to arms for the next generation as they craft their own activist and theatre-making practices in response to issues they are passionate about. The call is as urgent now as it was then.

CHAPTER 1

The Angel in the House and the Fallen Woman

In the winter of 1889 Elizabeth Robins was still struggling to break into the London theatre scene. Living in a boarding house and saving precious coins by walking long distances across London instead of taking the bus, she wore holes in her shoes, and suffered frequent colds. Oscar Wilde encouraged her to stay in England, took her under his wing and helped her get an agent. Some of the advice he gave over tea and cigarettes, however, may have done more harm than good to her career. Wilde advised his protégée against taking the lead she was offered in *A Fair Bigamist*, a woman-centred play written by a woman,[1] and instead directed her towards male actor-managers, introducing her to the celebrated and powerful Herbert Beerbohm Tree. Ten years older and married, Tree flirted with her career hopes for months but while he frequently sent her box seats to watch *him* perform, the parts he promised *her* never materialized.

In January, Robins was barely making ends meet playing the young widow Mrs Errol[2] in the saccharine drama *Little Lord Fauntleroy* at the Opera Comique (on Saturday matinees only). Robins's luck seemed to be changing when the successful playwright Arthur Wing Pinero admired her performance and invited her for a meeting. During their interview she described a preference for unconventional parts, and he fixed her 'line' as 'sympathetic Outcasts' (Robins, 1940, p. 176). As the company for his new play, *The Profligate*, was already engaged, he could only offer her the tantalizing but thankless work of understudying the coveted 'fallen woman' role of Janet Preece. The play ran for months, but never with Robins in the part she so desperately wanted to play. Registering her frustration, Robins confided to her diary, 'I would be made in London if I could play that part' (p. 183).

The vexations of Robins's early London career shines a light on some of the complexities of the Victorian double standard in relation to actresses. Codes of behaviour for men like Tree who owned theatres were infinitely freer and less dangerous than for the women who sought work in them. Being an actress, a profession still sometimes associated with prostitution, relied on pleasing men to get work and made keeping one's reputation tricky. Tree propositioned Robins to become his mistress and in refusing his sexual advances she forfeited the parts she might have played at The Haymarket. Robins likened the shock of the episode to being stung by a hornet, extrapolating the general precariousness of life for single actresses from the experience: 'I knew now how this might come to anybody, since it had come to me' (p. 243). This was by no means the only unwelcome sexual attention Robins received from men in her professional circle. In exasperation, she sometimes resorted to brandishing a pistol to deter them.[3] George Bernard Shaw punished her for rejecting his advances – mocking her as 'Saint Elizabeth' he did not cast her in his plays. Actresses, Robins frankly acknowledged, had to deal with 'considerations humiliatingly different from those that confronted the actor' (1932, p. 33). As a single woman, Robins also frequently experienced anonymous sexual harassment in public. A woman on her own, she wrote, could not 'be without fear' even in the open street in broad daylight and was not safe 'even in St. Paul's Cathedral'.[4] But while carefully guarding her personal reputation off stage, Robins knew that playing parts like the mawkish Mrs Errol would not make her a star; on stage she needed a part like the sexually transgressive Janet Preece to 'make' her. Like many women of her generation, Robins was caught somewhere between the moral standards of the sexually pure Victorian 'angel' and London theatre's *fin de siècle* fascination with the 'fallen woman'. To be an actress with a future, you needed to play a woman with a past on stage without becoming a woman with a reputation off stage.

THE ANGEL IN THE HOUSE AND THE FALLEN WOMAN

There's nothing left of what she was;
Back to the babe the woman dies,
And all the wisdom that she has
Is to love him for being wise.
                    (Patmore, 1890, p. 123)

'Separate spheres' had become a widespread middle-class ideology in the mid-Victorian period, famously typified in Coventry Patmore's wildly popular 1854 poem *The Angel in the House*,[5] which glorified the woman's total evacuation of self ('There's nothing left of what she was') in sub-servience to her husband. In upper- and middle-class 'separate spheres' ideology men and women didn't simply perform different gender roles, they inhabited different worlds: his the temporal and public, hers the spiritual and domestic.[6] The prominent philosopher and sociologist Herbert Spencer rationalized the gender and class divisions of Victorian society by describing it as a body with upper- and middle-class men ruling from the head, upper and middle-class women exerting benign influence from the heart and working-class men and women performing the menial work of the hands, while criminals, prostitutes and paupers made up the nether regions.[7]

In step with the new evangelical movement of the nineteenth century, the woman's domestic sphere was conceived of as the centre of purity and the higher sentiments while the male sphere encompassed the mate-rial world of industry and commerce. The Victorian man was defined in terms of public action, the woman in terms of domestic influence achieved modestly through piety, self-sacrifice and motherhood. From early in Victoria's reign, women were constructed as the moral guardians of the home and, by extension, protectors of the moral worth of the nation.[8] Estranged from paid labour, middle-class women were increasingly called on to turn their energies to softening the ugly aspects of industrial cap-italism through their angelic influence on men.[9] For women to exercise influence in this paradigm, they had to renounce independent public action, putting them in a complex and often contradictory relationship with power in the temporal world.

The rhetoric of 'separate spheres' advice given through books, pam-phlets, poetry, speeches and sermons was not, of course, as nuanced as women's actual lives,[10] but there were some very real social restrictions on what middle-class women could and couldn't do without ruining their reputations: pre-marital and extra-marital sex or romance were for-bidden, education was limited, and earning money was frowned upon. Employing notions of their angelic purity and talent for caretaking, some women used 'separate spheres' logic to extend their influence into the public realm through casual and organized charity work.[11] Much of this public work was rendered invisible, therefore permissible, through the nineteenth-century definition of work as a paid extra-domestic activ-ity (a definition that continues to make vast swathes of primarily female labour invisible). By the 1890s, public spaces like department stores,[12] women's colleges and theatres provided women with more access to the modern freedoms of the cities, blurring some of the boundaries of male and female spheres.

As more middle-class women benefited from legal and educational reforms, taking advantage of new opportunities for independence, a backlash rose to counter the instability of changes to social convention. The theatre became not only a physical site where men and women both participated publicly as consumers of culture, it became an ideological battleground where female transgressions could be thrillingly observed and symbolically punished, mining the excitement of a new order while pandering to the conventions of the old. Female characters in late-Victorian theatre were frequently polarized as either pure 'angels' or tainted 'fallen women', outcast from society through sexual transgression. As a dramatic character the fallen woman unsurprisingly held a much greater fascination for dramatists than the angel. Sin has always been more marketable than virtue and the *fin de siècle* obsession with 'the woman question' made issues of women's independence and sexual morality paramount. Because chastity was regarded as a woman's highest virtue, and because Victorians didn't draw clear distinctions between romantic seduction and sexual assault, the term 'fallen woman' could encompass anything from a deflowered ingénue to an unwed mother to a mistress, a courtesan, a prostitute or a victim of sexual abuse. In theatre, the fallen woman's fate was often a shame-driven suicide which allowed the audience to be titillated by her past and pity her wretched remorse without having to worry about her future. Fallen woman characters appear frequently in problem plays of this era, peaking in the mid-1890s in works such as Oscar Wilde's *Lady Windermere's Fan* (1892), Arthur Wing Pinero's *The Second Mrs Tanqueray* (1893), Janet Achurch's *Mrs Daintree's Daughter* (1894) and Constance Fletcher's *Mrs Lessingham* (1894). Variations on the fallen woman theme continued into the twentieth century with plays such as Clotilde Graves's *London Vendetta* (1906), Elizabeth Robins's *Votes for Women!* (1907) and Githa Sowerby's *Rutherford and Son* (1912).

Fallen women often share characteristics in common with the New Woman and many female characters in this period are both 'fallen' and 'New'. (Readers unfamiliar with the term 'New Woman' will find a detailed description at the start of the next chapter.) The fallen woman characters discussed in this chapter are sexual transgressors, while the next chapter focuses on social transgressors who are often, but not always, sexually active. Sos Eltis, whose book *Acts of Desire* is the consummate study of the stage history of the fallen woman, cites first-wave feminism's campaigns for expanded rights and opportunities for women as causative factors in the ubiquity of fallen woman plays at the turn of the twentieth century (2013a, p. 115). When linked to the independent figure of the New Woman, the fallen woman could serve as a reactionary anti-feminist warning, dramatizing the perils awaiting women who ventured beyond their proper sphere and took sexual liberties reserved for men.

PROFLIGATE MEN AND FALLEN WOMEN

I open this survey of the fallen woman where Robins started as an understudy – with Pinero's play *The Profligate*. Its two female leads are incarnations of the Victorian 'fallen woman' and 'angel' dichotomy as encountered through the past and present of the play's protagonist, Dunstan Renshaw, who seduces one and marries the other. The play opens on the morning of Dunstan's wedding to the angel, Leslie Brudenell. Dunstan calls in at the office of Leslie's solicitor, Hugh Murray. Dunstan, who is hung-over if not drunk, brags openly about his technique for seducing schoolgirls. Having learnt of the groom's disreputable past, Hugh decides he cannot in good conscience attend the wedding, a moral stance the other men find ridiculous: under the widely accepted terms of the double standard, there is no such thing as a 'fallen man'. As Dunstan heads for the registry office, the fallen woman, Janet Preece, comes to Hugh's office to seek help in tracking down the man who seduced and abandoned her. Though Janet doesn't know his real name (he used a seducer's alias), she makes a precise forensic sketch of Dunstan. Too late to save Leslie from marrying the profligate, Hugh condemns Dunstan for his treachery to both women and predicts that Leslie will find her 'heart a granary bursting with the load of shame your profligacy has stored there' (p. 39).

The second and third acts take place in the Renshaws' Florentine honeymoon villa. Under Leslie's angelic influence the profligate man has 'lost his dissipated look' and become 'gentle, watchful and tender' (p. 46), a change he acknowledges, saying 'I married her, as it were, in darkness; she seemed to take me by the hand and lead me out into the light' (p. 67). By extraordinary coincidence Janet arrives at the Renshaws' villa in a state of collapse with no knowledge that her seducer lives there – Dunstan is conveniently out of town for a few days. Leslie, who has no idea that Janet is her husband's discarded lover, nurses her back to health. After lying in a faint for three days, Janet wakes and marvels that she has 'died and come into a beautiful new world' where Leslie 'is the Angel' (p. 75). In this new world, Janet even imagines she might marry Leslie's brother Wilfrid who, unaware of her past, has fallen in love with her. When Dunstan returns, he and Janet face each other in horror, their secret revealed. The act ends with the disillusioned wife Leslie commanding Dunstan to 'Go!' (p. 104).

Dunstan returns to London, despairs of a reconciliation with his wife and drinks poison just before Leslie returns to him with words of redemption, 'We are one and we will make atonement for the past together. I will be your Wife, not your Judge' (p. 123). In Pinero's original version the play ends with Leslie's horrified realization that Dunstan is already dead. On the advice of actor-manager John Hare, however, Pinero stopped short of killing Dunstan in the London premiere production. Instead, the curtain closes on the conciliatory stage picture of a husband kneeling at his wife's side as she bows her head down to his. Though the profligate dies in one version and lives in the other, he is redeemed in both versions by his wife's forgiveness in keeping with the social norm of the double standard, where men err and women forgive. The subplot reinforces this: while Leslie forgives her husband, she decidedly prefers that the fallen woman Janet should emigrate to Australia rather than marry her brother.

Pinero scored his greatest commercial and critical success in 1893 with *The Second Mrs Tanqueray,* which established him as the most popular dramatist in England as well as making its leading lady, Stella Campbell (popularly known as Mrs Pat[13]), a star. A comparison of Pinero's earlier 'fallen man' play with this fallen woman play clearly illustrates the Victorian double standard: *The Profligate* asks if a man with a dissolute past can be redeemed and answers 'Yes'; *The Second Mrs Tanqueray* asks if a woman with a sexual past can be redeemed and answers 'No'. *The Second Mrs Tanqueray* opens on a heartily masculine scene as the widower Aubrey Tanqueray entertains friends to dinner at his chambers at the Albany[14] and confides his plan to marry a courtesan, Paula Rey. The other men tell him frankly that the marriage is a terrible idea. The act ends with Aubrey unexpectedly receiving word that his daughter Ellean is planning to leave her convent to come and live with him, introducing the great moral conflict – can he be a good father to a pure daughter if he is married to a woman with a past?

The Tanquerays' domestic life, an exile in the country necessitated by Paula's past, proves predictably unhappy for all of them: cut out of society, Paula is bored; the convent-bred Ellean instinctively shrinks from her tainted stepmother; and Aubrey lives in fear of Paula's corrupting influence on his daughter. To get her away from Paula, Aubrey allows Ellean to accompany a society friend on a trip to France, where she falls in love with the dashing Captain Ardale who accompanies the party back to England to ask for her hand in marriage. Paula discovers with horror that her stepdaughter's suitor is one of her own former lovers. Paula bitterly comments that Ellean 'could forgive *him* easily enough – but *me*! That's just a woman!' (p. 132). Ellean, more icy than angelic, does eventually thaw and attempt to show sympathy to the fallen woman, but she arrives too late, after Paula has jumped to her death from her bedroom window. Ellean ends the play by taking the blame upon herself: 'Killed – herself? Yes – yes. So everybody will say. But I know – I helped to kill her. If I had only been merciful!' (p. 137). The curtain falls without Aubrey offering to shoulder any of the blame, again conforming to the Victorian paradigm that it is for men to err and women to forgive.

The play was a huge critical and a popular success. The *Illustrated London News* called it 'without doubt the most original and startling piece of work which has been seen on the English stage in our time' (3 June 1893). *Punch* claimed that it marked 'an epoch in our dramatic annals' (10 June 1893), though more conservative critics worried that the play was not suitable viewing for young unmarried women.[15] William Archer pronounced the play 'modern and masterly' (TW93, p. 131), though he conjectured that a less melodramatic, more open-ended closing scene might have been bolder and more artistic, leaving the audience to forecast the Tanquerays' fates for themselves (p. 135).

Stella Campbell's performance as Paula, widely lauded as a work of genius, greatly contributed to the play's success. Indeed, in *The Saturday Review*, Shaw gave all the credit for the play's success to her acting and next to none to Pinero's writing (23 February 1895). Significantly, Campbell did not come from a theatre family and hadn't cut her teeth in the acting traditions and theatrical effects of melodrama with its semi-hysterical repertory of body language, 'the facial grimace, eye-rolling, teeth gnashing, heavy sighs, fainting, shrieking, shivering, choking' and hysterical laughter (Diamond, 1997, p. 10). For Campbell, 'a declamatory style, exaggerated gesture, rhodomontade in any form [were] ridiculous' (Campbell, c. 1925, p. 102). Campbell's inexperience with conventional stage formulas, gestures and tableaux gave her greater agility with realism where the focus was on the psychological complexity of character. 'I wanted nothing to interfere with the fundamental atmosphere of beauty, simplicity, and truth. Whatever the gamut, it must be within reasonableness, and the "bottom rock sane"' (pp. 102–03). As an actress ten years younger than Pinero and her co-star George Alexander, her sense of truth and beauty weren't always in line with theirs, causing her to sometimes feel 'snubbed' (p. 66) in rehearsals or find their suggestions anathema to her sense of realistic behaviour. In one scene, Pinero instructed Campbell/Paula to melodramatically sweep the ornaments off the top of the piano in a rage, to which Campbell says she 'replied in horror, "Oh, I could not make her rough and ugly with her hands, however angry she is"' (p. 69). The Alexanders insisted that Paula's hair remain stiffly quaffed throughout the play (Alexander's wife was Campbell's dresser) while Campbell 'argued that no woman could go through four acts of such tumultuous passions, eventually committing suicide, with a tidy head' (p. 69). In rejecting Pinero's grand gesture of rage on one end of the scale and Alexander's fastidious costume convention on the other, Campbell calibrated her performance within a gamut of 'reasonableness' more aligned to a contemporary woman's understanding of what was 'bottom rock sane' than prevalent theatrical conventions.

Though acting had become a more respectable profession for women towards the end of the century, no longer as casually equated with prostitution, parts like Paula Tanqueray still came at some cost to an actress's reputation. Though it made her a star, Campbell recalls that many held the attitude that she couldn't play the part so well if she 'did not know something of that kind of life' (p. 82), giving rise to rumours of a shady past and alcoholism (p. 90). In a curious twist of fate, two years after the play's success, George Alexander was arrested for soliciting a prostitute, causing a temporary scandal. Ironically, Pinero was called as a character witness.[16] Though such a blow to an actress's reputation would have been fatal, Alexander emerged from the incident without lasting damage to his social standing and went on to be knighted in 1911, illustrating the robust power of the double standard in both life and art.

In a turning point that could have resulted in a very different career for Elizabeth Robins, Pinero originally engaged her to play Paula Tanqueray only to ask her to drop her contract to make way for the less 'intellectual',[17] more emotive Campbell before rehearsals started. In a magnanimous letter

relinquishing her contract and congratulating Campbell, Robins acknowl-
edged the career sacrifice she was making, writing, 'There is to my mind
no woman in London so enviable at this moment, dear savage, as *you*'
(Campbell, c. 1925, p. 65). A few months later, Robins persuaded John
Hare to produce another fallen woman play, *Mrs Lessingham* by Constance
Fletcher,[18] and helped to substantially rewrite the final act for production.
(Though produced in 1894, *Mrs Lessingham* was actually written before
The Second Mrs Tanqueray, as William Archer attests in his review.[19]) The
play is most remarkable for its depiction of female sympathy between the
'fallen' and the 'pure' female characters, though this womanly compassion
fails to help the fallen woman achieve a happy ending. Gladys Lessingham,
played by Robins,' (Fig. 1.1) is a married woman who leaves a brutal
husband to live abroad with a young barrister, Walter Forbes. Their life
together lasts for five years until, resenting the sacrifices he has made
for her, Walter decides to return to England and his career without her,
remarking cynically, 'I've learned what it means to offer a woman your life
and be called upon for the small change every ten minutes' (p. 15). The
play begins five years after Forbes abandons Gladys. Gladys has just been
widowed and now, finally free to remarry, she is eager to reunite with Walter
in England, but discovers that he is engaged to a wealthy young aristocrat.
On learning of their past, Walter's fiancée Lady Anne convinces him to do
the honourable thing and marry Gladys, resulting in an unhappy marriage.
Unable to recapture her past happiness with Walter, Gladys determines
that his future should be with Anne. The play ends with Gladys's suicide,
the traditional fate of the fallen woman, freeing Walter to reunite with the
pure Anne. Gladys's sacrifice is in vain, however; Anne turns her devotion
to Walter's friend, Major Hardy. Though Fletcher denies her male protagonist a reunion with the angelic woman on the back of the fallen woman's
death, Anne's transfer of affection to Major Hardy – who regards women
as 'rudderless boats' (p. 35) – is hardly a feminist ending. Fletcher's sexually pure heroine ends with lines as passive as any authored by a man, as she
asks Major Hardy to take care of her, pleading 'I can't help myself, I am
not strong enough. Will you tell me what to do?' (p. 71).

The production at the Garrick received mixed reviews. While Shaw was
highly critical, Archer praised the author's dialogue as 'thoughtful, nervous,
natural' (TW94, p. 99). The reviewer for the *Annual Register* of 1894
commented that the piece was chiefly remarkable for the powerful acting
of Kate Rorke and Robins in the roles of 'two impossibly magnanimous

Fig. 1.1 Elizabeth Robins as Gladys Lessingham in *Mrs Lessingham*, 1894, reproduced from The Fales Collection by permission of Independent Age

women' (Burke, 1895, p. 126). Kerry Powell notes that the play ran for 33 performances, making it one of the most successful productions of a play by a female author in the late-Victorian period (1997, p. 135). Thirteen years later in 1907, as the suffrage campaign was turning militant, Robins would rework the genre in her play *Votes for Women!*, re-examining potential models of female solidarity between a 'pure' and a 'fallen' woman.

Already famous as a wit and an aesthete, Oscar Wilde rose to fame as a dramatist on the success of two fallen woman plays, *Lady Windermere's Fan* (1892) and *A Woman of No Importance* (1893). Wilde takes a great interest in models of antipathy/sympathy between women as test cases for the humanity of social morals. Wilde provides a unique spin on the ingénue character in *A Woman of No Importance*, by making her an American Puritan whose name, Hester, suggests the heroine of Nathaniel

Hawthorne's *The Scarlet Letter*.[20] Through Hester, Wilde engages directly with British purity feminism, a strand of feminism intent on breaking down prevailing codes of the sexual double standard not by relaxing morals around female sexuality, but rather by policing male behaviour. Hester takes a feminist stance in objecting to the double standard that allows men to go unpunished, but as a purity feminist she shows no mercy to fallen women: 'Let them both be branded' (p. 120).

The plot of *A Woman of No Importance* centres on the plight of a fallen woman, a mother who has dodged the shame of her past by posing as a widow. Twenty years on, Mrs Arbuthnot's former seducer Lord Illingworth unwittingly offers Gerald (his own illegitimate son) a socially advantageous position as his secretary. In the melodramatic climax of Act III, Mrs Arbuthnot sacrifices her reputation to save her son from coming under the influence of his libertine father, admitting the truth of her past in her famous cry, 'Stop, Gerald, stop! He is your own father!' (p. 143) before sinking slowly to the ground in shame. In the next act, Gerald insists that Lord Illingworth atone for the past by marrying his mother. Illingworth agrees, but she refuses to submit, stating flatly, 'There is no atonement possible' (p. 148). Gerald argues that marrying her seducer is a duty that she owes 'to all the other women in the world, lest he betray more' (p. 148). In a bitter comment on female solidarity, Mrs Arbuthnot counters:

> I owe nothing to other women. There is not one of them to help me. There is not one woman in the world to whom I could go for pity, if I would take it, or for sympathy, if I could win it. Women are hard on each other. (p. 148)

In the end Mrs Arbuthnot's salvation comes from an unlikely quarter, as Hester relaxes her puritanical views and offers a new kind of morality based on compassion and love. Running forward to save the fallen woman from the male-negotiated marriage, Hester physically embraces her, crying 'No, no: you shall not. That would be real dishonour, the first you have ever known' (p. 150).

The most original element of Wilde's play is in Hester's moral transformation from a conservative Puritan to a feminist solidarity figure, asserting 'In her all womanhood is martyred. Not she alone, but all of us are stricken in her house' (p. 151). Hester's conversion from judge to redeemer paves the way for an unusually happy ending to a fallen woman play. In a remarkable act of same-sex redemption, Hester proposes to take Mrs Arbuthnot away to 'better, wiser, and less unjust lands' (p. 150).

In this ending Wilde critiques the injustice of British social codes, while acknowledging their power; there is no question that the fallen woman can enjoy a happy ending in England. Hester's transformation may have been Wilde's own attempt to argue for a more humane, less hypocritical approach to sexual morality in an era where the old double standard was pitted against the new feminist purity campaigns which, though they were more gender equitable, were even more sexually conservative.

William Archer praised the sincerity and unconventionality of the confrontation between Mrs Arbuthnot and Lord Illingworth, calling it 'the most virile and intelligent' English dramatic writing of the day (TW93, p. 107). Archer found fault, however, with Mrs Arbuthnot's histrionic tone: 'But why all this agony? Why all this hatred? Why can "no anodyne give her sleep, no poppies forgetfulness"? With all respect for Mrs Arbuthnot, this is mere empty phrase-making' (pp. 108–09). Archer's criticism, though written rather patronizingly from a position of male privilege, picks up on the sometimes awkward join between Wilde's adaptation of conventional melodrama and his development of a new style without its moral absolutes. Tragically for Wilde, Victorian purity feminists were not nuanced in their morals. Working to reform the double standard and protect girls and women from exploitation in the sex trade, purity feminists pushed hard for the Criminal Law Amendment Act of 1885, under whose section 11, forbidding 'gross indecency' between men, Wilde would be tried, convicted, disgraced and imprisoned at the height of his fame in 1895, just two years after the West End success of *A Woman of No Importance*.[21]

PURITY FEMINISM

Purity feminism arose as a reaction against the Victorian double standard of punishing female sexual transgression but enabling male licentiousness, a practice made startlingly clear in the Contagious Diseases Acts of 1864–69 (CD Acts). The CD Acts, created with the aim of controlling venereal diseases in the armed forces, sanctioned forced medical examinations of prostitutes in garrison and port towns where soldiers and sailors suffered from high rates of sexually transmitted diseases (STDs). Though aimed at prostitutes, the CD Acts gave policemen the right to seize *any* woman in any town walking alone and force her into a medical examination. Women who struggled were sometimes straightjacketed. Examinations were carried out, often ineptly, with scalding metal instruments, sometimes causing internal injuries or miscarriages. Josephine Butler is the feminist leader most closely associated with speaking out publicly against the dangers both of venereal diseases and of the government legislation that attempted to control the spread of them through state regulation of women's bodies.[22] Purity feminists objected vehemently to the double standard of a bill that required women to submit to brutal medical examinations in order to prove to male customers that *they* were disease-free.[23]

Purity feminists bitterly objected to the conspiracy of silence between men and their doctors to conceal STDs from their wives. In his publication *On Gonorrhoeal Infection in Women* (1888), Dr William Sinclair admitted that British doctors frequently acted as willing accomplices, helping husbands to camouflage their gonorrheal discharge[24] in order to consummate marriages with brides in a state of ignorance. Although STDs had a devastating impact on thousands of women and their children, respectable women were meant to be completely ignorant of them. The 'holy war' of the purity campaigns was an exposé of these male conspiracies of silence. Butler denounced a system designed to ensure that the pleasures of sex were reserved for men while the unpleasant consequences were the responsibilities of women, pointing out that the men who carried diseases home to their wives would never submit themselves to the humiliation of forced medical examinations. The public attention garnered by Butler and her co-workers made a huge impact on the growing feminist consciousness in Britain. Susan Kingsley Kent submits that the campaign for the repeal of the CD Acts 'crystallized for women their status as sexual objects and catapulted many complacent, mild-mannered women into the public sphere to discuss a heretofore unmentionable issue' (1990, p. 9). The campaign was so controversial, however, that until 1877 feminists working in other areas such as education reform or suffrage felt compelled to withhold endorsement for fear of jeopardizing the gains they were making in their own fields – another example of the compartmentalization of issues in first-wave feminism.

Ethical issues relating to venereal disease appeared in London theatre by way of private subscription performances of European contemporaries Ibsen and Eugène Brieux. Ibsen confronted the issue of inherited syphilis in *Ghosts* (1881), and in *Damaged Goods* (1902) Brieux portrays collusion between a prospective bridegroom and his doctor. Both of these plays were translated into English and performed in London, but STDs weren't a topic British dramatists chose to take up in their own work, though St. John Hankin translated Brieux and Shaw wrote introductions for both Brieux and Ibsen. Writing during the most intense era of state and social censorship to occur at any time before or since on the British stage, it is not surprising that dramatists were disinclined to take up the subject of STDs. (They did, however, write about the equally forbidding and censorable topics of prostitution, abortion and infanticide.) Even Elizabeth Robins, who played nearly every Ibsen heroine, initially refused the chance to play the widow Mrs Alving in *Ghosts*, admitting that she found the play 'too dreadful for words' (1940, p. 258).

PROSTITUTION

Prostitution has always been one of the key symbols of women's subjugation, inequality, poverty and shame. Judith Walkowitz classifies the prostitute as the public symbol of female vice, embodying 'the corporeal smells and animal passions that the rational bourgeois male had repudiated and that the virtuous woman, the spiritualized "angel in the house" had suppressed' (1992, p. 21). In the Victorian era, the system was largely understood as class based, sacrificing working-class women to the lusts of upper- and middle-class men to maintain the purity of upper- and middle-class wives and mothers, though in reality many prostitutes catered to working-class men (Walkowitz, 1980, p. 23). Men who believed that sex was a normal and healthy bodily function for them, but something only to be passively endured by wives in the hope of children, could justify gratifying their lusts with an established sub-class of prostitutes without contaminating the purity of the mother – or future mother – of their children. In this capacity prostitutes were sometimes cast in a curiously heroic light as the guardians of middle-class women's purity. As the influential Victorian historian and political theorist William Lecky explained, but for the prostitute, 'the unchallenged purity of countless happy homes would be polluted', paradoxically making the prostitute 'the most efficient guardian of virtue' and 'the eternal priestess of humanity, blasted for the sins of the people' (1876, pp. 299–300). Not everyone agreed with Lecky's view. Ellice Hopkins, a leader in the social purity movement, scorned this argument, sarcastically suggesting that if prostitutes were martyrs of purity, 'brothels should be put next to churches' (quoted in Bristow, 1977, p. 98).

Middle-class England's general view of the prostitute was of womanhood debased by commerce, licentiousness, venereal disease and racial degeneracy. She was frequently characterized as a siren, temptress or harpy of unbridled voluptuousness who was, like Eve, responsible for her own fall from grace. While Lecky suggested that prostitutes could be seen as martyrs, feminists increasingly attacked prostitution as a source of literal contamination of middle-class wives and mothers in the form of venereal disease. Many purity feminists and some male social reformers like the Radical MP James Stansfield challenged notions of prostitutes as debauched or degenerate by nature, emphasizing their youth, poverty and vulnerability. While some philanthropists sought to reform prostitutes,[25] many believed them to be beyond redemption.[26] Evolutionists viewed the prostitute not only as a source of contamination of the present generation in terms of disease, but also as a degenerating influence on the race in terms of breeding. Victorian scientists cited the prostitute's supposed immodesty and voluptuousness as atavism – a throwback to a more primitive stage of evolution, equated with savagery. Though the two female sexualities were represented as worlds apart, the dividing line between them was feared as tenuous, engendering almost fanatical restrictions on middle-class women's dress and social mobility to enforce their sexual purity.

Feminists frequently compared marriage to prostitution as a trade in which men sanctioned women to earn their living. Success in both 'trades' relied on a woman's ability to attract men; both contracts were based on relinquishing rights over her body; neither trade offered legal protection against misuse by the man; and both came with the occupational hazards of venereal disease. Prostitutes and wives were both sellers in a buyers' market. The analogy was an effective one, lodging an arrow deep in the heart of the sacred bull of 'domestic purity'. Some feminists took this logic a step further, pointing out that prostitutes actually had more legal rights than wives: they could make contracts, bargain and receive wages for their work whereas, under coverture, married women could not. Feminist analysis of marriage as a trade led to suggestions that wives should receive salaries for housekeeping and child rearing as well as unemployment benefits if their position was terminated (in the event of a separation or the death of a husband). Martha Vicinus points out that the Edwardian suffrage campaign touched 'a responsive chord' in middle-class women in part due to the accounts of 'the horrors of prostitution' they had been exposed to during the Victorian prostitution-focused purity campaigns and the parallels drawn with the unequal legal position of wives and mothers (1985, p. 249).

The play from this era best known today on the theme of prostitution is George Bernard Shaw's *Mrs Warren's Profession* (written in 1894), though, due to censorship, the first licensed public performance in Britain didn't take place until over 30 years after it was written. For a censored play about prostitution it is remarkably sexless, treating prostitution more figuratively than factually as a vehicle for Shaw's Fabian economic ideas, battled out between a capitalistic brothel-owning mother and her accountant daughter. While Mrs Warren rages against the poor health of factory workers with Phossy jaw,[27] Shaw doesn't delve into any unpleasant details of the lives of prostitutes such as arrest, forced medical examinations, sexually transmitted diseases, physical abuse or unwanted pregnancy. The play is arguably extravagant in its depiction of Mrs Warren as a wealthy businesswoman. Walkowitz summarizes that for working-class women who turned to prostitution, the move was 'not one of opportunity and entrepreneurship, but rather of survival' (1980, p. 31), eking out a precarious living in a society in which 'sexual coercion was but one form of exploitation to which they were subjected' (p. 31). Shaw's plot revolves around the reunion of Mrs Warren with her daughter Vivie, who has grown up in boarding schools and attended university with little knowledge of her mother and no knowledge of where her money comes from.

The revelation of Mrs Warren's profession precipitates the drama. Though Vivie responds to the news without the expected moral outrage of a conventional Victorian woman, she expresses some conservative distaste for prostitution as well as some scepticism about her mother's economic justifications for her trade, asserting, 'The people in this world who get on are the people who get up and look for the circumstances they want, and, if they cant find them, make them' (p. 193). Mrs Warren scorns Vivie's notion that even the poorest woman can exercise self-determination, indicting British class and gender codes as wicked and arguing that women, especially working-class women, suffer from a deadly lack of opportunity. When Vivie argues that 'saving money and good management will succeed in any business' (p. 195), her mother challenges her sheltered idealism with working-class frankness, asking, 'where can a woman get the money to save in any other business?' (p. 195). Eventually, Vivie is won over and declares her mother to be wonderful, 'stronger than all England' (p. 197). The short-lived harmony is broken, however, by Vivie's discovery that her mother isn't just a woman with a past, but a woman with a present who continues to turn a substantial profit from the trade by managing several brothels. Crofts, whom Vivie condemns as a villain for investing money in an immoral trade without the justification of economic necessity, defends his 35 per cent interest in the business by comparing the plight of the average working-class girl unfavourably to that of the prostitute and by equating factory owners with pimps. Vivie accepts the criticism of society without condoning her mother and Crofts for profiting extravagantly by its evils. The ending of the play is a reversal of *A Doll's House*, with the mother's departing door slam signalling that she has been thrown out by her child.

Mrs Warren's Profession originated with Janet Achurch's idea to adapt Guy de Maupassant's story 'Yvette' for the stage. According to Shaw, he and Achurch each agreed to write their own version of the story (though it sounds rather like Shaw simply stole Achurch's idea). Though privately encouraging Achurch with her version, *Mrs Daintree's Daughter* (1894), Shaw attacked it professionally when he learnt that she had approached Lewis Waller at the Haymarket Theatre about producing it. By this time Shaw had finished his own version and preferred that Achurch should star as his Mrs Warren than as her own Mrs Daintree.[28] The most notable difference between these two versions of de Maupassant's tale is their styles: Shaw's is a comedy about a New Woman daughter; Achurch's is a tragedy about a fallen woman mother.

In her adaptation, Achurch doesn't avoid the seedy reality of the mother's business premises, which she is careful to describe as a gambling establishment rather than a brothel, presumably to avoid censorship. The house's function seems clear enough from the outset with stage directions that show Leila ('Mrs Daintree') turning on the red light to indicate the house is open. Three out of the four acts in Achurch's play are set in the sensual boudoir 'furnished luxuriously in the French style' (Act I, p. 2) where Leila conducts business. Far from presenting an image of a successful businesswoman, unscathed by her trade, Leila nervously smokes cigarettes and takes quinine and morphia to soothe her nerves. She retains a sense of morals, though she admits they are inevitably compromised: 'Oh, I have my scruples – only they are *my* scruples, not other people's. They are – what life has left me' (Act I, p. 12). By describing what Leila holds back and why, Achurch portrays her struggle for dignity: 'I am classed with all the other women who come to my rooms. I do things that are worse perhaps – but still, to keep my hands free, my lips untouched to caress the child' (Act I, p. 13). Leila is more victim than a business entrepreneur – her career is the consequence of her connections with at least two corrupt men. Where Mrs Warren controls her businesses, Leila is controlled by a male business partner, Geoffrey Howarth, who takes two-thirds of the profits and shoulders none of the risk.

Achurch's play opens with Leila determined to get out of the business and take her daughter Violet to another country, where she will never know of her mother's past. Howarth agrees to release Leila from the business, but only if she personally introduces a successor – he admits that he has a young girl in mind. Act II takes place on a farm in the country where Leila has been keeping her daughter in sheltered ignorance. Violet is 17 and eager for a more scintillating lifestyle. Leila is called away on urgent business, leaving the way open for Howarth, who has come to the country on a mission to seduce Violet into the business. When he propositions, 'You would like to have plenty of money and a beautiful house in town, wouldn't you?' Violet answers with greedy determination, 'I *mean* to have them!' (Act II, p. 25). The Act III curtain falls on the melodramatic tableau of Leila's shocked horror as Howarth introduces Violet to their clients as her successor. In the final act, Leila pleads with Violet to come away with her, but Violet is determined to stay and claim a stake in the business. Overcome with dread that her past is destined to become her daughter's future, Leila asks her daughter for a dose of quinine, but Violet mistakenly pours a fatal dose of morphia. Realizing her mistake, Violet weeps into her mother's lap, achieving cathartic redemption. Leila's dying lines are ecstatic, as she accepts that she can't escape her past but now hopes that her daughter will: 'It is best – the only way. (*Fondles Violet's head as it lies in her lap*) My darling's heart is reached at last' (Act IV, p. 12).

Shaw dismissed Achurch's ending as having the excessive pathos of 'something for a Bernhardt to star in' (quoted in Powell, 1998, p. 85), implying that her work was melodramatic and passé. As a successful actress of the new Ibsen-influenced realism, Achurch was well versed in embodying her heroines, so it is no surprise that her writing is more emotionally charged – some might say more emotionally connected – than the theatre critic Shaw's. As an author, Achurch enters the play from the leading woman's point of view and empathizes with her struggles, exploring means to express her emotional pain.

Like Shaw, Clotilde (Clo) Graves and Gertrude Kingston used comedy to make socio-economic critiques in their co-authored play *A Matchmaker* (1896), but rather than comparing prostitution to capitalism, they take the more radical step of comparing prostitution to marriage, casting doubts on the purity of the domestic sphere. The play teems with troublesome marriages, which run the gamut from unhappy to secret to bigamous. Mrs Lane, the title 'matchmaker' part written for Kingston, shares much in common with Jane Austen's Emma in her passion for and ineptitude at engineering suitable matches. Despite the obvious disaster and divorce strewn in her wake, Mrs Lane is undeterred in her hobby, wrangling fresh engagements by strategically sending unwitting couples off to admire her exotic Night Blooming Cereus – a romantic ploy that never fails to end in a proposal. The conundrum of the play is Margaretta Ridout's wretched marriage to the rich, profligate Lord Westbourne. Though Margaretta (played by Lena Ashwell) suffers no illusions about her profligate husband's past conduct or present character, in an original twist she neither judges nor forgives him, but instead judges herself for agreeing to the marriage. While she likens his mind to 'a stable loft' and his heart to 'a whiskey vault', she compares her own her heart to 'a broker's sale-room, flaring with artificial light' where everything has been 'trodden under foot, put up to auction, and sold to the highest bidder' (p. 74). In contrast to innocent female victims like Pinero's Leslie, who marries in ignorance, Margaretta admits agency in her own demise: 'Don't treat me as a victim any more! I struck a vulgar bargain vulgarly. I sold myself to Westborne, body and soul' (p. 74). This direct reference to prostitution caused special offence to at least one male critic who was appalled that the lines had been written by women (Powell, 1997, p. 140).

Prior to her marriage, Margaretta suffered disappointment in love when Archibald Rolles disappeared from her life just as their romance blossomed. Though Rolles wrote from abroad to declare undying love, his letter was fatefully intercepted by Margaretta's younger sister Georgina who concealed it and later rented it out to girls at her boarding school as a romantic entertainment. Despairing that Margaretta declined to answer his letter, the heartbroken anthropologist Rolles travels the world researching a comparative book of 'civilized' and 'savage' marriage customs in which he compares the bride's role in British marriage to human sacrifice (p. 25). Rolles returns from his travels to find Margaretta unhappily wed to Westbourne. Meanwhile, Westbourne is discovered to be secretly married to the German maid Wilhelmina, voiding the legality of his marriage to Margaretta. Margaretta suddenly finds herself in the precarious position of being unmarried, but no longer a maid – legally free, but sexually fallen. Westbourne offers to divorce his first wife so that he can make Margaretta an honest woman. Having sold herself once, however, she responds decisively 'I'd rather not!' (p. 110). The matchmaker, Mrs Lane, resolves the situation by sending Rolles and Margaretta off to admire the Night Blooming Cereus, resulting in their engagement. Through their use of comedy, the female writing team of Graves and Kingston offer a radical indictment of marriage as prostitution and acknowledge women's agency in brokering their own sales. The happy ending, however, did not please male critics. The reviewer for *The Theatre* called the piece 'a thoroughly invertebrate piece of work possessing little coherence and less cohesion' (1 June 1896), a common criticism of female playwrights' works, which were often disparaged as less ordered and well-structured than men's.

Adelene Votieri's *That Charming Mrs Spencer* (1897) dramatizes the plight of Kitty who, like Margaretta, is duped into a false marriage (prior to the action of the play), unwittingly making her a fallen woman. After the marriage misfire, Kitty sells herself on the stage at the Variety, dancing and singing to restore the fortunes of her aristocratic ancestral home and her spendthrift father Captain Mallooney before marrying Cecil Sebright, from whom she manages to keep her past relationship secret. Though Kitty demurs to Cecil's request that she retire from the stage once they are married, Cecil's father Sir George disinherits him for marrying a music hall star. Ever the plucky problem solver for the hopeless men in her life, Kitty goes undercover as a charming widow to trick Cecil's father into restoring his inheritance. When Kitty's past is revealed by her former seducer, the wicked Lord Kelvin, Cecil forgives her, reasoning, 'you were more sinned against than sinning' (p. 46). The play ends with Cecil's fortune restored and Lord Kelvin pursued by the police. Unsurprisingly, this play, with a uniquely pro-active female heroine, never made it to the London stage.

Harley Granville Barker's early play *The Marrying of Ann Leete* (1899) makes similar criticisms of marriage as fundamentally mercenary, but depicts it less as a market where women actively sell themselves than as a series of male business negotiations in which women have little agency. Barker displaces the world of the play from his own *fin de siècle* moment of 1899 to the close of the eighteenth century, evoking the reactionary and progressive cyclical overtones of *fin de siècle* epochs[29] while distancing his characters from nineteenth-century tropes. At the beginning of the play, Tory politician Carnaby Leete is arranging a marriage between his daughter Ann and the influential Whig politician Lord John Carp as part of his own plan to desert the descending Tory party in favour of the rising Whigs. Barker's choice of word and syntax in 'the marrying of' signals Ann's anticipated position as object in the marriage contract: 'the betting of Tatton's horse'; the 'letting of Markswayde'; and 'the marrying of Ann' are all conceived of as male business transactions. Alert and intelligent, Ann is depicted as an accomplice rather than a pawn in this political intrigue, pre-empting Carp's proposal with the business-like acceptance, 'Thank you very much; it'll be very convenient for us all' (p. 54). However, the idea of the political marriage takes on a more troubling corporeal reality when Carp, 20 years her senior, presses unwanted physical attention on her. When he 'kisses her full on the lips' she responds, 'I can't hate you enough' (p. 55) and 'I feel very degraded' (p. 55). When he asks with mock innocence, 'Ain't you to be mine?' (p. 55), she counters with an astute analysis of male prerogatives under British marriage laws: 'You want the right to behave like this as well as the power' (p. 55). Ann's window of opportunity to exert agency is compressed – the first three acts occur in the space of one day. At the end of the third act, Ann suddenly determines to escape the upper-class political marriage by instead marrying the gardener, John Abud. Her decision is as incomprehensible to the other characters as it is to the gardener himself. Barker does not treat the match as a romance. Ann's attraction to Abud seems to be simply that he is the gardener, associated with life. When they return to his cottage on their wedding night Ann asks to be treated 'not as a wife ... but as the mother of your children' (p. 81). Claiming his rights and status as her husband, the formerly humble servant asserts, 'Now I'm your better' (p. 81). When he puts his arms around her she instinctively 'shrinks', provoking his defiant, 'But I will. It's my right' (p. 82) before kissing her 'almost by force' (p. 82) after which she 'clenches her hands and seems to suffer' (p. 82). Having broken with social convention, Ann has the potential to become sexually self-aware, but her sexuality is inhibited by Abud's assertion of male power. Barker creates an uncomfortable empathy with Ann as she endures forced kisses, first from Carp, then from Abud, showing both men equally conscious and possessive of their rights over her body regardless of the class differences. At the end of the play, Ann tells Abud, 'we've all been in too great a hurry getting civilised. False dawn. I mean to go back' (p. 82) before climbing the steep stairs to her wedding bed, an ending that is neither happy nor hopeless.

Contemporary critics were confused by the play. *The Times* suggested it 'might more suitably be termed a practical joke' on the audience than a comedy (28 January 1902).[30] Barker's alternative Eden play, with its ambiguity and lack of romance, was not popular in its day,[31] but it hits a nerve of uncertainty that I think makes it one of the most provocative reflections on marriage in the era. Though Barker is the least dogmatic of the New Dramatists this early play captures aspects of the fear, disillusionment and doubt about relations between the sexes that characterize the Victorian/ Edwardian *fin de siècle*. Where audiences and critics were accustomed to considering individual characters with clear moral conflicts, Barker seems ahead of his time in using a much wider transhistorical lens to create an image of a fractured, limited and contradictory society – a fallen society, rather than a fallen woman or a profligate man.

SHIFTING MORALITIES AT THE START OF THE TWENTIETH CENTURY

Attitudes to female sexuality were changing quickly at the beginning of the twentieth century and variations on the fallen woman theme continued to appear, though usually with less clear-cut morals than in their late-Victorian predecessors. In 1900, just a few years on from the 'fallen woman' problem plays of the mid-1890s, the plot of Henry Arthur Jones's *Mrs Dane's Defence*[32] centres more on the suspense of whether the fallen woman's illicit sexual past will be uncovered than on the morality of her actions. Through the investigative efforts of a scandal-monger, Mrs Bulsom-Porter, 'Mrs Dane' (her real name isn't Dane and she was never a Mrs) is eventually found out and forced to end her engagement to her fiancé, Lionel. The harshest social condemnation is meted out not to Mrs Dane, but rather to her nemesis Mrs Bulsom-Porter, who is manipulated into signing a humiliating public apology despite the truth of her accusations. Lady Eastney calls out the hypocrisy of the double standard, asking 'aren't we all humbugs? Isn't it all a sham?' (p. 107). Gone is the melodramatic anguish of the fallen woman. Instead of throwing herself out of a window or drinking poison, Mrs Dane simply boards a train to London.

In 1902 Netta Syrett won the London Playgoers' Club competition for best new play with *The Finding of Nancy*, produced by George Alexander at the St James Theatre as part of the award. Syrett's script is a somewhat genre-confounding play, tragic in tone with a quietly happy ending and a heroine caught in scripts of behaviour between a fallen woman and a New Woman. In the first act Nancy is an impoverished middle-class woman supporting herself as a typist, who has to decide between becoming mistress to a married man or spending her life alone. She chooses companionship, if not exactly love, in a relationship with Will Fielding. Act II opens four years later on the Riviera under very different circumstances. Nancy has inherited a small legacy of her own, making her independent; meanwhile Will's institutionalized, alcoholic wife has died, leaving him free to remarry. Nancy's friend Isabel, a character who symbolizes the chaste but lonely spinster, presumes that Nancy will marry Will, but Will reminds Nancy of a past she is not proud of:

> *NANCY:* Oh Isabel! Theories are all very well, but there are things women never get used to. Foolish unreasonable things of course, but real to us, all the same. Ridiculous terrors; dreadful misgivings. Words that strike one like a blow. Even now, when I hear someone say 'She lived with him

for years' or 'she's his mistress' – you know the voice! I grow cold with
horror. I think, that's what *you* are, you are living with a man like that.
ISABEL: But that is not what you *think?*
NANCY: (quickly). No! only what I feel. And a man never understands
    that you can think one way, and feel another, without being fundamen-
    tally unreasonable.
ISABEL: Yes. Reason ahead, feet lagging behind. It's different for men I
    suppose. For ages they have been free.
NANCY: And so they take such matters easily, naturally. We can't do
    it, Isabel. There's age-long tradition against us ... training ... the old
    Puritan instinct. These things cling round us like grave clothes. We may
    take our freedom, but we can't take it lightly. Take it? We pay for it ... to
    the uttermost farthing. (p. 665)

When Will arrives at the holiday resort to propose, he sees that Nancy is
infatuated with a young man, Captain Egerton, and graciously bows out.
Because her past has been compromised, Nancy doubts that she ever really
loved Will until a telegram arrives which makes her think that he has been
killed. In her raw grief, Nancy publicly admits their relationship, ruining
her reputation while confirming, too late, her love for him. Thinking
she has lost Will forever, Nancy returns for one last look at the humble
rooms she shared with him. Will also returns and they reunite to resume
life together 'like the old married couple' Nancy acknowledges that they
'always have been' (p. 684). The woman with a past becomes a woman
with a future, though a future that is admittedly ambivalent about legal
marriage. Unfortunately for Syrett, the conservative critic Clement Scott
falsely suggested that Nancy's past was written from the author's lived
experience, resulting in Syrett's dismissal from her teaching job (Davis,
2012, p. 644). Syrett's challenge to conventional morality triggered
predictable critical outrage, causing the show to close after just one performance. Whether modelled in part from life (her own or someone else's)
or wholly fictional, this play explores both the moral and the mundane
dilemmas facing unmarried women who attempted a degree of agency
over their own sexuality at the turn of the twentieth century.

Ten years on from her social comedy *A Matchmaker*, Graves authored
one of the darkest fallen woman plays, *London Vendetta* (1906). Set in a
working-class tenement house, the play deals with the consequences of the
semi-incestuous child abuse of an orphan, Tina, by her adopted 'uncle'
and 'aunt' Paratti. At the opening of the play Tina marries an honest brick-
layer, Bill Kelsey, and thinks she has finally broken free from her abusers,

but when her past is revealed to her new husband a tragic series of events is set in motion. Graves took some care in establishing Tina's innocence and victimization by making the child abuse explicit. When Kelsey's mother accuses her, 'You fallen creature! You shame to me an' mine!' Convulsed with sobs, Tina pleads for mercy, recounting, 'They beat me 'an starved me ... They might 'ave cut me livin' 'eart out, if I'd known ... if I'd known ... I was doin' anything wicked. But I was only ... only [twelve³³] ... (her voice dies away)' (p. 36). Bill rejects his wife because of her past and vows to kill Paratti. In a bold act of self-sacrifice, Tina stabs Paratti to save Bill from avenging her and being tried for murder. Though Graves is careful to portray the child Tina as a victim, she depicts the adult Tina as unexpectedly masculine in her rescue of Bill and her visceral dispatch of the villain. Tina looks Paratti 'full in the face as she stabs him above the left collarbone' (p. 49) then pulls out the knife and says, 'Do you remember when I was ten³⁴ years old? [...] This is for that!' as she stabs him again (p. 50). The play ends with Tina bravely comforting Bill that things have worked out for the best, and asking the police to take her away. Though it is still the fallen woman, not her husband, who pays the price, Graves's denouement reverses the gender roles by having the woman rescue the man, sacrificing her freedom for his. Atypically, the husband's behaviour is measured by the traditionally feminine virtue forgiveness; Bill's anguished repentance over his harsh judgement of Tina's past makes this ending one of the most iconoclastic gender reversals in Edwardian theatre.

Margaret (Mack) Macnamara's *The Gates of the Morning* (1908), written in an idiosyncratic gothic, grotesque style, features a curious cast of flawed men and women who blur some of the traditional distinctions between saints and sinners. The first of two intertwining plots concerns Nancy Larne and Henry Mardale, a couple whose engagement was broken ten years previously (by a Miss Rowbins's revelation of her illicit past with Henry), and the question of whether or not they will reconcile and marry. The second plotline follows Nancy's niece, Alice, a fallen woman who has recently married a nonconformist minister, Samuel Wilson, who is keen to offload her illegitimate baby (not his) on relatives before taking Alice away to a new life in New Zealand. The play presents a marked difference between the behaviour and expectations of Nancy and Alice, women of two different generations. The older woman, Nancy, acts according to traditional codes and breaks off her engagement to Henry when confronted with his past relationship with Miss Rowbins, but continues to dream of a reunion on earth or in heaven, conforming to the womanly woman's ability to forgive and redeem a wayward man. Her desire to adopt Alice's child[35] rather than give birth to one is a sexually pure path to motherhood. Though Nancy throws herself into Henry's arms at the end of the play, her desire to marry him is confused and contradictory, particularly in relation to the actions of her younger and more rebellious niece, who openly admits that she chose to run away to become an actress and have affairs with men rather than dying an old maid. Alice doesn't bend to remonstrations from her mother about her past and stands firm against the will of her religious husband, making her the strongest character in the play and suggesting a new order that favours women with greater moral flexibility than Nancy's generation.

One of the most notorious 'sex scandal' plays of the prewar years was Stanley Houghton's *Hindle Wakes*,[36] first performed in 1912. The play deals with the aftermath of a weekend fling between a working-class Lancashire mill weaver Fanny Hawthorn and the prosperous mill owner's son Alan Jeffcote. Alan and Fanny meet by chance among friends on a holiday weekend at Blackpool and spontaneously decide to go to a hotel together. The play opens on Fanny's return and her parents' discovery that she has been 'ruined', precipitating a conference between the Hawthorn parents and the Jeffcote parents about what to do. Neither Fanny's nor Alan's mother believe that Fanny's part in the weekend is uncontrived – Fanny's working-class mother sees her behaviour as a risky but clever strategy to marry up and Alan's mother sees it less sympathetically as gold digging. In a cross-class alliance, both fathers agree that Alan must do the honourable thing and marry Fanny. In keeping with the silent suffering associated with the fallen woman, Fanny is never consulted about her wishes. She astounds everyone in the final act by refusing Alan, reversing the traditional gender roles: 'Love you! Good heavens, of course not! Why on earth should I love you? You were just someone to have a bit of fun with. You were an amusement – a lark' (p. 103). Though he admits he didn't love Fanny either, Alan is shocked to hear this kind of talk from a woman, objecting 'But it's not the same. I'm a man' (p. 103). While purity feminists challenged the sexual licence of men, Fanny instead claims sexual agency for women: 'You're a man, and I was your little fancy. Well, I'm a woman, and you were my little fancy. You wouldn't prevent a woman enjoying herself as well as a man, if she takes it into her head?' (p. 103). Casting a class aspersion against the nouveau riche, Fanny tells the wealthy manufacturer's son that he isn't man enough for her. At least some of Fanny's confidence might be attributed to the fact that women who worked in the Lancashire cotton mills earned the highest wages of any women in the country (Tilly, 1976, p. 461). The play was iconoclastic in its representation of an active, casual female sexuality and the portrayal of a woman who gains sexual experience without accepting that she is 'fallen' or allowing herself to be 'righted' by marriage.

The play caused a sensation when it was first produced by Annie Horniman's Gaiety Theatre in Manchester and became the most discussed problem play of the season when it transferred to London, arousing passions that led to script burning in the streets. The *Pall Mall Gazette* ran a column for several weeks devoted to responses and discussion, much of which centred on whether the actress, Edyth Goodall, should in good conscience have consented to play the part of the heroine Fanny, popularly known as the Girl Who Refused to be Righted. The *Church Times* defended the play, claiming that Houghton was being ironic, underscoring the distastefulness of profligacy and its defenders by voicing immoral views through a female character, but progressive critics who praised the piece interpreted the moral differently as a bold critique of the double standard.

To bring the chapter full circle, let's return once more to Elizabeth Robins, this time as a playwright. In 1913, 20 years after Shaw and Achurch wrote their prostitution plays, Robins wrote a phenomenally successful novel, *My Little Sister*,[37] dealing with sex trafficking or 'white slavery'[38] as inter-European sex trafficking was known. Robins's prewar work is far darker and more explicit than Shaw's or Achurch's plays from the 1890s. Unlike Mrs Warren who enters her profession through a calculated economic decision and goes on to become a business tycoon, or Achurch's fallen woman Leila who is led into a life of vice through the influence of a corrupt lover but retains a measure of agency and a partner's share in the business, Robins's female character Bettina is simply a victim. Bettina is a middle-class teenager who is abducted, drugged and enslaved in a brothel with locked doors and barred windows.[39] Unlike Shaw, who avoids any brothel scenes, or Achurch, whose brothel is veiled as a gambling den, Robins devotes an entire act to a disturbing and suspenseful brothel scene during which Bettina is drugged by the traffickers while her older sister Honor manages to escape with the help of an impulsive male ally.

Katie Johnson surmises that the full-length brothel scene and its indictment of upper-class male collusion and police complicity in prostitution (2015, p. 110) are the most significant reasons the play failed to make it to the stage in either New York or London despite the huge success of the novel, which went into a fourth edition within its first month. Robins, who personally visited police courts to research the piece, under-scores police complicity through Honor's incredulity in the following exchange which begins as an urgent conversation about tracking down the house her sister is being held in, but ends with a revelation of wider social horror:

> *INSPECTOR:* Well, we've got to make our enquiries ... but, as I say, we're bound to identify it in the end. It's sure to be on our list. Then we'll apply for a search warrant –
> *HONOR:* Your list – what list?
> *INSPECTOR:* Why, the list we have – the police list – of – of that sort of house.
> *HONOR:* (*Lifting her face*) That sort of house? Do you mean that there is more than one ...
> *INSPECTOR:* Well ...
> *HONOR:* Do you mean that there are many ... ?
> *INSPECTOR:* I'm afraid there are, Miss – you see, young ladies like you –
> *HONOR:* (*Staring at him*) Many houses where they take girls and – So many that you can't tell which – and you know it, and you *keep the list*! ...
> (*There is a moment's pause.*) (p. 163)

In the pause, Robins ensures that her audience has a moment to absorb the significance of the collusion between the state and prostitution rings. To underscore their complicity, Robins also doubles the upper-class barrister Mr Guy Whitby-Dawson with the brothel client 'The Tartar' who aids and abets the evil Madame Grey Hawk in her plan to ship 'the meat' (Bettina) from Hull to Hamburg, putting her beyond the protec-tion of British law. Robins's juxtaposition of the scene between Honor and the police inspector and a scene at Whitby-Dawson's legal chambers highlights corruption across class divisions within the judiciary.

In Robins's novel, the victim Bettina's only release is death. She dies and appears to her sister as a sort of guardian angel who comes 'to do for others what no one had done for her' (p. 344) through offering her own tragic demise as a cautionary warning to other young women – a function which the widely read novel, billed as based on a true story, seems to have served. Cicely Hamilton's theatre adaptation of Robins's novel ends trag-ically but spiritually, with Honor on her knees sobbing and praying both in grief and relief after she learns of Bettina's death. Taking the theatre adaptation back into her own hands,[40] Robins scripted a suspenseful fourth act in which Bettina is rescued just as Grey Hawk smuggles her drugged victim onto a ship. Robins's stage ending draws more from her background as a melodrama ingénue than on the psychological dialogic complexity of Edwardian problem plays. In its mix of gritty urban crime scene, dockside police raids and archetypal villains with names like Grey Hawk and The Tartar, it anticipates key elements of Noir. (Indeed the 1919 film version of *My Little Sister* may have been a proto film noir, but no known copy remains.)

At the beginning of Robins's London stage career, fallen woman plays like *The Second Mrs Tanqueray* traded on the titillation offered by glamorous actresses like Stella Campbell embodying fallen women on stage while playwrights and audiences considered the possibilities of their redemption or damnation comfortably from the stalls. In Robins's adaptation of *My Little Sister*, Bettina's story induces horror rather than titillation, and the possibilities of moral redemption or damnation lie with the male custodians of legal power. By making her heroine an innocent ingénue rather than a psychologically complex woman with agency, Robins might seem to have reverted to melodrama as regards dramatic form, but this formal tactic enabled her to skip over 'the meat' of the fallen woman's body and focus instead on the social issues of male corruption and complicity in the sex trade, a far cry from the individual villains of melodrama. The link between politics and art in this Edwardian writing is pronounced in comparison to works of the 1890s. In the 1890s women 'fell' through their own misguided or impulsive choices; in this Edwardian feminist plot it is the male legal system that is exposed as fallen. Robins shared a preliminary copy of the novel *My Little Sister* with Christabel Pankhurst prior to the publication of Pankhurst's tract *The Great Scourge and How to End It*, illustrating the circulation and cross-fertilization of women's work between the worlds of art and politics during the suffrage campaign.

* * *

In the space of a generation the salacious appeal of late-Victorian fallen woman dramas with the moral onus on the women had given way to Edwardian problem plays which challenged social codes ('aren't we all humbugs? Isn't it all a sham?'). The double standard was still a central social force, but it was increasingly contested on stage and off. Fallen women evolved from weeping repentants like Janet Preece, objects of pity or scorn, to more fascinating and psychologically complex characters, like

Paula Tanqueray. 'Angel' characters were no longer automatically reverenced, but increasingly scrutinized as prudish, uncharitable or simply unrealistic. Actresses like Janet Achurch, Stella Campbell, Elizabeth Robins, Lena Ashwell, Gertrude Kingston and Edyth Goodall made these parts even more compelling and nuanced than some of their male authors perhaps intended.[41] Their work, publicly embodying of these morally ambiguous heroines on the stage, contributed to the creation of a less rigid construction of female sexuality, making actresses primary collaborators in the emerging identity of the modern women.

Representations of men also challenged the ideology of separate spheres. The reckless Aubrey Tanqueray, the flippant Lord Illingworth, the daughter-bartering Carnaby Leete, the criminal 'uncle' Paratti, the bigamous Lord Westbourne, the ridiculous Captain Mallooney and the white-collar/blue-collar collusion of the police and the judiciary in Robins's sex trafficking play all cast doubt on male authority and privilege. As Eltis points out, 'The presence of such dubious representatives of male authority was an indication that English playwrights were engaging with wider issues of social order rather than simply producing sentimental dramas of individual experience' (Eltis, 2013a, p. 138). Even as many of the more conservative plays seem to argue for the importance of social structures as guard rails to keep women from ruining themselves, the public enactment and debate around them contributed to a re-imagination of the modern woman. The tension between agency and passivity for the female heroines lies at the heart of these fallen woman plays, a tension that is mirrored in the friction between artistic control and passivity in the work of female actresses and playwrights in a theatre world controlled by men. A fascination with the consequences of opening the Pandora's box of bourgeois female agency is likewise central in the New Woman plays, the subject of the next chapter.

CHAPTER 2

The New Woman

In 1890s Britain notions of the self-determined 'New Woman' were strongly associated with the work of Henrik Ibsen which was in turn closely linked with the actress-producer Elizabeth Robins. With its complex female protagonists, Ibsen's work went against the grain of the British actor-manager system where leading men sought star vehicles for themselves and often trimmed other roles to the bare minimum to avoid pulling focus from their own performances.[1] Believing that the commercial actor-manager system 'stultified art' (1932, p. 34), Robins put her faith in self-reliance and the development of the women's networks.[2] To make the kind of theatre she wanted to be part of, she became a producer. Two years after seeing Achurch's Nora, Robins and her collaborator Marion Lea each pawned a treasured possession in order to raise the funds to produce the 1891 English premiere of *Hedda Gabler*, putting themselves on the line as artists and investors. Robins directed the play and made her name starring in the title role.

Like *A Doll's House*, the production provoked a storm of commentary. Audiences and critics were astounded anew by the 'unwomanly' behaviour of Hedda and her even more violent departure from domestic life than Nora's, this time by way of a pistol shot rather than a door slam. In *The Times*, Hedda was characterized as 'a lunatic of the epileptic class' (21 April 1891), the *Saturday Review* called her 'a malicious woman of evil instincts, jealous, treacherous, cold hearted' (25 April 1891) and *The Observer* said: 'Hedda is about as disagreeable a product of wayward wickedness as the morbid imagination of a playwright or novelist has ever conceived' (26 April 1891). In the *Illustrated London News*, the conservative critic Clement Scott lamented that 'a woman more morally repulsive has seldom been seen on the stage' but praised Robins's performance as making 'vice attractive by her art' and stating, with mixed feelings, 'she has glorified an unwomanly woman' (25 April 1891). On the occasion of the final performance at the Vaudeville,

The Athenaeum paid tribute to Robins and Lea as 'clever, courageous, and persevering' producers who, 'in face of opposition scarcely short of persecution', brought *Hedda Gabler* to the London stage, enabling playgoers to judge the controversial work for themselves (6 June 1891). The production became so widely known that the feather boa Robins wore as Hedda set a fashion trend in London; Robins was famous (Fig. 2.1).

Robins went on to produce and star in many Ibsen plays,[3] including *The Master Builder*, which she received by post directly from Ibsen himself and read in Danish, act by act as he wrote them. Though William Archer[4] was Ibsen's principal English translator, Robins did substantial work on several Ibsen translations, particularly with an ear to making his heroines play on stage, nuancing the voices of these complex characters for their English premieres. More than any other actress or producer, Robins drove the Ibsen movement in Britain, bringing his works to the public as theatrical productions rather than literary publications. Though Ibsen's plays did not reach commercial West End London theatres until well into

Fig. 2.1   Elizabeth Robins as Hedda Gabler with Lövborg's manuscript, reproduced from The Fales Collection by permission of Independent Age

the twentieth century,[5] these independent productions and subscription matinees[6] indelibly imprinted Ibsen's influence on a new generation of theatre makers and critics. Archer aligned Ibsen with the rise of realism while Shaw styled him as a master of the social problem play. For Robins, who linked her career closely to his later more Symbolist works, Ibsen was 'first and foremost a poet' (Robins 1928, p. 7), whose work ushered in modernism and the modern woman.

Robins's success as an Ibsen actress was a double-edged sword. Creating the roles of Hedda Gabler, Hilde Wangel and Rebecca West for the London premieres made her reputation as a great actress, but the association with Ibsen caused a cul-de-sac in her career. Known for her independence and associated (via Ibsen) with the women's movement, Robins was, unsurprisingly, not the first choice of actor-managers when casting female co-stars.[7] Her seven years of devotion to Ibsen's work was also tied to the intimate relationship[8] she formed with William Archer who worked closely with her as a dramaturg on all her major productions, forming a somewhat exclusionary triangle between Ibsen, his principal translator and his foremost theatrical interpreter.

Even at the height of her acting career, Robins's preference for avant-garde, noncommercial theatre meant that her earnings were modest and her work interspersed with periods of unemployment. During these breaks from stage work she assiduously developed her craft as a writer, the career most closely linked to the image of the New Woman, reinventing herself as a journalist, novelist[9] and playwright to ensure financial independence. As both an Ibsen actress and a writer, Robins was the quintessential New Woman of the 1890s: she was single, financially independent, ambitious for her career, part of a new intelligentsia and (covertly) enjoying at least a romance if not a sexual relationship with a man to whom she was not married. Her loyalties were still the largely self-motivated devotions of an actress to a great part or a single woman to her own career rather than the family-centred loyalty of an 'angel' wife or the gender-based allegiances of the committed feminist she would become in the twentieth century.

THE NEW WOMAN

She Flouts Love's Caresses,
Reforms ladies' dresses,
And scorns the Man-Monster's tirades;
She seems scarcely human,
This mannish 'New Woman,'
This 'Queen of the blushless Brigade.'
        (*Woman*, 26 September 1894)

Undefined by her relationships with men as either 'Magdalene' or 'Madonna', the New Woman pushed the boundaries of female personal freedom and challenged conventional 'womanly' conduct by appropriating masculine privileges in the public sphere. She inspired some and outraged others in her pursuit of higher education and employment and in her harsh critiques of the double standard of sexual behaviour. The popular writer Sarah Grand, well known for novels featuring free-thinking (but pure-living) heroines, is credited with coining the term 'New Woman' in an 1894 article[10] in which she argued for a major expansion of the woman's sphere as a much-needed balancing influence on the Victorian patriarchy.

This New Woman became infamous in the press and literature of the late-Victorian era, peaking in the mid-1890s with novels such as Grand's *The Heavenly Twins* (1893), in which a sister enjoys rare freedom by impersonating her twin brother, Mona Caird's *The Daughters of Danaus* (1894), the story of a talented but thwarted female composer, and Ella Hepworth Dixon's *The Story of a Modern Woman* (1894), the loosely autobiographical story of a female journalist. Ann Heilmann notes a rise of feminist protest novels linked to the women's movement in the 1890s, and identifies one of the defining characteristics of New Woman fiction as 'its challenge to and subversion of the conventional dichotomies between literature and political writing, art and popular culture' (2004, p. 1). Stage manifestations of the New Woman appeared in plays such as Arthur Wing Pinero's *The Amazons* (1893), Shaw's *The Philanderer* (1893), Sidney Grundy's *The New Woman* (1894), Dorothy Leighton's *Thyrza Fleming* (1895) and Pinero's *The Notorious Mrs Ebbsmith* (1895). The degree to which these New Woman characters encouraged pro- or anti-feminist views can often be linked to the gender of their authors even when, like Shaw, they professed to be progressive advocates of women's rights. The New Women depicted on stage by male authors were generally more parodic and less persuasive in their feminist arguments than their more intelligent and nuanced counterparts in novels written by women. D.A. Hadfield observes that through these novels and the money women earned writing them, 'the New Woman was literally writing herself into existence' (2013, p. 113).

The New Woman of the popular press was more widespread as a literary phenomenon, circulated by anti-feminists to personify the dangers of women's emancipation through caricature, than she was a real social type. Fascination with this transgressive figure created what Gillian Sutherland has called a 'media feeding frenzy' (2015, p. 1) with frequent cartoons in popular publications like *Punch* depicting women in masculine attire smoking cigarettes, riding bicycles and/or wearing a graduate's cap and gown. In one *Punch* cartoon captioned 'The Problem Play', the New Woman (presumably an author) asserts, 'No! My principle is simply this – If there's a demand for these plays, it must be supplied!' to which the 'Woman not New' replies, 'Precisely! Just as with the Bull-fights in Spain', inferring that both the New Woman and the New Drama are uncivilized and fundamentally un-British. Other cartoons, like George du Maurier's 'The New Woman' (*Punch*, 15 June 1895), delight in joking about the New Woman's masculinity and her repellent effect on men of her own class; Jack declines taking tea with the tie-wearing cigarette-smoking women in the drawing room in favour of a cup in the servant's hall, the only place where he can still find 'female society'.

In the popular press, the New Woman was typically depicted as a bicycle-riding college student or graduate wearing 'rational dress'. Rational dress supporters advocated simplified garments[11] for women, such as the controversial 'divided skirt' for bicycling, to facilitate general freedom of movement as well as enabling athletic activities. The bicycle, a mode of personal transportation which came into popular middle-class usage in the 1890s and was dubbed 'the freedom machine', became symbolic of women's new physical and social mobility. Bicycles appear frequently in literature of the era as icons of female independence. In Kate Dixey and Lillian Feltheimer's comedic play *A Girl's Freak* (1899) the young heroines attempt to earn money to purchase bicycles by covertly renting out their father's rooms while he is away. In Annie Hughes's play *A Husband's Humiliation* (1896) the Wildfires, a married couple, argue when the wife arranges to meet alone with 'Mr Bicillus' (p. 7),[12] whom Mr Wildfire suspects of romantic feelings towards his wife, highlighting feared associations between physical and sexual freedoms. St. John Hankin pokes fun at reactionary attitudes to women's bicycles in *The Last of the De Mullins* (1908) when a mother blames her unwed daughter's pregnancy on her cycling:

> MRS. DE MULLIN: (*lamentably*) I believe it was all through bicycling.
> MRS. CLOUSTON: Bicycling?
> MRS. DE MULLIN: Yes. When girls usen't to scour about the country as they do now these things didn't happen. (p. 13)

In contrast to the traditional 'angel in the house' who stayed literally corseted in her domestic sphere, the New Woman wore a latchkey or a chatelaine as a symbol of her freedom to come and go between the public and the private realms as she pleased. In Leighton's *Thyrza Fleming* the power reversal between Theophila Falkland, a woman with 'close-cropped hair, manly attire, divided skirt' (p. 42), and her husband Bobby is epitomized through her firm control of the latchkey. Usually represented as middle or upper class, the New Woman rejected many of the conventions of femininity, often living and working on equal terms with men. Reading advanced literature, particularly Ibsen, smoking cigarettes and travelling unchaperoned were further hallmarks of the New Woman, qualities which could be equated positively with freedom or negatively with loose morals. The popular press delighted in buffooning the New Woman as both mannish and man-hating in cartoons, articles and satirical poems. Though the press certainly associated this figure with the women's movement, 'feminism' and 'New Woman' were not synonymous terms. In contrast to the gender-based politics and loyalties of feminism, which advocated broad social reforms for the greater good, the New Woman's signature statement was personal freedom. Clement Scott expressed his abhorrence of the supposedly selfish nature of the New Woman, emblematized by Ibsen's heroine Nora, in his attack in *The Theatre*:

> It is all self, self, self! This is the ideal woman of the new creed; not a woman who is the fountain of love and forgiveness and charity, not the pattern woman we have admired in our mothers and our sisters, not the model of unselfishness and charity, but a mass of aggregate conceit and self-sufficiency, who leaves her home and deserts her friendless children because she has *herself* to look after.
>
> (1 July 1889, p. 21)

Shaw parodies the associations between Ibsen and the New Woman in his play *The Philanderer* (1893). The main character, Leonard Charteris, a recognizable self-parody of Shaw, is an Ibsenist philosopher caught in a romantic tangle between two women, Julia Craven (based on Shaw's first lover, Jenny Patterson) and Grace Tranfield (based on the actress Florence Farr, with whom he had an affair in 1893). Charteris has been courting the supposedly 'advanced' but actually rather conventional woman Julia, but now wishes to break with her in favour of the authentic New Woman, Grace. When Julia refuses to be thrown over, Charteris lectures her: 'Advanced views, Julia, involve advanced duties: you cannot be an advanced woman when you want to bring a man to your feet, and a conventional woman when you want to hold him there against his will' (p. 67). Shaw's primary interest, thus, seems to lie in how the philandering man can exploit the New Woman's 'advanced views' for his own untrammelled sexual freedom.

William Archer loathed this play in large part because of Shaw's caricatures of Ibsenites as womanly men and manly women, describing the play as 'an outrage upon art and decency, for which even my indignation cannot find a printable word of contumely' (1899, p. 1) and lamenting, 'If Mr Shaw had racked his brains for a method of bringing Ibsen and all his works into ridicule and contempt, he could have hit on nothing better' (1899, p. 6). Shaw's friends Beatrice Webb, Janet Achurch and Stella Campbell were decidedly unimpressed with the play, finding it ugly, vulgar and offensive.[13] According to Frank Harris, Beatrice Webb was particularly 'disgusted by the sex-obsessed women' (Harris, 1931, p. 149), suggesting that Shaw's accomplished and intelligent female friends were much less interested than he was in the impact that the New Woman's 'advanced views' would have on male heterosexual freedoms.

Male authors like Grant Allen capitalized on the sensational appeal of the New Woman in novels like *The Woman Who Did* (1895) while belittling their New Woman characters as ridiculous and contradictory. A few years after coining the term 'New Woman', Sarah Grand commented on the ubiquity of negative stereotypes surrounding it, asking:

> Who is this New Woman, this epicene creature, this Gorgon set up by the snarly who impute to her all the faults of both sexes while denying her the charm of either – where is she to be found if she exists at all?
>
> (1898, p. 466)

More complex portraits of the New Woman appear in the characters of Rhoda Nunn in George Gissing's *The Odd Women* (1893) and Sue Bridehead in Thomas Hardy's *Jude the Obscure* (1895), though they also conform to some prevalent ideas about sexual coldness and an unfeminine lack of sympathy for others. Shaw, who attempted a career as a novelist before becoming a playwright, wrote five novels between 1879 and 1883 that feature proto-New Women characters.[14]

Male dramatists were more drawn towards explorations of how the woman question would affect heterosexual relationships than to investigations into the potential of women's education or women's evolving roles within the commercial and professional sphere. Female dramatists also favoured marriage and motherhood as subject matter and while as a group they devoted more time to representations of specifically feminist issues, they also largely bypassed the individual struggles of women entering colleges, universities and professions as a potential area for dramatic investigation. The absence of middle-class students and professionals in drama is marked, considering that between the censuses of 1861 and 1911 there was a 307 per cent increase in the number of women teachers, nurses, shop assistants, clerks and civil servants, and that within this same space of time women had infiltrated the male citadel of medical science and drawn considerable notice in the public press.

Though the majority of plays focus on upper- and middle-class characters, issues of women in the workplace are explored in greater detail by female authors in relation to lower-middle-class women. Netta Syrett's character Nancy, a secretary in a typewriting office, has to make hard choices between meat in her diet and furniture in her rented room on her salary of 80 pounds a year. Elizabeth Baker's plays *Chains, Lois* and *Miss Robinson* feature lower-middle-class female typists for whom office work is drudgery. As Linda Fitzsimmons notes, Baker's work explores the limited employment opportunities available to women and the exploitation they are subject to in the workplace 'while at the same time insisting on the need for women to have a decent alternative to selling themselves into marriage' (1992, p. 191). Cicely Hamilton's plays, as well as many of the suffrage plays like Inez Bensusan's *The Apple* (1909), portray and critique some of the injustices faced by lower-middle-class women in occupations such as typewriting and shop assisting. Feminist analysis of the hypocrisies of 'women's work' in relation to class divisions are also represented in many of the suffrage sketches, while women's entry into universities and professions passes relatively unremarked upon.

Where British theatre lacked truly positive representations of New Women, New Women novelists filled the void. Bright young career women abounded in novels written by women for women and girls. Like the college-girl genre, a new genre of career novels sprang up at the end of the century and remained immensely popular for decades. In her study of the phenomenon, Sally Mitchell lists the following titles as representative of the types of careers that featured in such novels: Mary Bramston's *A Woman of Business* (1885), Ellinor Adams's *Miss Secretary Ethel* (1898), Alice Williamson's *The Newspaper Girl* (1899), and a slew of books about female doctors and nurses, including Arabella Kenealy's *Dr. Janet of Harley Street* (1893), Ellen Clayton's *A Ministering Angel* (1895) and Annie S. Swan's *Elizabeth Glen, M.B.* (1895) (Mitchell, 1995, p. 27). These books, though fictional, were written largely with the intent of stimulating girls' imaginations as to the realm of possibilities opening to women. As Holloway points out, however, 'the reality of working life for young working women was often very different from the cheery bravado of the New Woman stereotype' (2005, p. 96) with long hours, low pay and lack of promotional prospects in comparison to their male counterparts. Basing their appeal on fantasy and adventure, these career novels were in many ways more suited to imaginative aspirational portrayals of women working outside the home than contemporary drama, which focused on realism within domestic settings.

New Women characters in novels and plays were often depicted (semi-autobiographically) as authors or aspiring authors. In actress-author Annie Irish's 1890 play *Across Her Path*, the heroine Barbara Ogilvie is discovered by smart upper-class society through the success of her modern novel, *Ambition*. *Ambition* enables Barbara to escape a troubled and impoverished past and find a rich husband. When a villainous unrequited lover arrives to sabotage her marriage through false sexual innuendo, Barbara disappears, but is rediscovered some months later by an avid woman reader when she publishes *Nemesis*. Barbara's ability to escape the villain twice, as well as finding and then recapturing love, through her abilities as a novelist gives the play a distinctly New Woman twist.

The popular and prolific playwright Sidney Grundy was quick to cash in on the public fascination with the figure in his play *The New Woman* (1894), which featured several female authors. Opposed to what he saw as the plotlessness of the New Drama, Grundy was not one of the progressive New Drama set, and his play is predictably reactionary in its representation of New Women.[15] It features a cabal of four cigarette-smoking feminist authors who have written books such as *Aspirations after a Higher Morality* and *Man, the Betrayer – A Study of the Sexes*. The authors' male hanger-on, Percy Pettigrew, is a caricature of the aesthete Oscar Wilde.[16] In the poster for the Comedy Theatre production, the New Woman appears true to type in dowdy dress, surrounded by a mess of papers, wearing a *pince-nez*. A latchkey is framed on the wall behind her and her smouldering cigarette has been lit at both ends, exposing her smoking as an affectation by implying that she can't tell the tobacco end from the filter. William Archer took exception to this joke at the New Woman's expense as a 'cruel injustice'.[17]

The play starts in the effeminately decorated chambers of Gerald Cazenove, the *raisonneur* who suffers from what his uncle the Colonel diagnoses as 'intellectual measles' (p. 4) and a lack of manliness in his connection with the unsexed New Women: 'They have invented a new gender. And to think my nephew's one of them!' (p. 5). In the first act, Gerald and Mrs Sylvester (Agnes) are collaborating on a book on the ethics of marriage when Gerald confesses that he has fallen in love and hopes to be married himself. Agnes warns that marriage would be a foolish hindrance, while his aunt Lady Wargrave forbids the marriage on class grounds: Gerald's beloved is Lady Wargrave's maid Margery. In contrast to the middle-class New Women with whom Gerald associates, working-class Margery affirms that she is perfectly ready to swear to 'obey' as part of her marriage vows. Gerald reconsiders his formerly 'advanced' views on mutual sympathy between the sexes, breaking off his intellectual attachment to Agnes with classic separate spheres logic: 'Strength requires gentleness, sweetness asks for light; and all that is womanly in woman wants all that is manly in man' (p. 44). Grundy's happy ending exiles the New Women and their views and restores the conventional marriage of a manly man to a womanly woman.

In his review, Archer refuted the idea that Agnes Sylvester was a New Woman at all: 'She is any woman of brains pitted against any woman of beauty; and even her brains we have largely to take on trust' (TW94, p. 230). Even the conservative critic Clement Scott found Grundy's portrayal of the New Woman heavy handed and simplistic, suggesting:

> [I]f we are to discuss the 'New Woman' let her be fairly discussed. Mrs Sylvester might have been a true as well as a New Woman and thus shown us the earnest side of the movement in contrast to the ridiculous side of it.
>
> (*Illustrated London News*, 8 September 1894)

Offering a sexist counterpoint to the many female-authored New Woman novels and plays published in 1894, the year Lyn Pykett has described as 'the annus mirabilis of the new woman' (1995, p. 137), Grundy's play chimed with mainstream audiences, making *The New Woman* one of the biggest box office hits of the year.

The Notorious Mrs Ebbsmith

In 1895 Pinero followed the success of *The Second Mrs Tanqueray* with a New Woman play, *The Notorious Mrs Ebbsmith,* in which a politician turns his back on society and his career to live in a free union with a New Woman who was played by the now famous 'Mrs Pat' (Stella Campbell). The play opens in Venice, where Agnes (widowed) and Lucas (married) are embarking on the joint project of radical marriage critique and reform. Lucas, who has given up the promise of his political career to escape an unhappy marriage, seems committed to Agnes's feminist political ideals at the beginning, but sensuality is at the root of a developing crisis. Prior to meeting Lucas, Agnes was a radical feminist platform speaker, warning women of the dangers of marriage. When she first enters, Agnes's dress is described as 'plain to the verge of coarseness' and her face as 'at the first glance almost wholly unattractive' (p. 67). When Lucas kisses her on the lips, she 'makes no response, and after a pause gently releases herself and retreats a step or two' (p. 78) to which he remarks on her growing coldness. Agnes proposes that their relationship should evolve into a higher form of love, 'devoid of passion' (p. 78), fuelled instead by the mutual project of radical political writing and speaking. Her vision is more in keeping with the conservative ideals of purity feminism than Lucas's ideas of a partnership between a man and woman, which at first appears to be a radical endorsement of free love but later looks more like the established male prerogative of keeping a mistress. His response to her proposal of an asexual relationship encapsulates the prevailing cynicism around calls for male chastity. The rift between Agnes's ideal of Lucas as a 'new man' and his true nature as a sensualist widens with the arrival of a revealing gown he has ordered for her. She examines it with aversion: 'A mere strap for the sleeve, and sufficiently *décolleté*, I should imagine. [...] Rustle of silk, glare of arms and throat – they belong, to my mind, to such a very different order of things from that we have set up' (pp. 82–83). When Lucas's wife and the Duke of St Olphert, the representative of patriarchy, arrive from England to persuade Lucas to return to his home and career, Agnes resorts to wearing the dress to appeal to his lust. As an actress, Campbell apparently took the point of Agnes's degradation further than Pinero intended when she appeared wearing the silken gown as if it were a hair-shirt and played the bitter and ironic notes to the exclusion of all others, drawing criticism from Archer.[18] Despite Agnes wearing the gown with 'a heavy, almost sullen, look upon her face' (p. 98) Lucas delights in it, implying that he is looking at her *décolleté* rather than her expression.

Ultimately, Lucas abandons the 'madness' of their progressive plans with a wave of the hand: 'No more thoughts of reforming unequal laws from public platforms, no more shrieking in obscure magazines' (p. 105). In the end Pinero avoids the tragic pathos of suicide and instead sends Agnes to a bleak fate in a vicarage. Though Pinero attempts to create a more complex female character in this play, the slippage between Agnes Ebbsmith's identity as a New Woman, a fallen woman and a hysteric[19] (as she appears when she flings a Bible into the fire and burns her hand retrieving it) undermines the progressive possibilities of the New Woman. The promise of Agnes's potential glory as a leader of women turns to shame in her love for a hypocritical man. Despite hearing of her off-stage past as a New Woman platform speaker, what the audience actually sees is Agnes's transformation from a dowdy New Woman to a repentant fallen woman.

The play met with more mixed reviews than *Tanqueray*. The *Quarterly Review* described Agnes as 'the cold theorist, the blue stocking misbehaved, Girton astray' (October 1895). Shaw opens his review with the simple, damning line 'The play is bad' and goes on to lambast Pinero's dramaturgy as sensational '"character actor" nonsense' (*The Sketch*,[20] 27 March 1895). For Campbell, Agnes was a frustrating role, which strained her relationship with Pinero as she attempted to play against the part as written. The first three acts, she said, 'filled me with ecstasy. There was a touch of nobility that fired and inspired me, but the last act broke my heart' (Campbell, c. 1925, p. 98). Though she believed that Agnes, with her revolt against conventional morals, was 'a finer woman, and the part a greater one, than Mrs. Tanqueray' (p. 99), the script and the production were stacked against the New Woman's righteous political indignation, instead reinforcing the conventional shame and despair of the fallen woman. Campbell didn't find the 'Bible-reading inertia' of the final act to be a realistic character progression for Agnes, reasoning 'for her earlier vitality, with its mental and emotional activity, gave the lie to it – I felt she would have risen a phoenix from the ashes' (p. 98). Campbell regarded Pinero's 'rounding off of plays to make the audience feel comfortable' as 'a regrettable weakness' (p. 99) and longed for a fourth act, in which Agnes would emerge again as a commanding public speaker, rather than 'creeping back into the shell of a narrow morality' (p. 99). This tension between the roles real New Women actresses wanted to play and the parts male dramatists wrote for them was a central conflict of the 1890s, leading some, like Robins, to believe that they would have to take on both writing and producing if they wanted to truly change representations of women in theatre.

Thyrza Fleming

In Dorothy Leighton's drama *Thyrza Fleming* (1894) a manly New Woman cousin and a womanly New Woman mother battle over the future of the innocent young Pamela Rivers. Pamela leaves her husband Hugh within hours of their wedding, when the arrival of a mysterious letter signed 'T' leads her to believe he has a mistress. The plot shares many similarities with Sarah Grand's *Heavenly Twins,* most notably the young wife's refusal to consummate the marriage, shielding herself from a husband she deems morally and sexually tainted.[21] Pamela has a ready-made familial refuge in her cousin, an ardent advocate of purity feminism with the evangelical name Theophila. Where Grand's heroine Evande is an original thinker who stands alone, Pamela acts under the influence of the unsympathetically drawn New Woman who has instilled her 'dangerous notions into Pamela's empty head' (p. 42). With her close-cropped hair, manly attire and comedic back-slapping manner, the New Woman Theophila threatens male privilege not only by proselytizing young women like Pamela, but by actively policing the behaviours of men. Theophila's network of female detectives attack the double standard head-on by investigating prospective husbands' pasts in a deliberate attempt to stop pure women from marrying impure men.

The manly, man-hating New Woman cousin is a one-dimensional comedic character in contrast with the tragic romantic figure of Pamela's New Woman mother, creating what Carlson has identified as 'a battle of genre' (1999, p. 271) in this play. Though she made the New Woman's claim to personal freedom by walking out on her husband and child when Pamela was only a year old, Thyrza Fleming (her assumed name) is drawn more sympathetically than the stock New Woman character. Thyrza is less like fallen women with illicit pasts in dramas by Henry Arthur Jones, Pinero or Wilde than she is like Ibsen's Nora. Rather than leaving her husband for another man or because a past sin has been discovered, Thyrza says, 'I simply left him to be free' (p. 33). Thyrza's rationale for walking out on her family incorporates elements of feminism in her rejection of patriarchal authority, calling her husband's ideas of a wife's duty 'hideous'. She rejects her husband's assertion of ownership over her through his restrictions on her actions, books, friends and pursuits. But unlike Nora, who offered audiences a rejection of the status quo and an open ending for the future, Thyrza's story paints a bleak picture of life beyond the family. In the opening scene, Leighton invokes Ibsen when Pamela says 'I won't be treated like a doll' (p. 15), only to undermine female assertions of independence through Thyrza who stands as witness to the misery that feminist thinking will bring:

> I wanted freedom; I thought I owed a higher duty to myself than to my child, for I hated her father and thought I was right in leaving him. But now ... I am heavily punished, and I suppose it was all a mistaken view of duty, and I am reaping what I sowed. I begin to see dimly that the true self of a woman

never can be developed at the expense of those who look to her for love and tenderness, and that self-development is generally an excuse for self-indulgence. God knows I've learnt this lesson hardly, but ... (sighs and gets up) I've learnt it at last! (p. 63)

In a spectacular act of collusion with Hugh, who turns out to have been Thyrza's love interest of 15 years,[22] Thyrza becomes his advocate in trying to win her daughter Pamela back from the New Women and their 'modern clap trap' (p. 56). Thyrza's arguments run along classic separate spheres lines as she urges Pamela, 'Isn't it a greater thing to keep a man's love and respect and to bring him the realisation of his ideal, than to follow your own isolated notions of morality?' (p. 56). Ultimately Thyrza's conservative endorsement of the double standard and her passionate attempts to reconcile Pamela and Hugh makes her story a tragic and cautionary vision of what happens to women who pursue self-interests.

Two years prior to *Thyrza Fleming*, Mrs Erlynne, a similarly New Woman/fallen woman in Wilde's 1892 play *Lady Windermere's Fan*, urges her daughter to stay with her husband and fulfil the womanly duties that she herself shirked. Though in both plays the absentee-mother rescues the daughter from her own fate, there are key differences in the resolution. After restoring Pamela and Hugh's marriage, Thyrza immediately reaches for a revolver to end her life in the self-destructive tradition of the fallen woman. She is saved by Pamela, who, having overheard the truth of her parentage, returns and 'flings her arms round her, with a wild cry' of 'M o t h e r !' (p. 67). In contrast, Mrs Erlynne keeps the secret of her maternity, and despite admitting to feelings for her daughter, asserts, 'I have no ambition to play the part of mother [...] I want to live childless still' (p. 54). After restoring order in her daughter's house, Mrs Erlynne rejects a repentant ending for herself, marries into the aristocracy and goes to live abroad, making Wilde's ending less conservative than Leighton's.

EDUCATION AND INDEPENDENCE

One of the primary goals of the New Woman was freedom, which was strongly associated with education and the financial independence of careers. Rigorous academic education, however, wasn't available to most girls at the college or even secondary school level. Girls' education had fallen to a particularly low standard in the early and mid-Victorian era, especially in private middle-class schools where it was fashionable to promote 'accomplishments' such as needlework and piano over academic subjects like English or mathematics. Parents paid enormous sums to sham schools that turned out semi-literate daughters, cultivated only in 'the arts of attraction'. In Bessie Hatton's play *Before Sunrise* (1909) a father rebuffs the idea that his middle-class daughter is insufficiently educated as ridiculous: 'Caroline is well educated. She can play and sing nicely, writes a neat ladylike hand, speaks a little French, sews and embroiders, and no one expects any more from a woman' (p. 210). Education, which might have been an escape from the monotony of life in the gilded cage, was frequently only a modified extension of it. Many of the wealthiest families did not send their daughters to school at all.[23] Working-class girls were actually more likely to receive a foundational education from certified teachers. Middle-class girls were often schooled in private houses by untrained spinster daughters and sisters as an informal social solution to genteel poverty. By the latter half of the century, liberals and conservatives alike agreed that girls' education should be reformed; the controversial question was how and to what purpose.

In 1869 the pioneering education reformer Emily Davies[24] and her friends Barbara Bodichon and Lady Stanley founded Girton residential college for the education of women with a view to sitting the Cambridge Tripos. Cambridge University's mathematical Tripos was considered to be the most intellectually demanding examination in the world, with students competing annually for the coveted title of Senior Wrangler. In 1881 Cambridge formally admitted women to the examinations alongside the men. The most spectacular early triumph for women's education came in 1890 when Philippa Fawcett[25] took the highest honours in the Cambridge mathematical Tripos, putting the university in the contradictory position of denying formal admission or degrees to pupils who were verified as stars by its own system.[26] Fawcett, who could not receive a degree herself and therefore could not be Senior Wrangler, was announced in the public assembly as 'Above the Senior Wrangler', triggering telegrams and newspaper reports around the English-speaking world. Fawcett's achievement inspired many young women to pursue higher education, as well as inspiring Shaw's character Vivie Warren.

Edward Aveling's comedy *My Niece*[27] was published in the same year as Fawcett's famous result. Set in the garden of Mrs Hazeldine's finishing school in Brighton, the piece captures some of the paradoxical feelings about female students in its depiction of a group of girls notionally preparing for the Cambridge exams but actually more interested in romantic intrigues. Male characters voice typical backhanded compliments ('she's very pretty for so learned a girl' (p. 13)) while the young women make obnoxious gaffes that undermine their credibility as well educated. Ironically, Aveling's fictional schoolgirls bear no resemblance to the fiercely intelligent women of his own social circle, including Annie Besant, Beatrice Webb, Olive Schreiner and his lover Eleanor Marx with whom he translated her father's work *Das Kapital* and co-authored *The Woman Question*.

Despite the progress of reformers such as Davies and the growing number of girls pursuing higher education, serious study was still largely regarded as unfeminine. Defenders of the status quo like Harry Campbell, who published *Differences in the Nervous Organisation of Man and Woman* in 1891, predicted that true women would be ravaged by study, implying that women who excelled at scholarship were somehow unsexed. Conservative educators and doctors like Hughes Bennett, Henry Maudsley and Robert Sprague wrote copious articles to discredit the campaign for female education, couching their warnings to girls and their parents in terms that suggested that they did not object to education for women out of any unfriendly desire to bar them from learning, but simply from a profound concern for their physiological well-being. These self-proclaimed protectors of women's health cautioned that the delicate feminine psychological balance would be distorted and possibly destroyed by studies which would rob energy from the ovaries to fuel the brain. The physiological danger was double: the neglected ovaries would atrophy, causing irregular periods, uterine disease, amenorrhoea, dysmenorrhoea, chronic and acute ovaritis, and prolapsed uteri, shrivelled breasts, sterility and even cancer; meanwhile the brain would become over stimulated, which could result in neurasthenia, hysteria, insanity, hypochondriasis and emaciation.[28]

The education aspect of the woman question generated some of the most interesting and intense debates of the era as well as some of the most caricatured representations of women. Late Victorian and Edwardian period plays treating the subject of female education are rare, despite the fact that educated women were a forceful presence in real life. When they do appear, their studies are often the subject of jest or mockery. In Pinero's 1891 play *The Times*, the character Lucy Tuck has been studying at Newnham College, Cambridge with dire consequences to her health as noted by her aunt: 'Poor Lucy has broken down woefully at Newnham. Her feminine intellect has drawn the line at Latin Prose and left her rubbing menthol into her brows from morning til night' (p. 29).

Lucy admits that despite leaving Newnham she has been suffering from a headache for two years as a result of her studies, and worries that it makes her 'appear unsociable' (p. 29). Though Pinero's characters stop short of speculating on whether Lucy's fertility remains intact, her 'unsociable' appearance implies that education has decreased her chances of marriage. In relation to the severity of contemporary medical warnings, Lucy Tuck gets off lightly with her two-year headache and off-putting visage. The end product of female education, reactionary doctors warned, would not be educated *women*, but rather educated 'monstrosities', as imagined by Dr Henry Maudsley, 'something which having ceased to be woman is not yet man' (1874b, p. 477). Fifteen years later and well into the suffrage campaign, the general sentiment that womanliness and scholarship were like water and oil still held sway. In Harley Granville Barker's play *Waste* (1907), the protagonist, Henry Trebell, reportedly 'father' of the greatest scheme for education reform in British history, remarks, 'I've never met a clever woman ... worth calling a woman' (p. 175).

The dangers purported to jeopardize the health of female students didn't end with the physiological damage to individuals; because the 'price' of women's education was described almost exclusively in terms of thwarted motherhood, eugenicists warned that widespread women's education could bring about 'race suicide' (Sprague, 1915, p. 158). In addition to medical concerns over the fertility of educated women, eugenicists feared that if women were allowed to pursue higher education and enter the professions, then the crème de la crème would choose these formerly male prerogatives over marriage and motherhood. The only legitimate children brought forth, then, would be those of the lower orders of society, thus polluting and degenerating the national stock.[29]

In *Mrs Warren's Profession*, Shaw's Vivie Warren plays to some of these fears of the 'unsexing' effect of a college education. Vivie is instantly recognizable as a New Woman with her iconic bicycle, serious-looking books, business-like dress and chatelaine. Not only has Vivie attended college and taken exams at Cambridge, but she has recently tied for Third Wrangler in the maths Tripos. These are the established trademarks of the New Woman, but Shaw goes further, endowing Vivie with a freakishly strong handshake and an attitude towards life that is presented as the cool, unsentimental, self-sufficient mindset of a confirmed bachelor, 'permanently single ... and permanently unromantic' (p. 222). Vivie not only smokes cigars (a habit Frank points out that nice men have abandoned), she blows smoke wreaths. Her office desk is cluttered with ash pans and snowed under by heaps of papers and books. In short, Vivie is more of a 'man's man' than any of the male characters in the play, affirming reactionary fears more than symbolizing progressive visions.

Vivie's lack of feminine sympathy is the aspect of her personality most disturbing to the other characters. She is outspoken, critical and prefers work to society. During the first private interview between mother and daughter it is the brothel magnate Mrs Warren who is shocked by her daughter rather than vice versa. Mrs Warren, who expects that her tears will be greeted with sympathy and tenderness from another woman, especially a daughter, is aghast when Vivie responds by checking her watch and enquiring at what hour they will breakfast. Crofts and Frank want a wife and Mrs Warren wants a loving daughter, but Vivie is more interested in actuarial calculations, conveyancing and the stock exchange than any of these personal relationships. Vivie craves work, attesting that she would 'open an artery and bleed to death' (p. 184) rather than drift through life with no purpose or grit. In her rejection of three suitors and her mother, Shaw depicts his Cambridge-educated woman as cold, masculine and not particularly sympathetic. In the end, Vivie determines to shut herself off in a world of papers and ledgers with a female business partner pointedly named Honoria. While this ending leads some to speculate on the possibility of a lesbian relationship, I read the female partnership of Fraser & Warren as less significant in its sexual implications than in the relative 'purity' of its economic foundation. Fraser and Warren are middle-class women who work for themselves in their chosen field. They are not exploited by the pimps of industrial labour, and they do not exploit other female workers.

INVERSION PANIC

Early in the twentieth century, reactionaries would use the works of sexologists like Havelock Ellis and Richard von Krafft-Ebing to present a further social danger facing women in higher education: sexual 'inversion'. Although Ellis, the most prominent British sexologist, described 'inversion' as congenital,[30] he also warned that it could be acquired by women with latent proclivities.[31] This second, more nebulous category was composed of women whom he described as having a 'genetic weakness' for the advances of the invert, although not actually inverts themselves. Ellis categorized this class of women as 'homosexual' and claimed that homosexuality was an attribute that, unlike inversion, was acquired and therefore preventable. The congenital invert, he assured, was rare and should be treated humanely.[32] The welfare of women with submerged susceptibilities, however, should be proactively safeguarded by society; in the 'unwholesome environment' of an all-girls' boarding school or college, these women would succumb to the seductions of the congenital invert whereas, safely confined within traditional institutions, the homosexual would overcome her susceptibility.[33] Because any female might harbour latent homosexuality, all women were potentially at risk in women's schools and colleges.

Claims issued under the cloak of medical science to question the health and morality of educated women were difficult for feminists to refute with equal authority. In fiction, however, women could create and disseminate representations of a college culture where attractive young women from varied backgrounds and classes lived and worked together in happy industrious communities. The heroines of these novels simultaneously enjoy the freedom of having their own private rooms for study and entertaining as well as the stimulating communal experiences of dining halls and lectures. A whole genre of college-girl novels sprang up, many of them serialized in magazines, providing multiple new role models for girls. In these stories, tremendously popular among young women of all classes, the heroines are generally smart, beautiful and athletic. In Edith Nesbit's[34] short story 'The Girton Girl' (1895), Laura Wentworth is a handsome and learned super woman who can gracefully ride, sing, swim, dance and pull an oar or a trigger as well as she can construe Aeschylus. Above all, she is fiercely protective of her independence: 'The right not to marry is what we want' (p. 755). In an intriguing plot twist, Laura both subverts and conforms to gender type when the man who loves her swims out to sea to drown himself in despair over her anti-marriage stance and she heroically swims out to save his life, then marries him. Although many of her traits and talents are masculine, this heroine and many like her have more in common with Greek Goddesses than with negative stereotypes of bluestockings[35] or spinsters. The college-girl novel thus allowed a new generation of young women to imagine themselves in entirely new scripts of behaviour.

While these novels created an important imaginative space for young women, feminists needed more concrete scientific evidence in their arsenal to withstand the attacks of reactionary authorities. Feminists strategized that it was time for women to produce their own experts. In a pioneering study in 1887, Eleanor Sidgwick,[36] herself one of the first students of Newnham College, Cambridge, devised a questionnaire to study the health of college women as compared with that of their sisters or cousins. The results of this study, published as 'Health Statistics of Women Students of Cambridge and Oxford and of their Sisters', claimed that the college women were in better health than the control group of women who had remained at home and furthermore that 'as mothers of healthy families we have seen that the students are more satisfactory than their sisters' (Sidgwick, 1890, p. 91). Studies like this were invaluable to the cause. One of the first feminist imperatives was to enter the medical profession and discredit the scientific explanations so frequently used against women. When women attained the status of lecturer, doctor and lawyer they would, it was hoped, be able to argue their own positions with convincing authority. Mary T. Bissell, a pioneering woman doctor, authored one such treatise, called 'Emotions Versus Health in Women', in which she maintained that far from presenting a danger to women's health, education could prevent the 'excessive emotional disturbance' (1888, p. 510) of idleness.

Bessie Hatton's 1909 play *Before Sunrise* is set four decades in the past in 1867, and opens with a patriarch noting with satisfaction the defeat of John Stuart Mill's amendment to include women's suffrage in The Second Reform Act. On the day of this pivotal moment in feminist history (the first suffrage societies were formed in the wake of this event) Hatton depicts a crossroads in a young woman's life. Caroline can either marry a profligate man or live with another woman and pursue a career. Caroline is encouraged to pull the stays in her corset tighter for her philandering suitor Tom and when she breaks down in tears of pain, her mother threatens her with the life of an old maid. At this juncture, handsome Mary arrives offering feminist advice and opportunity. In contrast to Caroline's physical and mental anguish, Mary brings an air of hope and excitement as she happily announces that her book has been accepted by a publisher and dreams of the great things women will accomplish in the not too distant future – which for the 1909 audience is the present. Mary acknowledges that women 'are handicapped at present', but predicts that they will make 'magnificent headway in great professions, as doctors, writers, artists' and take 'high honours at the colleges and universities of their country' (p. 213). Mary equates Caroline's painful corset with ideological evils, declaring that women's 'minds are enveloped in moral stays, just as our bodies are pinched and tortured to take on an unnatural and ugly shape' (p. 215). Mary warns Caroline's mother of Tom's licentious past, causing her to faint, apparently not so much in disgust at Tom's sexual history as at Mary's social impropriety in bringing it up. Caroline's parents regard Caroline's female friend Mary with a suspicion that echoes medical fears of inversion, calling Mary a 'bluestocking' (p. 210) and a 'mannish young woman' (p. 211). Mary offers a same-sex counter-proposal to Caroline, inviting her to come and live with her in Paris and encouraging her to seek employment as a teacher. Despite worries that her education is wanting, Caroline delightedly accepts Mary's offer, but the play ends on a tragic note as Caroline's mother sends Mary away and physically places Caroline in Tom's arms as the curtain drops. By setting Caroline's story half a century in the past, however, Hatton encourages the 1909 audience to see their own time as 'the wonderful dawn of the new era' (p. 213) foretold by Mary.

Nearly 20 years on from creating Vivie Warren, Shaw wrote *Fanny's First Play* (1911) in which an updated Cambridge student, Fanny O'Dowda, hires actors and invites critics to a play she has anonymously authored. *Fanny's First Play* was fantastically popular, the longest running of any of Shaw's works in his lifetime with 622 performances. Like Shaw, Fanny is an active member of the Fabian Society[37] and in another consciously self-referential gesture, she also is an aspiring playwright. The presentation and critical reception of Fanny's play within the play cleverly mirrored the real play's London debut.[38] In this play within the play, the young middle-class heroine, Margaret Knox (played by Lillah McCarthy), goes to prison for two weeks for knocking out two of a policeman's teeth. In gaol she meets several suffragettes and by the time she is released she has received an education that changes her outlook on life completely. Though in the play the character Margaret is not herself a suffragette, the critic Trotter extrapolates that the play's author, Fanny O'Dowda, is:

> FANNY: [...] I did a month with Lady Constance Lytton; and I'm prouder of it than I ever was of anything or ever shall be again.
> TROTTER: Is that any reason why you should stuff naughty plays down my throat?
> FANNY: Yes: it'll teach you what it feels like to be forcibly fed. (p. 181)

Fanny dilutes her own political opinions and experiences in the fashioning of her fictional self, Margaret Knox, a strategy often used by female dramatists. Though she is not in the running for Senior Wrangler in the Tripos, Fanny is much more engaged with the world at large. The most significant element of Fanny's education comes not from Cambridge, but from her involvement with the suffrage campaign and a month in prison.

WOMEN AND WORK

Once educated, what types of work could or should women pursue? This question was the source of much debate and angst in Victorian and Edwardian Britain. Emily Davies proposed that women needed to test their capacities through experience, pursuing the trades and professions of their choosing, allowed to succeed as well as to fail. In her article 'Women and Work', Langham Place Group member Barbara Bodichon predicted that women 'will rather prefer those nobler works which have in them something congenial to their moral natures' (1857, p. 64), speculating that the arts, the sciences and education would most strongly attract them. Fifty years later, actress and author Cicely Hamilton took the less romantic, more constructionist view that there was no inherently natural occupation for either sex, only work that men preferred and work that they did not, arguing: 'woman's "natural" labour in any given community is the form of labour which the men of that community do not care to undertake' (MT, p. 112). Social Darwinist F. Howard Collins put it bluntly: 'the stronger sex forces the weaker to do all the drudgery' (1889, p. 418).

By Hamilton's reasoning, domestic work was the form of labour British men least cared to undertake. The central London employment statistics for 1891 show that women engaged in domestic service accounted for roughly half the female workforce.[39] While the middle-class 'woman of leisure' was confined to the domestic realm through culture, thousands of working-class women were confined to the same realm as servants. Married women also engaged in domestic service through the lower-middle-class custom of taking in lodgers, which provided a way of earning income without working in public. By the turn of the century, however, the age of domestic service was in decline and women were taking up more visible public occupations such as shop work, factory work, clerical work, nursing, millinery, dress and shoe making, and food production. A woman's career options were significantly narrower than those of her male counterparts, but she was moving gradually into the public sphere, and public perceptions of 'a woman's place' were shifting.[40]

While the real numbers of women in the workforce did not rise substantially, the number of women in non-domestic vocations increased dramatically and with it public consciousness of working women. In a sign of growing anxiety about social change, an Inter-departmental Committee on Physical Deterioration was established in 1903 to investigate the per-ceived deterioration of the race supposedly caused primarily by married women working (Holloway, 2005, p. 79). Despite alarm over working wives, by the 1911 census only 9.6 per cent of the married female population of the UK was employed in paid work. The major changes in employment would come a few years later as women took on a wide variety of men's jobs during WWI, radically altering the constitution of workplaces and notions of the woman's sphere and creating tensions between patriarchy and patriotism. Patriarchy struggled to maintain power over the family while capitalism sought to reap the benefits of cheap unorganized women's labour. Despite feminist aims for greater gender equality, women ultimately entered the public workforce less through the efforts of feminism than through the necessity of war and the profiteering of capitalism.

Beyond bit part domestic servant roles, female employees make fairly rare appearances in the drama of the era in comparison with the conspicuously increasing appearances they were making in real life. When they do appear, they are often marginal characters or their professions are peripheral. Then again, male professionals are also relatively invisible. William Archer identified the lack of interest in work generally as a snobbish trait in British drama compared with continental drama, noting that 'while German playwrights pass and repass freely from high life to middle-class life and low life, the English playwright concerns himself exclusively with the manners and the emotions of the idle rich' (quoted in Wilson, 1951, p. 15). Doctors and lawyers appear primarily when feeling the pulse of a Lady or making the will of a Lord. In England working people – the charwoman, the landlady, the greengrocer – were the characters of farce and music hall. Serious dramatic literature generally lacked representations of working life in favour of leisured drawing room scenes, one of the limitations of British theatre that advocates of the New Drama sought to challenge, as they championed and often translated work from the continent dealing with a wider sphere of human experience. William Archer translated a 13-volume edition of Ibsen's plays as well as plays by Maurice Maeterlinck and Gerhart Hauptmann; Elizabeth Robins translated or finessed translations of many of the Ibsen roles she played as well as translating works by Ibsen's contemporary Bjørnstjerne Bjørnson; and St. John Hankin and Charlotte Payne-Townshend Shaw (Shaw's wife) translated Eugène Brieux. Edith Craig's production company the Pioneer Players prioritized plays in translation including works by Herman Heijermans, Paul Claudel, Nikolai Evreinov and Anton Chekhov, usually translated by Craig's partner Christopher St. John (Christabel Marshall). Despite the general lack of attention to employment in British drama, there are some interesting examples of working women in the drama of the period.

Typewriting was a rapidly expanding field, often associated with the New Woman, treated by J.M. Barrie in *The Twelve-Pound Look* (1910). From the 1880s, feminists were quick to spot the typewriters coming onto the market as the key to a whole new field of skilled labour. Women set up typing schools in their homes, or in larger premises if they had the capital, with the aim of creating an 'army' of typists, rushing women into the field before male clerks had time to claim it. Typewriting offered better hours, less physical strain and higher pay than jobs in shops or factories. *The Young Woman* career guide magazine featured typewriting as one of the most promising and suitable professions for girls, not unlike the lady-like accomplishment of piano playing with the fair typist's 'fingers dancing quickly over the tiny ivory keys' (quoted in Mitchell, 1995, p. 36) with a musical effect. The number of women employed in clerical work rose from 6,000 in 1881 to over 20 times that number (125,000) in 1911.[41] Women typists became an established civil service pay grade in 1894 as a result of a petition by female employees for better pay and permanent status. In the 50 years leading up to WWI the number of women office workers increased by a factor of 500 (Steinbach, 2004, p. 41). The play-wright Elizabeth Baker wrote *Chains* in 1909 while working as a typist for *The Spectator*. George Gissing's novel, *The Odd Women*, provides the most thorough fictional account of typing as the New Woman's new vocation.

In contrast to the gritty realism of Gissing's novel, J.M. Barrie's *The Twelve-Pound Look*, written in the midst of the militant suffrage campaign, is a comedic parable. The play opens on the soon-to-be Sir Harry Sims rehearsing to receive his knighthood. The typist, sent by the Flora Type-Writing Agency to type form replies to letters of congratulations, turns out to be Harry's ex-wife Kate who disappeared mysteriously many years before. Harry is shocked, then delighted, by this turn of events, instinctively feeling that the situation will provide the perfect opportunity to make his first wife jealous. Kate, however, is 'self-reliant and serene' (p. 7), nimble in her work, confident in her manners and has an easy sense of humour. In contrast, Barrie provides extensive directions for Lady Sims, whose lines and movements are punctuated by the notes: 'nervously', 'abashed' (p. 5), 'in her nervous way' (p. 7), 'almost with the humility of a servant' (p. 9), 'with a dread fear that she has vexed her lord' (p. 13) and 'faltering' (p. 37). A photograph from the Little Theatre production depicts a comedic contrast: Kate, played by the glamorous leading lady Lillah McCarthy, looks smart and modern in the rational dress of the New Woman while Lady Sims, played by character actress Cicely Hamilton, is encumbered by a parodic excess of finery including a conical princess hat with a veil and a dress with a long train.[42] As Harry speaks of his current wife auctioneer-like, with the pride of possession, he arouses Kate's anger rather than her envy. She accuses him of crushing her successor's spirit: 'That dear creature capable of becoming a noble wife and mother – she is the spiritless woman of no account that I saw here a few minutes ago. I forgive you for myself, for I escaped, but that poor lost soul' (pp. 34–35). It never occurs to Harry that the one thing which Kate envies her successor is motherhood; he is quicker to point out that Lady Sims has four footmen than that they have two children. Far from the scenario Harry has hoped for, it is Lady Sims who 'gazes with a little envy perhaps at a woman who does things for herself' (p. 8) and watches Kate work, 'half-mesmerised' (p. 10). Finally, portentously, Lady Sims enquires how much a typewriter costs. Barrie's play is constructed more as a warning to men and husbands than a call to arms for women and wives. The warning, 'If I was a husband – it is my advice to all of them – I would often watch my wife quietly to see whether the twelve-pound look was not coming into her eyes' (p. 35) implies that middle-class men who have taken women's financial dependence for granted are going to have to compete with the common virtue of self-sufficiency on offer to the increasing number of middle-class women entering the professions.

The Twelve-Pound Look is unique in depicting a divorced couple. Though England did eventually make divorce possible,[43] feminists were well aware that British divorce laws were behind the times in relation to the rest of Europe and America. The law was full of obstacles[44] and extremely expensive, making it a 'privilege of the rich'.[45] Shaw also treats divorce in some of his plays. In the original ending to *The Philanderer* (1893), the ill-suited couple, Julia and Paramore, decide to go to South Dakota for a quick low-profile solution, underscoring the draconian nature of English divorce laws. Paramore is warned that even in South Dakota he should be careful of Queen's protector officials:[46] 'In this country, if it can be found that a divorce has been arranged to promote the happiness of the parties concerned, it is cancelled as immoral' (p. 158). On advice from his friend Lady Colin Campbell, who told him to put the third act in the fire, Shaw abandoned the divorce act and ended the play with a conventional engagement scene.[47] Fifteen years later Shaw revisited his opinions in favour of more relaxed divorce laws in *Getting Married*, but made his criticisms of the status quo palatable to audiences by reconciling the divorcing couple after airing the arguments.

St. John Hankin's comedy *The Last of the De Mullins* (1908) challenges the patriarchal status quo by comparing the decline of an aristocratic family – in land, wealth, heirs and spirit – to the prosperity of their break-away daughter Janet, an unmarried mother. In both business and family matters, Hankin represents upper-class decline as a joint product of dwindling capital and inflexible scripts of behaviour. His New Woman Janet De Mullin, who gives herself the surname 'Seagrave' and passes herself off as a widow, exemplifies the middle-class virtues of industry, investment, thrift and invention. A successful entrepreneur, her triumphs are built on a combination of hard work and calculated risk-taking. She increases a £400 legacy, inherited from an aunt, into £500 in a few years by investing in the railway, an industry that symbolizes nineteenth-century industrial progress. Though she is reliant in the first instance on the capital bequeathed by her aunt, she does not invest it in safe government bonds, but rather puts it to work, generating her own capital. When the opportunity arises, she uses her funds to become the controlling partner of *'Claude et Cie'*, the hat shop she formerly worked at as an employee. Once in control of the business, Janet refuses to honour the unspoken code of middle-class leniency towards unpaid upper-class bills. She sues half the British aristocracy for their outstanding accounts, yielding nearly £1,200 to start a new business, one that will cater exclusively to middle-class women 'who are not too haughty to pay for a hat when they see a cheap one' (p. 48). Janet is not entirely a self-made woman, but Hankin depicts her most substantial gains as products of industry and acumen. By rejecting patriarchal values, Janet frees herself from the conventional shame of the fallen woman or the stigma of working in the public sphere. Her son Johnny and her middle-class business are both sources of pride:

> JANET: [*firmly*] Yes, Aunt Harriet, I like it. And I'm proud of it.
> DE MULLIN: [*sharply*] Nonsense, Janet. Nobody can possibly be proud of keeping a shop.
> JANET: I am. I made it, you see. It's my child, like Johnny. (pp. 71–72)

Unlike Vivie Warren, who pursues her career at the expense of romance, or Kate Sims, who pays for her freedom by forgoing motherhood, Janet De Mullin's strongest argument for independence is identifying a link between her thriving business and her healthy child. Like Barrie, Hankin represents an upper-class woman aspiring 'down' into the middle class in order to escape a life of superfluousness. Janet's social shift, in economic and ideological terms, is a gender shift as well as a class shift, moving from the position of an upper-class woman to that of a middle-class man: she owns the shop.

Like Vivie Warren, Janet owes her independence largely to the financial support of another woman and goes into partnership with another woman, forgoing a 'middle man', so that the women work for themselves. In Janet's case, the business caters to women and is supported by women, creating a semi-separatist economy. The implications of tapping into a female economy were revolutionary. As the American businessman Eustace State in *The Madras House* (1909) observes, the middle-class women of England and America are 'potentially the greatest money-spending machine in the world' (1994, p. 183). The possibilities of women harnessing female spending power for their own economic gain was a progressive vision. Shop work was a rapidly growing area of employment for women. Industrialization led to the mass production of many household and personal goods including 'ready-made' or 'ready-to-wear' clothing, bringing with it a new age of consumerism and department stores catering for all classes of customer. In the 30-odd years between the launch of the fashionable Liberty department store on Regent Street in 1875, the palatial new Harrods in Knightsbridge in 1905 and Selfridges on Oxford Street in 1909, the number of shops in the country more than doubled.[48] Wealthy ladies interested in supporting employment opportunities for women helped bring about the rise of female shop assistants by letter campaigns to store managers specifically requesting to be served by women.[49] The sector grew exponentially as an employer of women from the late-Victorian era through the Edwardian period. Because shopping was highly stratified by class, from humble local corner shops to the glittering behemoths of the West End, it could accommodate suitable employment for women of different backgrounds. Middle-class women, who had formerly been most restricted, were now able to work in smart department stores without being regarded as unladylike. By 1914 shop assistants were the largest single group of middle-class women workers in the country.

Elizabeth Baker's play *Edith* (1912) features a strong central female character who works her way up from shop assistant in 'a wretched little milliner's shop' (p. 280) to become the owner of a fashion chain that stretches across England and into Europe. The play deals with the comedic fallout from Edith's father's will, which leaves his prosperous business to Edith rather than her brother, throwing the family into outrage and panic. Edith's brother Gerald, who never liked the family business and would have sold it in a poor deal, is so deeply affronted at having been passed over for a girl that he can't see the business logic of his father's decision. His ignorance of his sister's success confirms him as hopelessly out of touch with the fashion industry, as she observes: 'If you knew enough of your trade, Jerry, you'd know that the name of "Marie Première" stands for the last word in smartness' (p. 288). Like Vivie and Janet, Edith chooses another woman as her partner in yet another instance of a separatist economic business model.

Cicely Hamilton's most commercially successful drama was *Diana of Dobson's* (1908), one of the longest running plays by a woman in the Edwardian era with 141 performances. The heroine of *Diana of Dobson's* (played by suffragist actress manager Lena Ashwell) is a young middle-class woman who has been made destitute by the death of her father and is now a shopgirl in the employ of a London drapery establishment. At Dobson's she works 14 hours a day, six days a week, for a pittance salary, 'for the use of my health and strength – five bob a week for my life' (p. 12). The play's most daring theatrical innovation is the setting of the opening scene, which takes place in the women's dormitory of Dobson's as several shopgirls undress for bed. Hamilton subverts a potentially titillating tableau of female bodies undressing, instead depicting a distinctly unerotic illustration of the dehumanizing reality of the 'living-in' system. Diana and her co-workers cannot be read simply as so much nubile young flesh, tantalizing in their nightgowns – they are exhausted and quarrelsome workers coming off a 14-hour shift. Critics noted the 'realism and serious interest' of Hamilton's 'exposition of the living in-system' (*The Musical Standard*, 22 February 1908) while still speculating, somewhat cynically, that the undressing scene would help to make the play a success at the box office. Despite its feminist message, *The Academy* critic deemed it 'sufficiently realistic to please even Peeping Tom' (22 February 1908). Sheila Stowell identifies a separatist strategy at work in Hamilton's complete exclusion of men from the first act, allowing her 'to establish a female perspective safe from male interruption' (1992a, p. 183).

Hamilton, who researched the work by attending shop assistant union meetings, portrays Diana's situation as providing mere subsistence wages, grim food and cheap dormitory lodging. The controversies of the 'living-in' system were a matter of contemporary public debate, with the Amalgamated Union of Shop Assistants organizing a protest meeting at the Queen's Hall on the same night the play opened (Dymkowski, 2004, p. 115). Contemporary shopgirls complained bitterly of the 'living-in' system, pointing out that some paupers in workhouses were better fed and better housed. Employees felt doubly cheated under the system because not only were half their wages withheld for room and board, but the facilities and meals provided were of markedly lower quality than the market rate (Holcombe, 1973, pp. 112–13). Like her real-life counterparts, Diana has to pay fines for any perceived workplace transgression and is constantly threatened with dismissal. In legal terms shopgirls enjoyed more independence than married women but in day-to-day living, they often fared worse than their married counterparts. Subsistence wages and the 'living-in' system meant that shopgirls were far more restricted in their movements, their society and their ability to influence their environment than a wife in her home. Ultimately shopgirls were as financially dependent on their employers as a wife on her husband and, unlike a wife, a shopgirl could be sacked when her looks faded. The bleakest example of this in the drama of the period is Miss Tassey, a 45-year-old shop assistant in Elizabeth Baker's 1910 play of the same name, who is discharged by her employer because she is getting too old for counter work. With no job, no pension, no husband and no future in the only trade she knows, Miss Tassey kills herself.

Amidst a scene of grumbling after work at Dobson's with the other exhausted shopgirls, Diana receives a letter with the news that she will inherit 300 pounds from a distant relative, causing a sensation. Against everyone's advice Diana determines to seize what may be her only opportunity to taste freedom, and spend the money on one luxurious month of travel abroad. In the next act, Hamilton depicts a Cinderella transformation between the exhausted, short-tempered and shabbily dressed Diana of Dobson's and her newly created persona, the wealthy young widow Diana Massingberd, on holiday at a fashionable Swiss resort. Out of the shop environment, Diana is instantly sought after by the eligible men, enabling the rags-to-riches opportunity of rejecting a proposal of marriage from her former employer. Sir Jabez, who lives luxuriously off the profit of exploited female labourers, is made ridiculous by condescendingly explaining his trade to Diana. His justification for underpaying his workers is a standard conservative capitalist argument:

> In every healthy state of society the weakest goes to the wall, because the wall is his proper place. If a man isn't fit to be on top, he must go under – if he hasn't the power to rule, he must serve whether he likes it or not. (p. 32)

The majority of Sir Jabez's 'shiftless chaps', however, are women like Diana, and Sir Jabez's capitalistic logic clearly marks a distinction between attitudes of chivalry towards the middle-class woman as opposed to her working-class sisters, who must perforce 'go to the wall' in an industrial labour market. Joel Kaplan and Sheila Stowell point out that this conversation between two people in the garment industry, one an owner and one a labourer, is cleverly centred on 'dress', as Diana's rose-pink evening dress renders her visible for the first time: 'Indeed, so complete is the identification of the "girl" with the "garment" that the entrammeled Sir Jabez, while he woos its wearer, surreptitiously "feels the quality of goods in her sleeve"' (Kaplan and Stowell, 1994, p. 112).

In the creation of Diana Massingberd, Hamilton reverses the standard gender dynamic of courtship by making the young Captain Bretherton and his family anxious for a match as a means to secure an income for him. When he proposes, Diana confesses her true economic circumstances and Bretherton indignantly accuses her of being an adventuress, provoking a cutting outburst from Diana who in turn accuses him of being an adventur*er*. She defends her integrity and lays down a challenge:

> *DIANA:* When you thought I had married an old man for his money, you considered that I had acted in a seemly and womanly manner – when you learnt that, instead of selling myself in the marriage market – I have earned my living honestly, you consider me impossible. And yet, I have done for half a dozen years what you couldn't do for half a dozen months.
> *BRETHERTON:* And what's that?
> *DIANA:* Earned my bread, of course – without being beholden to any man and without a penny at my back. (pp. 51–52)

Diana leaves the hotel having held her own against both the leisured classes and the profiteers of industrial capitalism. Unfortunately, this is strictly a moral victory; Diana's money is spent.

The next act, set a few months later, provides yet another reversal when Bretherton appears again as a homeless manual labourer living rough on the London Embankment, having taken up Diana's challenge to support himself for six months. When he meets Diana by chance, Bretherton is anxious to demonstrate that he is now a worthy suitor. His social experiment has taught him that he can indeed afford to marry for love and he proposes to her again. Diana, who has been 'half starved for days', asks without irony, 'under the circumstances, don't you think that you are putting too great a strain upon my disinterestedness?' (p. 62) which is about as close to heterosexual romance as Hamilton gets. While Bretherton's character transformation makes him more attractive, Diana accepts his offer of marriage more in the spirit of an unemployed worker accepting a good job offer than of a woman in love. The pair celebrate their engagement as friends, sharing coffee and sandwiches on the Embankment among the homeless. Hamilton's argument on the evils of female economic dependence is forceful enough to withstand being completely glossed over by the happy ending. The engagement between Diana and Captain Bretherton is not depicted as a romantic idyll, but as a mutually beneficial contract and a step forward in relations between the sexes in terms of honesty. Writing in the *Sunday Times*, J.T. Grein hailed *Diana of Dobson's* as:

> exactly the type of play which we have been yearning for, it depicts life of today, it cuts into the lower stratum, it is hallowed by a touch of romance ... the greatest merit of all ... is the veracity, the simplicity, and directness of the play.
> (16 February 1908)

In *Chains* (published in 1911) Elizabeth Baker critiques the destructive effects of female economic dependency on romance, but dispenses with the conventional romantic comedy ending of an engagement. Maggie (played by suffragist Sybil Thorndike) is a lower-middle-class shop assistant who throws her shop collar and apron to the floor and dances on them when she receives a proposal that will rescue her from the work, despite not being particularly fond of the middle-aged widower Walter. After their engagement, Walter expects an affection that Maggie cannot naturally give, creating an awkward sexual tension as he holds her hand and she looks at it 'imprisoned in his' (p. 53). Maggie eventually breaks off the engagement, saying she was a fool 'to throw up one sort of – cage – for another' (p. 75). Though her act is a liberation of sorts, Maggie's economic situation means that she is still not and probably never will be free.

Inez Bensusan's[50] play *The Apple* (1909) is a bleak indictment of how women's lives are compromised for the sake of men both at home and at work. At the beginning of the play Helen, who works as a typist in an office, has been propositioned and groped by her boss, Mr Dean, who is also her father's boss. Helen has reached breaking point, thrown a ruler at Mr Dean and quit her job. She tells her sister Ann, 'I've awakened to a sense of the injustice of it all. I'm going to rebel. I'm going to fight for my rights, your rights, equal rights for us all' (p. 144). Helen determines to emigrate to Canada for a new life, but relies on her share of the legacy left by her grandfather to fund her passage. Her brother Cyril, however, lays claim to the shares of his three sisters in order to make a wealthy marriage. Mr Dean comes to the house to tell Helen he has smoothed the way for her to return to work, and renews an offer to make her his mistress. During his visit to the house, Mr Dean convinces Helen's father that all of the inheritance should go to Cyril, 'the apple' of her father's eye, leaving Helen no means to escape. Cyril and Mr Dean exit together, stepping out freely into the night as Helen ends the play trapped at home, trapped in her job, and trapped in an abusive sexual relationship.

New Women in the Theatre

Though it was a difficult career to break into, acting could offer women wages potentially higher than they could earn in any other trade. In the late-Victorian era, associations between actresses and prostitutes still lingered, but they were waning. The adored Ellen Terry helped to do for actresses what Florence Nightingale[51] had done for nurses, elevating the profession to new respectability through her personal celebrity and popularity. (Terry effected this change in popular attitudes specifically through her stage presence as the quintessential 'womanly woman', not through private example, since she was actually twice divorced and the mother of two illegitimate children – Edith Craig and Edward Gordon Craig.) While the rise in respectability of the profession made the stage more alluring to women in some respects, the terms upon which these wages were paid bore some uncomfortable resemblances to those dictated by prostitution, with work dependent on youth and looks. As late as 1898, the established critic Clement Scott said, in an interview with the evangelic periodical *Great Thoughts,* 'It is really impossible for a woman to remain pure who adopts the stage as a profession', and, adding insult to injury, 'a woman who endeavours to keep her purity is almost of necessity foredoomed to failure in her career' (1 January 1898). A furore of indignation, including many angry letters from actor-managers uniting to bar him from their theatres, caused the *Daily Telegraph* to dismiss Scott from his post, despite his swift retraction.

Tracy C. Davis identifies the salient question for the status of the trade as a whole as being 'whether women were able to acquire the reins of management, raise capital, and to take charge of the means of production'. The answer Davis arrives at is a qualified no: 'Even women at the apex of the hierarchy', she writes, 'operated under restricted conditions' (1991, p. 50). By contrast, Baz Kershaw notes the continuing if not growing power of the actor-manager as evidenced by the series of knighthoods bestowed on them, including Henry Irving (1895), Squire Bancroft (1897), Charles Wyndham (1902), John Hare (1907), Herbert

Beerbohm Tree (1909), George Alexander (1911) and Johnston Forbes-Robertson (1913) (Kershaw, 2004, p. 37). In contrast to this host of knightly actors, Davis notes that the first woman to be honoured such for services to theatre, Geneviève Ward, had to wait another generation before she was appointed D.B.E. in 1921 at the age of 84.

Cicely Hamilton's *Diana of Dobson's* might never have made it to the stage if it weren't for the popular actress Lena Ashwell going into management for herself at the Kingsway Theatre. A key point of Ashwell's agenda was finding plays with more interesting female roles than were typically on offer in male-dominated commercial theatres. In an interview with the *Illustrated Sporting and Dramatic News*, she explained:

> [U]nder the prevailing system I cannot get the characters I am ambitious to appear in, and my ambition will not be satisfied until I have a theatre in London at which I can produce serious works, and prove there is a big public for them.
>
> (3 September 1904)

Ashwell went into management with the express aim of producing plays by unknown and/or female authors and challenging the commercial ring of actor-manager 'aristocracy'. She was specifically inspired by German municipal theatres with their local and state government funding and endowments – still a dream in England. As well as originating the role of Diana, Ashwell also played the pro-suffrage characters Lady Killone in J.B. Fagan's *The Earth*[52] (1910) and Annys Chilvers in J.K. Jerome's play *The Master of Mrs. Chilvers* (1911), attesting to her eye for strong, unconventional female roles. Gertrude Kingston and other actresses also took on theatre management as a way of exerting control over the parts they chose to play. In her autobiography Kingston reflected, 'It is a sober reality that in the stage world I have been granted few opportunities of exhibiting what I had in me to give' (p. 182). Claire Hirshfield notes that actress-managers like Robins, Ashwell, Kingston and Craig 'who chose the uncertain path of activism were in part inspired by an understandable distaste for the insipid heroines they had often portrayed on stage' (1985, p. 150).

Viv Gardner and Susan Rutherford have pointed out that women played key roles in experimental British theatre, with Florence Farr running a season of plays at the Avenue Theatre in 1894, playwright Dorothy Leighton serving on the management of the Independent Theatre, and Elizabeth Robins founding and running the New Century Theatre. Gay Gibson Cima argues that Robins's contribution as a producer 'compares favourably with that of the Independent Theatre', generally regarded as the major experimental theatre of the era, noting that the Independent premiered only two of Ibsen's works while Robins introduced five and that Robins's productions played to wider audiences with better financial success than the Independent's (1980, p. 160). Lillah McCarthy also assumed a managerial role when she took over running the Little Theatre in 1911 and was an associate manager, with Harley Granville Barker, of the Savoy in 1912. Edith Craig formed the avant-garde Pioneer Players in 1911 and in 1913 Inez Bensusan started the Woman's Theatre with the aim of promoting more progressive representations of women. Theatre management, however, especially theatre management that valued short runs of new works over long runs of star-vehicle potboilers, was extremely difficult to sustain. Ventures by actress-managers certainly brought more diverse women's roles to the stage, but though impactful these enterprises were often short-lived.

Annie Horniman was arguably the most innovative and successful female theatre manager of her day both in terms of business aptitude and artistic vision. Horniman was dedicated to producing new plays by British dramatists in short runs and looked to a repertory system that interspersed classics as the most suitable means to promote better standards of acting as well as make productions of new works economically viable. She promoted naturalistic acting and opposed the star system. Throughout her professional life she demonstrated a brilliant eye for spotting new talent, anonymously backing the first production of a Shaw play, discovering Stanley Houghton and fostering the work of W.B. Yeats, with whom she founded the Abbey Theatre in Dublin. Despite her genius as a dramaturg and theatre manager, Horniman was repeatedly cast as a 'lady bountiful' rather than a collaborator or business manager. When she announced the launch of a Manchester repertory theatre, the press described the venture as 'more or less the hobby of Miss Horniman, a wealthy lady who loves to dabble with drama' and rejoiced that Manchester would share with Dublin 'the fortune which that good fairy, Miss Horniman, is bestowing upon the theatre' (*Manchester City News*, 20 September 1907). A week later, Horniman gave an interview attempting to construct a more professional public image: 'I want this scheme to be a financial success and an artistic success. I want to see plays produced that it will be worth paying to see, from the point of view of the public' (*Manchester Courier*, 28 September 1907). The press, however, continued to depict her as a benefactress rather than businesswoman: 'Miss Horniman has come to us very much in the nature of a lady bountiful. She has a pocket full of good plays and a basket full of highly efficient actors and actresses' (*Manchester Evening Chronicle*, 26 October 1907). When Horniman hired Ben Iden Payne to direct a repertory company for the Gaiety, the *Yorkshire Herald* and the *Manchester Courier* erroneously announced that Horniman's theatre was to be known as 'Mr. Iden-Payne's Company' (*Yorkshire Herald*, 15 January 1908) and 'Mr. B. Iden Payne's Repertoire Company' (*Manchester Courier*, 16 January 1908). Even as the mistake was corrected in one paper to 'Miss Horniman's Company, under the direction of Mr. B. Iden Payne' (*Irish Times*, 29 February 1908), three newspapers persisted with 'Mr. Iden Payne and his Company' (*Era, Carlisle Patriot* and *Cumberland News*, all 29 February 1908). When Horniman insisted both publicly and legally on her role as owner-manager, rather than the lady bountiful behind Payne, Manchester City Council turned on its 'good fairy' and refused to grant a drinks licence to a female proprietor. This denial was tantamount to a financial death blow to the new theatre, as theatres made a substantial proportion of their revenue through the sale of drinks and the Gaiety could not be expected to cover costs, much less operate at a profit without a drinks licence. Horniman was thus forced into the role of philanthropist, running the theatre at her own expense for three years until she was eventually able to obtain a licence in 1911.

* * *

In their introduction to *New Woman Plays*, Linda Fitzsimmons and Viv Gardner observe that women in the New Woman plays don't 'articulate any "New" philosophy, they are shown living out the problems created by traditional views of women' (1991, p. xi). Pinero's Agnes Ebbsmith looks as though she will break the mould and deliver a new vision through her political speaking and writing, but like so many heroines she gives up her convictions for a man who proves less worthy than she supposed. Dorothy Leighton's character Thyrza Fleming starts as a renowned actress whose retirement will be 'disastrous for the dramatic world' (p. 24), which sounds more fulfilling than being the long-suffering wife of a tyrannical husband, but the repentance and misery she confesses to over the course of the play only serve to reinforce the patriarchal status quo as she implores her daughter not to break with convention but instead to try and 'see things from a wider point of view – from the man's side for instance' (p. 56). Where the New Woman plays of the 1890s primarily focus on the struggle for sexual freedom, making the 'New' easy to conflate with the 'fallen', Edwardian drama concentrates much more on women's struggle for legal and political equality. Plays from the 1890s exhibit pronounced anxiety about how increased education and independence might affect middle-class women's femininity and sexuality, resulting in 'cold fish' like Shaw's Vivie Warren who rejects sexual relationships completely or Grundy's man-hating, yet man-chasing, female authors. Julie Holledge proposes that 'It is significant that when the "New Woman" plays were in vogue in the 1890s, the suffrage campaign was making little headway in parliament' (1981, p. 35). With the debate on 'the woman question' revolving around (male) unease about female sexuality, women were in a no-win situation – they were damned if they did, damned if they didn't conform to 'separate spheres' expectations of sexual morality.

By 1907 the self-motivated New Woman of the 1890s had been eclipsed by the rise of the gender-loyal Edwardian suffragette. Rather than expressing sexual angst about the 'unsexing' of female students or wage earners, drama written during the height of the militant suffrage campaign emphasized women's growing independence and education as an argument for political and legal equality. The female characters in the Edwardian plays examined in the latter part of this chapter and the chapters which follow are marked in their contrast to their Victorian predecessors. The successful author Mary from Hatton's *Before Sunrise*, with her career in Paris, heralds a bright future of opportunity in education and employment as well as freedom from sexual oppression, far from the ridiculous capers of Aveling's finishing-school girls or the nervous breakdown of Pinero's Lucy Tuck. Shaw's Cambridge-educated playwright character Fanny, more human and more political than Vivie, obviously delighted the audiences that kept the show running for over 600 performances.

With prominent suffrage actresses Lillah McCarthy, Cicely Hamilton and Dorothy Minto headlining the cast, the run of *Fanny's First Play* conflated theatrical and political narratives: the actresses performed doubly in their parts as characters and their public roles as stars of the Actresses' Franchise League (AFL), anticipating Brechtian *gestus* in their layering of character and actor. This doubling of feminist-character with feminist-actress is a hallmark of many Edwardian productions, such as the popular AFL personality Lena Ashwell's starring role in *Diana of Dobson's*. Ashwell also played Kate in the 1910 production of *The Twelve-Pound Look* at the Duke of York's Theatre and the following year McCarthy and Hamilton co-starred as Kate and Lady Sims in the Little Theatre production. The cast lists from the Edwardian plays considered in this chapter suggest a modern movement in which art, artists and politics are intricately crosshatched – a pattern even more evident in the chapters that follow.

In contrast to Victorian playwrights like Pinero and Jones, Edwardian male playwrights like Barrie, Hankin and Barker write female characters whose lives don't revolve entirely around sex and the past, but focus instead on independence and the future. Kate gives up a husband and the possibility of children in order to pursue an independent career and Janet becomes a successful businesswoman and mother without need of a husband or a business partner. In the 1913 conclusion to *Way Stations*, Robins celebrated the change, noting that 'the sensitive observer will mark the enlightening effect on men of the new standards. They begin to speak of women in public with less flummery; they write of her with an accent less cock-sure, and yet more worthy of assurance' (WS, p. 349). She specifically points out that Barrie's *Twelve-Pound Look* 'is since Militancy' (p. 349), noting the impact of the suffrage movement on converting male writers and reining in the 'fatuity' (p. 349) of their depictions of women.

Where the Victorian New Woman stood for her own rights and freedoms, the Edwardian suffragette stood for the rights of womankind and by extension humankind. The suffragette crossed class boundaries in her pursuit of social justice and, like a soldier, a martyr or a mother, was prepared to make grave personal sacrifices for others. Where the New Woman had been an individualist, the suffragette was a feminist. Pushing back against unwomanly caricature, feminists co-oped the traditional iconography and rhetoric of motherhood as part of their argument for extending womanly influence into the public realm. The next three chapters examine the interlinked political and dramatic representations of single women, motherhood and women's suffrage.

CHAPTER 3

Odd Women

In 1899 on the brink of the new century Ibsen published his final play, *When We Dead Awaken.* Both Elizabeth Robins and William Archer were greatly disappointed in the script. Uninspired to produce it, Robins called the work and Ibsen's fading voice 'wreckage on a giant scale'.[1] That summer Robins and Archer also ended the clandestine romantic relationship they had shared for nearly a decade. Few details survive to shed light on the exact nature of the break, apart from Robins's diary entries recording an upsetting exchange of letters that left her profoundly unhappy for several days,[2] but their frequent meetings, which had been such a fundamental part of their lives throughout the 1890s, became scarce. With the centre of her artistic and personal life in London shifting, and with the nineteenth century and the Victorian era both drawing to their close, Robins made an extraordinary decision.

In 1900 Robins set out on a journey to the gold fields of the Klondike in search of her youngest brother Raymond, a journey to one of the roughest, most dangerous spots on earth which she undertook alone in full Victorian dress and picture hat. Robins's friend W.T. Stead, the newspaper editor and controversial pioneer of investigative journalism, advanced her £300 for the trip, which she repaid by publishing feature articles for his paper. During her travels from Nome up the Yukon River, Robins taught herself photography and kept detailed diaries containing sketches of life among miners, missionaries and Inuit. She visited gambling dens in Nome, went to prospecting camps in the Klondike by dog sled and spent her birthday in the Arctic Circle. Her brother Raymond had gone in search of gold and, she feared, lost himself along the way. She found him and managed to persuade him to return from the wilderness. By the time she arrived in Seattle to begin her long journey back to London, Robins was experiencing the first wretched symptoms of typhoid fever. She lay deathly ill in Seattle General

Hospital for two months and suffered acute post-typhoid symptoms for a further two years. During her convalescence, she began work on a novel, *The Magnetic North* (1904), blending a fictional narrative with her harrowing lived experience of the Alaska-Klondike. It is curious that in between the hit-and-miss critical and financial success of her New Woman novels of the 1890s and her decidedly feminist Edwardian writing, this male quest novel (more akin to Joseph Conrad or Rider Haggard than Sarah Grand or Mona Caird) was the biggest blockbuster of Robins's career. Ironically this was also the first novel she openly published as a woman, using her own name instead of the male nom de plume C.E. Raimond. Robins's gold prospecting adventure story went into seven reprints in four years and was admired by notable literary personalities such as Mark Twain, some of whom compared her eye for detail to Émile Zola's. Her actor's skills of keen character observation and an ear for dialogue stood her in good stead as a novelist, bringing this remote part of the world to life for thousands of readers. This success marked a turning point, making her significantly more financially secure.

Robins played a few more roles in London before retiring from the stage in 1902 at the age of 40 and becoming a full-time writer. Even after she retired as an actress and ended her relationship with Archer, Robins evidenced no desire to marry. Her publisher William Heinemann proposed to her repeatedly, but her answer to him and others was always no. Like many of her female contemporaries, Robins resolutely maintained her independence as a single woman as a key part of her identity. When financial success as a writer made it possible to buy a large country house in Sussex, Robins began to share her life more and more with other women as her writing became overtly feminist. In 1909 she met the young Octavia Wilberforce, great granddaughter of William Wilberforce, figurehead of the Abolitionist Campaign in Britain. A year later when Octavia's father opposed her ambition to become a doctor and insisted instead that she marry, Robins helped fund Octavia's medical studies. Octavia moved in with Robins the same year; they lived together for 42 years until Robins's death. Many have speculated as to whether their relationship was one of platonic companionship or something more romantic.[3] Though Robins had been married for two years in her twenties, and though she lived the second part of her life in a domestic partnership of some kind with another woman, her lifestyle in the twentieth century looked very much like that of a 'glorified spinster' – arty, educated, attractive but unavailable to men, outwardly chaste and financially independent through her own labour.

ODD WOMEN

While popular Victorian rhetoric depicted marriage and motherhood as a woman's ultimate goal, or in the less romantic words of Cicely Hamilton, 'as inevitable as lessons and far more inevitable than death' (MT, p. 29), marriage was statistically impossible for thousands of women at the turn of the century. The British population was significantly gender dispropor-tionate, owing in part to male deaths in the Crimea and more so to a mass exodus of mostly male emigrants to further reaches of the Empire. Women suffered the worst effects of the imbalance; not only were thousands denied the vocation of marriage and motherhood that separate spheres ideology told them was their destiny, many were also deprived of the home and finan-cial security a husband was supposed to provide. Single women without private means struggled to find adequate ways of supporting themselves. Though these plights unfolded as a series of quiet crises enacted in private homes, the problem was national in scale. It was the age of the spinster.

As unmarried women, spinsters held a tenuous but nevertheless legiti-mate position in society. Victorians and Edwardians were sometimes vague as to the usage of the term, but an unmarried woman could generally be described as a spinster on the basis of age, sexual morality and class. Over the course of the nineteenth century, the age when women were classi-fied as spinsters gradually shifted from the early twenties to 29 or even the early thirties. Unlike the overnight transformation of a woman's status from Miss to Mrs, the epithet of spinster crept gradually over a woman's identity somewhere between the ages of 25 and 35, by which age it was assumed to be permanent. Although spinster status came about gradually, a breach of chastity could instantly transform a woman from a respectable (if pitied) spinster to the social exile of the fallen women. If she wished to hold onto her vulnerable but socially sanctioned identity as a spin-ster, sex and motherhood were forbidden. 'Spinster' also had an implied middle- or upper-class connotation. Working-class women tended to be identified by their trades and could not expect to be kept in a state of eco-nomic dependence and sexual purity if they failed to find husbands. While unmarried upper- and middle-class women became spinsters, haunting the drawing rooms of fathers and brothers, unmarried working-class women either worked, went to the workhouse or slipped into another ready-made category of single women: prostitutes.

In 1861 the census showed that there were more than 400,000 unmarried women over the age of 34 in Britain. By 1901 the number had doubled and it continued to increase steadily until WWI. At the turn of the century one in three women were single at any given time, and one in four remained single throughout their lives. Those who sought to retain the middle-class social structure of traditional Victorian marriage were understandably alarmed by these figures. Spinsters were labelled 'surplus', 'superfluous', 'redundant' or 'odd' women. The commonly used term 'odd women' suggested something more unsettling than a simple statistical imbalance, implying that these women were somehow abnormal or deviant. Unlike married women, who at least in theory had husbands to champion their causes in the public arena, the spinster had no public representation, especially if her father was deceased. Often dependent upon the goodwill and economic support of their nearest male relative, the spinster's domestic status was subservient, effectively denying her both public and private forums.

The question, for liberals and conservatives alike, was what to do with this surplus of women. Some (men) proposed restoring demographic balance to the population by encouraging women to emigrate. W.R. Greg, for example, saw the difficulty as 'chiefly mechanical' in his observation that 'It is not easy to convey a multitude of women across the Atlantic, or to the Antipodes by any ordinary means of transit' (Jeffreys, 1985, p. 87). Spinsters were thus spoken of in terms of a gross national surplus product in need of exportation, though the proponents of this theory did not trouble themselves, as a commercial exporter would, to investigate whether or not once exported there would be a market for these 'goods'. Spinsters themselves, most of whom showed no desire to leave the country, largely ignored this call to emigrate and focused their energies instead on challenging the concept of superfluousness. In her article 'How to Provide for Superfluous Women', Jessie Boucherett countered with a tongue-in-cheek suggestion that more *men* over the age of 21 should leave the country in order to create greater employment opportunities for women: 'It is in the power of the Government to put facilities in the way of emigration; but something more than facility is required, because men who ought to emigrate very often prefer to remain in England' (1869, p. 35). By and large, men chose to ignore spinsters. St. John Greatorex, the liberal MP in Robins's play *Votes for Women!*, admits dismissively, 'that kind of woman doesn't interest me, I'm afraid' (p. 147). Despite the fact that many policy-makers supported middle-aged daughters or sisters, the plight of the single woman remained an issue that could easily be swept under the carpet.

The declining popularity of marriage appreciably contributed to the growing number of spinsters. Though marriage was an accepted and expected part of life, as a legal institution marriage underwent an intense period of public scrutiny from the mid-Victorian period until the First World War, a period of change in laws and public opinion unrivalled until the recent LGBTQ marriage equality debates and reforms. In response to Mona Caird's 1888 essay 'Marriage' pronouncing the institution 'a vexatious failure' (p. 197) the *Daily Telegraph* put the question 'Is Marriage a Failure?' to their readers. They received 27,000 responses. Readers gave copious examples of the ways in which marriage indeed *was* a failure, signing themselves by epithets such as 'LOST BEYOND REDEMPTION', 'A VICTIM TO BAD TEMPER', 'SHATTERED NERVES', 'INWARD GRIEF', 'A CRUSTY BACHELOR' and 'A PERPLEXED CURATE'. The romanticized rhetoric of separate spheres was increasingly challenged by darker counter narratives from the lived experiences of both women and men. In addition to questioning romantic rhetoric, many women were challenging the law. The popular aphorism 'my wife and I are one, *and I am he*' was very nearly a literal description of husband and wife under the British legal system in the nineteenth century. Entering marriage, a woman forfeited her rights to own property, receive inheritance, keep her own wages, sign contracts and sue or be sued in a court of law. She also relinquished rights over her own body, including sexual consent, reproductive rights and guardianship over her children. The eighteenth-century judge Sir William Blackstone, who wrote *Commentaries on the Laws of England* (1765), explained that:

> the very being or legal existence of the woman is suspended during the marriage, or at least is incorporated or consolidated into that of the husband; under whose wing, protection and *cover* she performs every thing; and is therefore called in our law-French a *feme-covert*. (p. 442)

Mona Caird speculated that contemporary marriage had its roots in earlier evolutionary stages in which male hunters had raided villages, abducting 'brides'. This, she stated, represented 'the origin of our modern idea of *possession* in marriage. The woman became the property of the man, his own by right of conquest. Now the wife is own his by right of law' (1888, p. 189). Criticisms of married women's lack of legal standing led many feminists to compare marriage to slavery. Langham Place Group members like Barbara Bodichon who published in *The English Woman's Journal* during the American Civil War made direct comparisons in works such as 'Of Those Who are the Property of Others' (February 1863).

Progress in expanding married women's legal rights was one of the main achievements of mid-nineteenth-century feminism, restoring married women to some of the legal rights they had held as unmarried women, such as the right to own property. Upper-class society hostess Caroline Sheridan Norton (granddaughter of the playwright Richard Brinsley Sheridan) became one of England's first feminist legal reformers, success- fully campaigning for two key pieces of legislation for married and divorced women: the Custody of Infants Act of 1839 and the Matrimonial Causes Act of 1857.[4] The Married Women's Property Act (also partly credited to Norton's efforts for legal reform, though she did not herself take part in the campaign) was perhaps the single most effective feminist inroad into the English law. Barbara Bodichon's essay 'A Brief Summary, in Plain Language, of the Most Important Laws Concerning Women' (1854) helped to initiate the campaign, which won significant victories in 1870 and 1882. These Acts brought about a colossal reallocation of English property; a shift in material wealth second only to the dissolution of the monasteries and abbeys under Henry VIII.

Despite these legal gains for married women, marriage rates contin- ued to fall markedly from the late-Victorian era until WWI. Many feminist historians including Sheila Jeffreys, Lillian Faderman and Patricia Hollis have directly linked the decline of marriage and the subsequent rise of the Victorian spinster – a rise in terms of numbers, visibility and self- confidence –to a dramatic reappraisal and redefinition of women's rights and opportunities in the late nineteenth and early twentieth century. The earliest stages of the organized feminist movement in Britain focused largely on the plight of single women and, even later, when feminists broadened their objectives, the women's movement largely comprised and was led by spinsters. Spinsters, for example, comprised 63 per cent of the membership of the enormously powerful Women's Social and Political Union during the suffrage campaign.

It is worth noting that while the Victorians and Edwardians certainly saw connections between spinsters and feminism, the image of Victorian spinsters that has filtered down through the years is often that of the rather pathetic old maid. While first-wave feminism was largely devoted to reforming conditions of education and employment opportunities for (white) unmarried women, second-wave feminism of the 1960–80s chiefly addressed the concerns of (predominantly white) middle-class wives and mothers, and this bias during the prolific era of second-wave feminist histor- ical scholarship shaped the way subsequent generations have remembered the first wave. The impressive number of spinsters involved in Victorian feminism has often been overshadowed in historical accounts by married counterparts, such as Josephine Butler and Emmeline Pankhurst (who began a political career in her own right only after she was widowed).

Despite her ubiquity, the spinster received relatively slight attention in the theatre. Given that actor-managers still controlled most theatres and selected plays first and foremost as vehicles for their own celebrity, this is no surprise. Spinsters are not uncommon in the New Drama, but, unlike their numerous counterparts in the novel, they are rarely main characters; a spinster with more than a couple of good lines in the course of a play is rare. Maud Rogers's one-act *When the Wheels Run Down* (1899) is unique in focusing its plot on the eleventh-hour romantic reunion of a 45-year-old spinster, Priscilla Dormer, with a suitor who returns after 15 years at sea. This middle-aged spinster romance, however, was produced for one night only.[5] In drama, spinsterhood was not represented as a lifestyle choice offering the positive alternatives to marriage that thousands of women increasingly found attractive in real life, such as autonomy, economic self-sufficiency, professional vocations, and solidarity and/or primary relationships with other women. Spinster characters in dramatic literature instead usually fulfil an atmospheric function, serving as symbols of waste, futility and sacrifice. In *The Voysey Inheritance* (1905) Barker's spinster character 'Poor Honor', is a classic example: 'In a less humane society she would have been exposed at birth' (p. 102). Alice, the only character who pays much attention to Honor, begins to describe her generously as having the patience of a saint, but reconsiders and settles on 'the patience of a ... of an old maid' (p. 104). Violet, the spinster daughter in Hankin's *Return of the Prodigal* (1905), is condemned by the customs of the nouveau riche marriage market to live quietly with her parents. Meanwhile, her brother Henry becomes a partner in their father's firm and marries into the upper class while her brother Eustace roams the world adventuring. In contrast to the prospects and concerns of both her respectable brother and her ne'er-do-well brother, Violet's life of knitting socks for charity and providing background piano music for other people's conversations is redundant and hopeless. When her prodigal brother Eustace suggests that her life is enviably leisurely, she disabuses him of the idea:

> You are free. I am not. You think, because I stay quietly at home doing the duty that lies nearest me and not crying out against fate, therefore I've nothing more to wish for! Would *you* be happy, do you suppose, if you were

in my case? I live here in Chedleigh from year's end to year's end. Mother never leaves home. She doesn't care to pay visits. So I cannot either. I may sometimes get away for a few days, a week, perhaps, but very seldom. And as mother grows older I shall go less. Soon people will give up asking me when they find I always refuse. And so I shall be left here alone with no friends, no real companionship, merely one of the family obliged to know the people they know, visit the people they visit, not a grown woman with interests of her own and a life to order as she pleases. (p. 88)

Honor and Violet represent waste and premature decay. Even in the works of unmarried feminist dramatists such as Hamilton and Robins, spinsters yield centre stage to recently engaged ingénues, wives or women with pasts. The dramaturgy of spinsterhood, however, is fascinating. Harley Granville Barker's Huxtable sisters from *The Madras House* provide the most quietly disturbing characterizations of wasted womanhood, Frances in Hamilton's *Just to Get Married* depicts spinsterhood as morally hon-ourable but economically challenging, and Shaw's Lesbia from *Getting Married* provides the most assertive personification of a 'glorified spinster'.

WASTED WOMANHOOD

A common characterization of the Old Maid was that of a restless spectre, condemned to a purgatory of perpetually watching but never participat-ing in the joys of womanhood. Lisa Tickner observes that in contemporary newspapers, magazines and cartoons, 'the Spinster is almost always thin, lacking in the curves appropriate to pleasurable femininity, motherhood and charm' (1987, p. 164). In a *Free Review* article titled 'Stagnant Virginity', columnist Hope Clare claimed to be able to distinguish married women from spinsters upon a single glance into a railway carriage by the spinster's despairing, sexually frustrated glances at male passengers (January 1897, p. 413). An anonymous contributor to the first issue of *The Freewoman* magazine captured society's ability to both pity and fear the spinster:

> I write of the High Priestess of Society. Not of the mother of sons, but of her barren sister, the withered tree, the acidulous vessel under whose pale shadow we chill and whiten, of the Spinster I write. Because of her power and dominion. She, unobtrusive, meek, soft footed, silent, shame-faced, bloodless and boneless, thinned to spirit, enters the secret recesses of the mind, sits at the secret springs of action, and moulds and fashions our emasculate society. She is our social nemesis.
>
> (quoted in Jeffreys, 1985, p. 95)

The alleged dull despair or jealous puritanism of the spinster served the dual purpose of dehumanizing and disempowering the notion of a single woman as a free agent, while reaffirming the normality and health of married women.

The first act of Barker's *The Madras House* (1909) takes place in the home of the Huxtables, a respectable family who live in the middle-class suburb of Denmark Hill in a home likened to a chaste prison for their spinster daughters, aged from 26 to 39. In the Huxtable domestic scene, Barker amplifies the traditional stereotype of the unobtrusive 'superfluous' woman into a powerfully visual theatrical presence by having not one, but six spinster characters. Through this technique, Barker emphasizes the dreary aspects of the spinsters' situation while retaining their traditional background placement and spectral quality. In his lengthy stage directions, Barker takes pains to point out that what glimmers of talent or inclination the daughters might have possessed are all but extinguished by the stifling atmosphere of their middle-class household. Emma, for example, 'would have been a success in an office and worth perhaps thirty shillings a week' (1994, p. 97), but having a daughter working for wages would lower the social status of her family. Julia, who was considered a genius with watercolours, was 'sent to an art school where they wouldn't let her do water-colour drawing at all' (p. 96), and Jane who has twice been proposed to by not quite desirable young men, has not been allowed to marry, being considered too young at 26 to know her own mind. For the most part the Huxtable daughters' names are immaterial, as their characters are all so underdeveloped that even their parents find it difficult to tell them apart (and Barker himself confuses them in his manuscript[6]). The difference between one Miss Huxtable and another is likened to the difference 'between one lead pencil and another, as these lie upon one's table after some weeks use; a matter of length, of sharpening, of wear' (p. 96). Though individually any one of the Huxtable daughters could blend into the background, it is impossible to ignore the presence of six spinsters in one drawing room. Thus, through multiplication of the numbers rather than exaggeration of the stereotype, Barker is able to make the unremarkable remarkable, or to foreground the background.

Barker provides a carefully detailed description of the chaste fortress that defends the virginity of the six spinster daughters, significantly all still of child-bearing years. The drawing room, described as a 'family museum', has been arranged according to the tastes of Mrs Huxtable whose maiden name, Tombs, suggests that the room is in fact a family mausoleum.

The chief ornament of the drawing room is a gilt clock, slowly ticking away hours and days. The clock, rather like the girls, stands out from the other furnishings in that it has a pulse, but where the clock remains solid, enshrined beneath a dome of glass, the girls are slowly growing older, marking the passing of time with their own subtle but sure decay. The focal point in Barker's precisely detailed set design for this act is the window through which the sisters gaze at the Crystal Palace. The Crystal Palace, an emblem of the wealth, progress and glamour of the age, acts both as a symbol of the fairy-tale romance of the possibilities beyond the drawing room and as a testament to the solid materialism of that industrial world.[7] It is, at once, the site of girlish fantasy and a fixed, reliable point in the urban landscape, used to predict the weather. Barker creates a subtle but keen image of arrested development when Jane and Julia, who have stepped out to admire the view, find themselves locked out on the balcony. With their faces to the window, they tap on the pane, but Mr Huxtable, busily engaged with the other men, declines to break off his conversation to let them in. They remain in this symbolic limbo throughout much of the scene, excluded from both public and domestic life.

The Huxtable daughters are expected to comport themselves with the decorum of adults though they are denied any but the slightest experience of adult concerns or responsibilities. Emma tells Philip what she thinks is an amusing anecdote; her sister Julia kept a man's shirt collar that came back from the steam laundry by mistake and her mother cried over the incident for a whole day, thinking it showed evidence of 'a wanton mind' (p. 118):

> PHILIP: I don't think that's at all amusing, Emma.
> EMMA: (*in genuine surprise*) Don't you?
> PHILIP: How old is Julia?
> EMMA: She's thirty-four. (*Her face falls too*) No ... it is rather dreadful, isn't it? (p. 118)

Emma concedes that the story of Julia and the purloined, perhaps fetishized, man's shirt collar has disturbing undertones. The incident indicates that at least one of the Huxtable women is suffering from a lack of romantic or sexual attention. Barker does not pathologize the Huxtable girls in the extreme terms of 'ovarian insanity' or 'old maid's mania' found in contemporary medical warnings (discussed later in this chapter), but these incidents suggest that the confined glass house is an atmosphere conducive to germinating strains of spinster's psychosis.

Despite the obvious discontent and claustrophobia of the young spin-sters' situation, Philip's suggestion that they leave Denmark Hill shocks Emma. Her wide-eyed 'Where to?' prompts a sigh from Philip, who concedes, 'Ah, that's just it' (p. 119). There is nowhere for them to go. Constantine Madras views the situation with disgust, primarily as a waste of potential motherhood rather than as a waste of the women's personal talents or ambitions and castigates their father for not having drowned them all at birth. He suggests polygamy to Mr Huxtable as a solution: 'how much pleasanter for you ... and how much better for them ... if you could still find a man ready for some small consideration to marry the lot!' (p. 197). In his column for the *Saturday Review*, Max Beerbohm noted that the spinster daughters of the Huxtable House 'are as the chemicals which in certain experiments do but "act by their presence" – inobtrusive figures, yet philosophically significant' (19 March 1910). *Common Cause* applauded the work, saying 'all friends of women owe Mr. Barker their most grateful thanks' for revealing 'the conspiracy of society against a woman's self-development and self-expression' (7 April 1910).

Githa Sowerby's drama *Rutherford and Son* (1912), set in the indus-trial north, depicts a rare volcanic eruption of dormant rage from a spinster daughter towards a patriarch. When the nouveau riche capitalist Rutherford discovers that his unmarried daughter Janet has been having a cross-class affair with the foreman at his glassmaking factory, he reacts as if Janet has stolen from him, more devastated by the homosocial betrayal of his foreman Martin's loyalty than the heterosexual betrayal of his daugh-ter's virtue. Janet unleashes the pent-up rage of years of silence:

> *JANET:* Oh, you've no pity. ... [She makes a movement to go, then turns again as if for a moment.] I was thirty-six. Gone sour. Nobody'd ever come after me. Not even when I was young. You took care o'that. Half of my life was gone, well-nigh all of it that mattered ... What have I had of it, afore I go back to the dark? What have I had of it? Tell me that. Tell me! (p. 174)

Seeing his daughter's idle domestic confinement as a mark of his class ascendency, Rutherford responds angrily: 'I brought you up for a lady' (p. 175). He understands Janet's position in terms of class privilege – 'you might ha' sat wi' your hands afore you from morn till night if ye'd had a mind to' (p. 175) – rather than social or sexual imprisonment. Janet reads his demands as a patriarch in darker terms, reminding him with disgust, 'you got me – me to take your boots off at night', a comment that speaks to the degradation of her status in the household, as well as to her father's ignorance of what 'a lady' should be called on to perform. Though Janet is prepared to leave her rich father's house for a life in the village with a working-class husband, Martin's ultimate loyalties remain with her father and, apart from a kind word from her sister-in-law Mary, she leaves the house outcast and alone.

THE PERILS OF POVERTY

The death of a father could spell economic disaster for a middle-class woman with no means of income. Generally speaking, unmarried daughters were strongly discouraged from any sort of paid labour and advised to occupy themselves with charity work, such as the domestic acts undertaken with comedic zeal by Margery Denison in Hankin's comedy *The Charity that Began at Home* (1906). More formal charity schemes also abounded, such as the Spinsters Mutual Improvement Society parodied in Margaret Young's comedic play *Honesty: A Cottage Flower* (1897), established 'with the object of bringing into direct contact the classes and the masses, to the benefit, it is confidently believed, of both' (p. 10). Charity work re-enforced the status quo by emphasizing the socially superior status of upper- and middle-class families without contradicting the general commercial devaluation of women's work, a code that rested on the assumption that middle-class women would never have to support themselves.

While male writers like Barker and Hankin depicted the redundancy, frustration and stultification of upper- and middle-class daughters and sisters living marginal lives in the patriarchal homes of fathers or brothers, female writers like Edith Lyttelton and Antonia Williams dramatized the struggles of single lower-middle-class women providing for themselves and sometimes other dependant mothers or sisters, combining some of the ethical problems of the fallen woman with the economic perils of the spinster. In Antonia Williams's 1907 drama *The Street* the protagonist Margaret Martin is forced into selling herself to a predatory landlord to keep herself, her widowed mother and her fair and fragile sister Violet from the street. The action takes place over the course of one evening in the all-female family's living room and centres on Margaret's attempts to save Violet from her own fate. Having 'ruined' the 27-year-old daughter Margaret, the landlord's eye has fallen on her 18-year-old sister; he proposes free rent for Mrs Martin and Margaret in exchange for Violet coming to live with him (unmarried). He attempts to seduce Violet with wine, then threatens the family with eviction when she refuses him. When Violet returns from this off-stage trauma she is virgo intacta, but she has

lost her innocence and glimpsed into the hell Margaret has endured, something she sensed but didn't fully understand before, remarking 'today –
I am feeling – as you looked, Margaret' (p. 86).

Though Margaret has the moral fortitude to sacrifice herself for her
sister and her mother, she does not have the material means to support
them, and so the women's salvation relies on the male protagonist, John
Castleton, who offers Violet's impoverished would-be-husband Owen a
job so that they can marry and then proposes marriage to Margaret himself.
Considering herself 'damaged goods', Margaret refuses Castleton's proposal despite her genuine affection for him. Undaunted, he acknowledges
Margaret's past but vows that he loves her not despite it, but because of it:

> CASTLETON: Listen. You might come to me and say: 'For those I love, I
> have parted with honour and hope'.
> MARGARET: Mr. Castleton!
> CASTLETON: You might even come to me and say: 'For their sakes I must
> sell myself again to the most pitiless blackguard who ever lived – '
> MARGARET: [brokenly]. Don't – I – I – can't –
> CASTLETON: Wait! Do you know what my answer would be? Greater love
> has no man! You have done the impossible. You have reconciled death
> and life. You have made heaven of hell. You have proved that the body
> is nothing where the spirit is all. You have touched with your own hands
> the pitiful human, and made it divine.' (pp. 128–29)

Castleton, a male character written by a female author, demonstrates an
unusually nuanced and empathetic grasp of the complex challenges facing
women without means in a predatory misogynistic world. Even more atypically for a male character, he regards a fallen woman's past sacrifice as a
badge of courage that promises future domestic happiness. Williams provides a fuller, more hopeful redemption for Margaret than most fallen
women in drama, but though it ends with a conventionally happy double
engagement, the abiding impression of *The Street* is of the dangerous vul-
nerability of unmarried women without means who, though they may
possess agency in terms of self-sacrifice, find their ultimate fates resting on
the actions of men.

Edith Lyttelton's *Warp and Woof* (1908) also depicts the perils of poverty
for unmarried women by dramatizing the oppression of lower-middle-class
fitters in the dressmaking trade who are literally worked to death in the
service of upper-class customers oblivious to the human cost of their
gowns. Like Williams, Lyttelton gives her heroine Theodosia a pale and
pretty younger sister to protect. The crisis of the play revolves around the

younger sister's fate and the sacrifices Theo may be called upon to make to protect her, including the sacrifice of her virtue. Theo, who is full of life and vigour, and her frail sister Phoebe both work for Madame Stéfanie, who drives them 'like slaves' (p. 177). Lyttelton underscores the cruelty of their servitude by dramatizing a surprise visit from a labour inspector whom the unscrupulous businesswoman Madame Stéfanie dupes by hiding her workers in a locked room, concealing the fact that she is forcing them to work illegal hours without food or rest. Theo is tormented by worries about her sister, whom a doctor has warned has a life-threatening condition and should be moved to a warmer climate, a cure far beyond their means. In addition to her immediate anxiety about Phoebe's health, Theo longs for the prospect of some joy in their lives 'instead of this grind, grind, grind all day and all night', lamenting 'I like gardens – I like balls too – I want to be young – and gay – and happy. I've only got one life, and I'm missing everything – it calls me, calls me' (p. 181). Theo's only possible escape from the servitude of the dressmaking shop is a proposition from Madame Stéfanie's friend Percy who offers to make her his 'sweet friend' (p. 183), but she rejects him vehemently: 'We'll live our own lives! We're honest anyway ... and we want to keep honest ...' (p. 183).

When Phoebe coughs up blood, Theo is forced to take money from Percy to pay for a doctor. In a reverse sacrifice, Phoebe dies before Theo fulfils her side of the bargain. Just as Theo accepts Percy's bank note, a woman arrives to tell Theo of Phoebe's death and her last words: '"Theo, Theo, come back," she said, "come back" – just as if she saw you – and then her eyes dropped, and she fell into my arms – dead – dead' (p. 204). The play ends with Theo dropping the bank note to the ground. She calls out to her sister, 'Phoebe – Phoebe – I've come back' (p. 206) before sinking to her knees and breaking into convulsive sobbing. Lyttelton's bleak closing tableaux drives home the grim reality that for a woman without means, keeping her honour may become a matter of life and death.

CHANGING ATTITUDES TOWARDS CELIBACY

The Victorian biological determinist view that sexual relations required an active or 'katabolic' male and a passive or 'anabolic' female constructed sex drive as uniquely male, and consequentially branded women who exhibited sex drive as 'unnatural' or 'unwomanly'. Many early feminists agreed with this theory. Spinsters, such as Christabel Pankhurst, who advocated a policy of women's sexual abstinence as a means of reforming male behaviour, made an explicit connection between sex and politics in their slogan 'Votes for women, chastity for men!' According to Pankhurst's logic (the logic of Victorian essentialism) to shout 'chastity for women' would have been redundant – it was men, not women, who needed to exercise self-control. Feminists sought to shift popular ideas about sexuality from the belief in an irrepressible male sexuality to a new social constructionist position to argue that 'unnatural' diseases such as syphilis and gonorrhoea had been brought about by men's false representation of their sexuality as an appetite over which they had little control or responsibility.

In the meantime, anti-feminists were preparing a new line of attack: where female chastity and spirituality had formerly been praised and naturalized in Victorian ideology, fears in a declining birth rate and concerns over the rapid growth of the women's movement led to a new pathologizing of celibacy and an increasingly sexualized definition of 'happily married'. Almost every female 'disease' was linked back to some disorder of the reproductive system, such as Dr T.S. Clouston's identification of 'Ovarian Insanity', or 'Old Maid's Insanity' (1904, p. 530). Dr Henry Maudsley maintained that sexual hallucinations were 'the characteristic features of a form of insanity of old maids' and were engendered 'in the same way as visions of banquets occur in the dreams of a starving person' (1874a, p. 76). Clouston pathologized a celibate life as 'unnatural' in his warning of nature's revenge on unmarried women:

> [U]nprepossessing old maids, often of a religious life, who have been severely virtuous in thought, word, and deed, and on whom nature, just before or after the climacteric, takes revenge for too absolute a repression of all the manifestations of sex, by arousing a grotesque and baseless passion for some casual acquaintance of the other sex whom the victim believes to be deeply in love with her, dying to marry her, or aflame with sexual passion towards her, or who has actually ravished her after having given her chloroform. Usually the clergyman is the subject of this false belief.
>
> (1904, pp. 530–31)

Earlier in the nineteenth century doctors had affirmed that men, not women, needed sexual release to maintain their health, a claim made largely as a justification for prostitution and unassailable conjugal rights. Now doctors switched tack and claimed that women also faced medical crises if deprived of sex, though women's symptoms were more often described as psychological rather than biological in nature. Unlike bachelors who were expected, if not encouraged, to find sexual outlets via prostitution or affairs, the spinster was certainly not advised to pursue extra-marital sex for the sake of her health. Instead, male sex reformers, psychologists and physicians promised a future of emotional support and sexual delights to women choosing heterosexual marriage over single life. Divorcing women's rights from their political and economic context, anti-feminists suggested that woman would find more freedom and happiness within the heterosexual pleasures of marriage than through demands for political power. By redefining the issue of female autonomy in sexual terms, feminist detractors were able to portray chaste women's rights activists as the physically and mentally diseased puritanical enemies of healthy sexually active married women.

Feminist theories of male sexuality at the turn of the century were a bricolage of biological determinism in relation to male sexual drive and behaviourism in relation to men's conduct. While feminists generally regarded men as essentially more lustful, they argued that men could and should be socially conditioned to control their impulses. While feminists articulated radical new theories to deal with what they saw as the immoral excesses of male sexuality, most of them took the high ground in relation to their own conservative notions of female sexuality. Some feminists, like Olive Schreiner and members of the Men and Women's Club,[8] including Eleanor Marx, Edward Aveling and sexologist Havelock Ellis, advocated greater sexual freedom for both men and women. Ellis argued that while in earlier ages women had been credited with an unduly large share of the sexual impulse, his own generation tended to 'unduly minimize the sexual impulse in women' (SPSIII, p. 227). While agreeing with dominant male discourse that described female sexuality as more passive than male, Ellis characterized women's sexuality as more varied than men's (in one woman over time as well as comparatively between different women) and thus harder to pin down. For Ellis, women's erogenous 'sphere' was 'larger and more diffused' and their arousal more complex, periodic and subject to circumstances (SPSIII, p. 256). Female doctors like Louise Atkins and Elizabeth Blackwell asserted that men and women were not fundamentally different in the strength of sexual feeling, claiming that chastity, not child-bearing, was injurious to women's health. Most feminists, however, maintained the received essentialist view that men had stronger (and baser) sexual appetites.

Mainstream feminism was anxious to retain, for political purposes, the notion of women as the morally superior sex, using this as a key argument for extending women's influence beyond the home and into government. Prominent feminist leaders like the Pankhursts hotly rejected any variations of 'free love' philosophies as damaging to the women's cause. Pointing to the allegedly low moral standards of men as the cause of prostitution and venereal disease, feminists reasoned it would be a tactical error for women to allow themselves to sink to 'male' behaviour. The chastity of formerly ignored spinsters was, thus, suddenly a matter of startling importance to many different groups, conservatives and suffragists alike insisting on the crucial importance of their celibacy while small minority groups such as the Men and Women's Club encouraged a new degree of sexual freedom. Many women were prepared to 'go without' for the sake of an ideal purity, while others did not conceptualize themselves or their lives in terms of repressed sexuality; either way, the private decisions of these single women began to take on increasing political significance.

In the second act of *The Madras House*, which takes place in a live-in drapery establishment similar to Hamilton's *Dobson's*, Barker depicts a traditional 'old maid' as the company's unspoken enforcer of sexual purity. In keeping with purity feminism, Miss Chancellor radiates sobriety. She knows the value of her 'type' to employers who wish to adopt the living-in system and require women like her to oversee it. She lives, works and speaks as an old maid is expected to, without complaint, looking on spinsterhood 'as an honourable state, as my Bible teaches me to' (p. 146). Her high moral tone and watchful eye, however, are not appreciated by the younger employees whose behaviour is policed. As in Macnamara's *The Gates of the Morning*, Barker depicts a generational clash between the values of a traditional Victorian spinster and a progressive Edwardian unmarried woman in which the older woman's righteous chastity doesn't come off as a wholly attractive quality nor the younger woman's desire for sexual experience as totally depraved. Where early feminists articulated clear objections to the unscrupulousness of men who both seduced and judged women, purity feminism created unique tensions between unmarried women with different views on sexual agency.

The Glorified Spinster

Independent from ties to husbands or responsibilities towards children, spinsters came to occupy central positions in the fast-growing women's movement by the end of the nineteenth century. The most politically threatening, and therefore most publicly ridiculed image of spinsterhood to emerge, was that of the 'glorified spinster' (a moniker from an 1888 *Macmillan's Magazine*[9] article that caught on), drawn from the ever-multiplying ranks of self-supporting women, feminists, 'bluestockings' and suffragists. The glorified spinster might belong to all or none of these categories; her primary distinguishing characteristic was her refusal to interpret her single status as a tragedy, defining herself as a woman 'plus something' (independence) rather than 'minus something' (a husband). Although there were overlaps between the image of the 'glorified spinster' and the New Woman, New Women were typically depicted as younger and while some advocated chastity, being a New Woman did not necessarily preclude the possibilities of sex, marriage or even motherhood. In a letter to the *Daily Telegraph* a woman signing herself 'A GLORIFIED SPINSTER' explained 'The glorified spinster reads Spencer and Mill; she earns her own living; she dwells in rooms by herself; she lives honestly, dresses plainly; and as she is thrown on her own resources for amusement, she cultivates her intellect' (Quilter, 1888/1984, p. 54). Financial and emotional independence were key to the identity of the glorified spinster; the letter writer asserts with pride, 'there does not exist on this earth a more respectable character than a woman who can stand alone and make her own way in this big, dreary world' (p. 54). Walkowitz emphasizes the significance of the glorified spinster's 'new urban female style of being at home in the city' (1992, p. 63), making her one of the contributors to the coalescing figure of the modern woman. Though many spinsters proudly adopted the term, some *Telegraph* readers found the words 'glorified' and 'spinster' incompatible. Replying anonymously in *The Spectator*, one such respondent suggests that 'spinster mutilated' (Littell, p. 801) would be a more appropriate term, arguing that it is 'a mutilation of the feminine nature to live the self-dependent life without the power of constantly entering into the feelings and the wants of others' (p. 803).

In *Getting Married*, before Shaw's glorified spinster even appears on stage, Shaw flirts with her lack of interest in men and implies the possibility of an alternative sexuality through her name: Lesbia. The play begins with General 'Boxer' Bridgenorth's tenth proposal to his spinster sister-in-law, which is promptly refused. When Mrs Bridgenorth asks the general why he refers to the woman he has been proposing to for 20 years as 'your sister', rather than calling her by name, he responds: 'Better call her your sister than try to call her L – [*he almost breaks down*] L – well, call her by her name and make a fool of myself by crying' (p. 111). Despite the promise of her name, Lesbia shows no more interest in women than she does in men. Lesbia is of the type of spinster Shaw classifies as 'voluntary'; she is in possession of 'character and good looks and money and offers' (p. 118). In the play's preface Shaw states: 'We must recognize two classes of old maids: one, the really superfluous women, and the other, the women who refuse to accept maternity on the (to them) unbearable condition of taking a husband' (p. 51). Israel Zangwill's novel *The Old Maid's Club* (1892) also set out the notion of 'voluntary' spinsterhood years earlier in the fictional club charter, which stated that no woman could join the group unless she could prove that she had refused a conventionally agreeable proposal of marriage. The 'voluntary' standing, then, was still judged by male standards. Alice Maitland in Barker's *The Voysey Inheritance* also enjoys numerous proposals without feeling the need to accept: 'When it's a question of money I can understand it .. but if one can provide for oneself or is independent why get married!' (pp. 105–06) Lesbia and Alice, it should be noted, are wealthier than typical personifications of the 'glorified spinster' who was usually depicted as a frugal working woman who 'in spite of the smallness of her resources' manages to attend the theatre, see exhibitions and travel, 'extracting the greatest possible amount of pleasure out of every shilling'.[10]

When questioned by the general as to whether she feels compelled by 'the natural appetites', Lesbia retorts, 'an English lady is not the slave of her appetites', complaining: 'That is what an English gentleman seems incapable of understanding' (p. 121). This could be interpreted as a positive representation of a celibate lifestyle, or equally as a recuperative reinforcement of the notion of women's supposedly superior morals and weaker sex drive. Lesbia shares her deepest personal objection to marriage with Shaw's own wife Charlotte, a refusal to recognize conjugal rights as a legitimate requisite to the marriage contract. There is no explicit discussion of this point in the play, but Lesbia's simple remark, 'I have not stated my deepest objection to marriage; and I dont intend to. There are certain rights I will not give any person over me' (p. 179) is a clear reference to the issue.[11] While Freud might theorize on Lesbia's horror of pipes and cigars, Shaw does not represent his glorified spinster as the victim of old maid's psychosis. Far from suffering from personal delusions as to her own desires, as some of the married characters do, Lesbia demonstrates a rare insight into and acceptance of her own character.

Lesbia's regret is not the lack of a man in her life, but rather the lack of children. Instead of forbidding unmarried women to procreate – through customs, laws and economics – Lesbia argues:

> I believe it would pay the country very well to pay me very well to have children. But the country tells me that I cant have a child in my house without a man in it too; so I tell the country that it will have to do without my children. (p. 119)

When she does consider an 'alliance' with the general it is only on the conditions that she would be able to: keep her own house; be allowed to independently decide every question concerning herself and her children; and most importantly be able bar him from the house for at least two years each time a child is born. In the end, she reaffirms her position that marriage is too high a price to pay for motherhood: 'I am an English lady, quite prepared to go without anything I cant have on honourable conditions' (p. 181). Explanation by example was not an uncommon form of protest made by many women of this generation who conceptualized themselves as 'on strike' against unfair marriage laws. Lesbia is an ideal candidate for Shaw's own proposal, put forward in the preface to the play, to solve the problem of surplus women 'by legitimizing the children of women who are not married to the fathers' (pp. 48–49), thus separating the institutions of marriage and of motherhood. This proposal, though favoured by many progressives, had some serious shortcomings in an economic climate where financially independent women were a very small privileged minority. This is discussed further in the next chapter.

Spinster Travellers

Also part of a small privileged minority, one of the most fascinating and inherently dramatic figures to emerge in the Victorian and Edwardian public imagination was the spinster traveller. Unmarried women with means and independence like Marianne North, Edith Durham and Mary Kingsley moulded the image of the Lady Explorer, setting out to the furthest reaches of the Empire and beyond. The iconoclastic Lady Explorer became an irresistible figure of fun to journalists and members of the Royal Geographical Society back home:

> A lady an explorer?
> a traveller in skirts?
> The notion's just a trifle too seraphic:
> Let them stay and mind the babies,
> or hem our ragged shirts;
> But they mustn't, can't,
> and shan't be geographic.
>   (*Punch,* 10 June 1893, p. 269)

Although there were only a handful of spinster explorers, they inspired an immense number of articles and caricatures in contemporary magazines and papers. Expeditions led by women, publicized in the British press, functioned as some of the most dramatic contemporary examples of women claiming the male sphere in its broadest sense: the Empire. While a man could undertake exploration for exploration's sake, many women explorers justified their travels on pretexts of missionary work or health cures. The famed Scottish traveller Isabella Bird (known to successive generations of feminists through Caryl Churchill's iconic play *Top Girls*) pleaded the 'necessity' to her health of pursuits which sound unlikely for an invalid – travelling through the Hawaiian Islands on horseback, climbing mountains and visiting active volcanoes (Bird, 1894, p. vii).

As Dea Birkett points out, one of the most striking chords in the writing of female travellers is the desire to be alone.[12] Travelling alone functioned as a means of developing individual identities divorced from the defining relationships of spinster daughters or maiden sisters. Once freed from the British domestic setting and its restrictions, spinster travellers often fiercely adhered to aspects of womanly propriety, many of which were particularly impractical in the new environments they encountered. Mary Kingsley, for example, reported that she stomped through tropical forests in a high-necked, mutton-chop-sleeved blouse and a long black skirt. This phenomenon, Birkett argues, was not a clinging to the role of Victorian lady, but rather a strategy by which female travellers embraced their identity as members of a race of white colonizers. In this case the strict dress code was not, as at home, designed to enforce gender barriers, but rather to enforce class and colonial barriers, iconographically allying the female traveller with the masculine face of British Imperialism. Despite their outright disruption of dominant scripts of womanly behaviour, most female travellers internalized stereotypically masculine attitudes to the point that they were, ironically, significantly behind the times in their attitudes towards their own sex, having a heavily vested interest in denying allegiance to other women so as not to threaten the status they enjoyed abroad as honorary white men. In this way, the famed spinster travellers were mirage-like visions on the frontiers of feminism: alluring from a distance, evaporating on closer inspection.

Though the Lady Explorer fascinated and entertained the public, she does not figure in the drama, though there were several direct links between the progressive dramatists and women travellers.[13] The closest character to a female traveller in the New Drama appears in Shaw's *Misalliance* (1910). The dashing Polish acrobat Lina Szczepanowska[14] (played by Lena Ashwell), whose work takes her around the globe, enters dressed in flying clothes and goggles after crash-landing her plane into the greenhouse of a country home. In the course of her brief visit four different men fall under her spell. She rescues the head of the household from a gunman, instructs the men in gymnastics and promises to 'make a man' of the snivelling upper-class son, Bentley. When Mr Tarleton, a self-made millionaire, offers to make her his mistress, she takes down his details in a little book, with the explanation: 'Thank you. I keep a list of all my offers. I like to know what I'm considered worth' (p. 68). Lina soon longs to escape the English country home environment, which she perceives as unhealthy and effeminate. 'All the conversation here is about love-making. All the pictures are about love-making. The eyes of all of you are sheep's eyes. You are steeped in it, soaked in it [...] It is disgusting. It is not healthy' (p. 111). When the younger Tarleton proposes, Lina is affronted and indignant at the suggestion that she needs marriage or money. Like a glorified spinster, she is proud of earning her own living and fails to see how she could possibly be improved by marriage: 'I am strong: I am skilful: I am brave: I am independent: I am unbought: I am all that a woman ought to be' (p. 112). The lengthy business of instruction on how to pronounce the name Szczepanowska underscores the innate foreignness of Lina and the essential Englishness of the others. Though the English characters are smitten by her exotic charms, Shaw suggests that English society, with its stuffy homes and its sheep's eyes, is not capable of producing, or even pronouncing, a Szczepanowska.

Unnatural Passions

At a time when the notion of women's moral and sexual purity was a cornerstone of feminist arguments, and at a time when women in public were still associated with prostitution, the Achilles heel of the women's movement was obvious. The simplest, most devastating way to attack feminism was to attack the sexual morality of feminists themselves, an assault greatly aided by the writings of male physicians, sex reformers and educators who, by the turn of the century, claimed to have detected an insidious new threat to British family life and the stability of the nation's future: the invert. In order to reaffirm the inherent 'naturalness' of traditional social order, conservatives set about stigmatizing unmarried feminists as unnatural or 'inverted'. Feminists, who had proudly boasted of their sexual purity might, instead, be sexual deviants. Love and friendship between women, romanticized and socially applauded earlier in the century, now became suspect and dangerous. Unmarried women, such as the early suffrage leaders Frances Power Cobbe and Mary Lloyd, could no longer live together (as many did) without the taint of suspicion. Even staunchly conservative anti-suffrage women, such as the bestselling novelist Marie Corelli,[15] who shared a house with Bertha Vyver, could no longer be innocently regarded.

Havelock Ellis, one of the most influential sexologists, regarded 'inversion' as congenital, thus recommending a certain pity or tolerance for inverts, but (as discussed in Chapter 2) also paradoxically warned that that the women's movement had brought about an increase in homosexuality among women with a weakness for the advances of inverts. The women's movement, then, not only made demands that threatened the order of the traditional British household, but was recruiting a new race of sexually degenerate women. Contrary to its specious claims of purity, the women's movement was now denounced as a breeding ground for lesbianism. Passionate relationships between women were pathologized as 'beyond the bounds of sanity', and as one of the most serious 'dangers to young people' (Scharlieb, 1909, pp. 175–76). Unnatural passion, one doctor claimed, 'can always be distinguished from true affectionate friendship between women, by its jealous, exacting and extravagant tone' (Browne, 1917, p. 102), stigmatizing the newly constructed figure of the female invert as psychologically unstable.

Richard von Krafft-Ebing, author of *Psychopathia Sexualis* (German publication 1886; English translation 1892), characterized the female invert as a 'masculine soul, heaving in the female bosom' (1886/1965, p. 335). He describes the female invert almost solely in terms of her desire to pursue traditionally male activities or her lack of interest in traditionally female activities, rather than in terms of sexual desire:

> The female urning may chiefly be found in the haunts of boys. She is the rival in their play, preferring the rocking-horse, playing at soldiers, etc., to dolls and other girlish occupations. The toilet is neglected, and rough boyish manners are affected. Love for art finds a substitute in the pursuits of the sciences. At times smoking and drinking are cultivated even with passion. Perfumes and sweetmeats are disdained. The consciousness of being a woman and thus to be deprived of the gay college life, or to be barred from the military career, produces painful reflections.
>
> (Krafft-Ebing, 1886/1965, pp. 334–35)

Through Krafft-Ebing's dissemination of the notion of the 'mannish lesbian', women who rejected traditional gender roles and sought social and economic equality could now be branded as cross-dressing sexual perverts. Krafft-Ebing laid particular emphasis on cross-dressing as proof of inversion, which could encompass anything from full male drag to wearing the divided skirts designed to facilitate bicycling, conflating sexual orientation, gender identity, fashion and expediency. Krafft-Ebing's work acted as the tremor that caused an avalanche of articles on this new subject; between 1898 and 1908 there were over a thousand articles and books on homosexuality published in Germany alone. Groups, such as the Scientific-Humanitarian Committee, devoted to explaining the 'third sex', were formed. Women who lived with other women were unlikely to think of themselves as radical transgressors prior to *Psychopathia Sexualis*, but the sexologists' flurry of publications on inverts provided conservatives with a tool for casting unmarried women at large as unnatural deviants. What began as a new area of investigation for medical men became more and more public, providing an extremely effective weapon against the political demands of women.

'Inverts' are not readily apparent in the drama. Though Shaw, male, married, and notorious for irreverence, took the licence to joke on the subject, naming his glorified spinster 'Lesbia', having his Caesar consecrate a new conquest with 'Lesbian wine' and possibly hinting at a female partner for Vivie Warren, other dramatists avoid references to this topic. As a married man, Shaw could afford to preserve Lesbia Grantham as a strong-minded old maid of England, call his Polish acrobat a 'man-woman' and depict Vivie Warren as a whisky-drinking cigar smoker without fear of being cast as an invert himself. By contrast, Cicely Hamilton, a spinster feminist with lower-class sympathies and lesbian friends, possibly lovers, opted for heteronormative happy endings. Growing fear of transgressive female behaviour made voluntary spinsterhood difficult to represent on stage without potentially tarnishing the newly emergent feminist images of female students, professionals and suffragists.

Looking for explicitly lesbian characters or storylines in the dramatic literature of this period would be like looking for 'spinster' or 'fallen woman' characters in twenty-first-century drama, because the terms are not socially commensurate in the different eras. Women who have sex before marriage today are not 'fallen' and single women are not spinsters. Likewise, although there were many women in the Victorian and Edwardian era who preferred romantic or sexual relationships or domestic partnerships with other women, they may not have identified as lesbians. Turn-of-the-century British culture did not tolerate overt homosexual relationships and homosexuals did not typically identify with labels that would socially destroy them. Oscar Wilde sued the Marquess of Queensberry for criminal libel for calling him a 'somdomite' [*sic*]. In a climate of angst regarding the role of women and the medical pathologizing of inverts, it would have been difficult for women to be open about same-sex relationships, even to themselves. Whether or not specific relationships between women were physically consummated remains largely in the realm of conjecture unless the women themselves, like Hamilton's friend Radclyffe Hall, took the unusual step of making their sexuality explicit to a wider public,[16] or unless new evidence, like the diary of Mary Blathwayt, is discovered posthumously.[17] Until very recently the majority of LGBTQ people have continued to consider it in their best interests to be secretive or at least discreet about their relationships. Britain's Clause 28, which forbade local authorities from any services, publications or educational material that showed homosexuality in a positive light or that could be seen to promote 'the acceptability of homosexuality as a pretend family relation-ship',[18] was not repealed until 2000 in Scotland and 2003 in the rest of the UK. Marriage equality has only been legalized in the UK and the US since 2014 and 2015 respectively. It would be naïve, then, to equate a lack of direct evidence about what women did in bed with each other at the turn of the last century with an assumption that there wasn't a range of rela-tionships ongoing between women, from romantic friendships to lovers to life partners. To see possible representations of same-sex relationships between women in Edwardian dramatic literature, however, we must do what marginalized people have always done: read between the lines.

Hamilton's popular suffrage play, the *Pageant of Great Women* (1909), was produced with considerable creative input from Edith Craig, founder of the Pioneer Players. Craig's female life-partner Christopher (aka Christabel) St. John appeared in the *Pageant* as Hannah Snell, an eighteenth-century woman who served in both the army and the navy, somehow miraculously managing to maintain her disguise as a man despite being wounded 11 times to the legs and once to the groin. Hamilton played the female soldier Christian Davies who served for decades in the army in the late seventeenth century, killed a sergeant in a dual over a woman and even paid child support to a prostitute who claimed 'he' was the father of her child. The physical appearance of Hamilton and St. John in drag playing notorious sexual outlaws would certainly have suggested homosexuality to those who were looking for it, as did the inclusion of heroines such as Sappho.[19]

Unlike Shaw's financially independent Lesbia, the heroine of Hamilton's play *Just to Get Married* (1910) is by no means a 'voluntary' spinster, though she nearly breaks off an engagement to live with another woman. Georgiana Vicary is a 29-year-old orphan, dependent on her aunt and uncle. The visit of an eligible family friend, Adam Lankester, puts the entire household on tenterhooks, especially Georgiana who dreads her upcoming 30th birthday and describes herself as 'an unfortunate spinster who sees her last chance of matrimony trembling in the balance' (p. 15). Unlike Julia Huxtable, Georgiana does not evince any symptoms of the supposed ills of celibacy. Her concern to marry is economic rather than emotional, sexual or maternal. Georgiana sees marriage as the only alternative to a future of ignominy and poverty, speculating that euthanasia might be more humane than spinsterhood:

> [I]f you haven't married, you've failed. There's nothing else – and people look down on you. And as you get older there's no one to care about you – and you just don't matter. It's so dull and miserable – no sort of a future. I dread it so. [...] Poor relations don't count for much even when they're nice looking; but when they're old and ugly – well, they oughtn't to be allowed to get old and ugly. It would be ever so much more merciful to take 'em to the Dogs' Home and smother 'em painlessly. (pp. 57–58)

Georgiana shocks her old friend Frances by confessing that love doesn't figure in her reasons for wanting to marry Adam. Frances, who has chosen art and independence over marriage, baulks at Georgiana's lack of morals. When Adam proposes, Hamilton portrays a sad contrast between his joy and Georgiana's polite resignation. Her mortification intensifies with each love letter and gift Adam sends her until finally, the day before the wedding, she decides that spinsterhood is preferable to deceiving a man who genuinely loves her. Hamilton evokes sympathy for both men and women whose relations are warped by the financial dependency of women. Georgiana breaks off her engagement by confessing, 'the night you asked me to be your wife, when you took me in your arms – the first time you kissed me – I was sick with shame – sick!' (p. 57) Though he is hurt, Adam comes to see the situation from Georgiana's point of view and they part as friends, on honest terms for the first time.

The next development in the plot could be seen, and arguably was seen by some feminist contemporaries, as a potentially same-sex ending. After breaking off her engagement to Adam, Georgiana decides to run away to London to live with Frances. Though this wouldn't have suggested a romantic relationship to all members of the audience in 1910, I wager it would have to Cicely Hamilton's network of friends. Although a same-sex denouement would have more closely resembled her own life, Hamilton opts for a conventional happy ending with a twist: Georgiana chances upon Adam in the waiting-room at the train station and in a gender role reversal she asks him to marry her. From a business point of view, the happy hetero ending was a good decision – the show ran for 61 performances in London at Gertrude Kingston's Little Theatre, enjoyed a national tour and made a successful transfer to New York in 1912. The commercial happy ending was not, however, universally appreciated by audiences and critics. The critic for the feminist paper *The Vote* noted a cool audience reception on opening night, suggesting that they might have preferred an alternative ending: 'At the end of the second act the enthusiasm was tremendous – but the third act was evidently a little harder to accept' (19 November 1910). Even *The Times* expressed reservations about the ending, but noted:

> The first two acts were so good, so shrewd in observation of personal details [...] so deadly in their indictment, so adroit in their mixture of witty comedy with dead earnest tragedy [...] that a feeble third act could not destroy their merit.
>
> (9 November 1910)

By December the third act was referred to by Marjorie Strachey in the *Englishwoman* as 'that terribly abused happy ending' (quoted in Whitelaw, 1990, p. 128). Hamilton's biographer Liz Whitelaw comments, 'It reads as though Cicely knew she had to end the play like this but that all her instincts told her that Georgiana would have been better off setting up house with Frances' (1990, p. 128). While her Georgiana ends up with Adam, plenty of women in Hamilton's circle *were* setting up house with Frances.

Hamilton stands out among dramatists in exploring the economic hypocrisy of traditional courtship in heterosexual romantic relationships in depth, creating her own sort of 'socialist rom-com' genre in *Just to Get Married, Diana of Dobson's* and *Jack and Jill and a Friend* (1911). The focus on heterosexual romance rather than a celebration of voluntary spinsterhood may be somewhat ironic in light of the fact that Hamilton lived and worked among a powerful network of women who had lifelong relationships with other women and, according to her biographer, was a lesbian herself (Whitelaw, 1990, pp. 1–6; pp. 109–14). Hamilton's emphasis might also be seen as a strategy calculated to bring her key ideas to a wider forum and as a keen awareness of the material circumstances under which her theatre work was produced and received. Anna Andes suggests that rather than reading the endings of Hamilton's comedies as surrendering to convention, a dramaturgy of male conversion can be seen at work: 'the man is converted by the woman to her way of thinking about marriage, a conversion that is required in order to bring about a resolution that allows marital harmony to ensue' (Andes, 2015, p. 504). Diana, Georgiana and Jill all break convention not by rejecting marriage, but by being honest with their suitors about their circumstances, honesty that enables the men to change their perspectives from romantic chauvinism to realistic friendship – friendship which may enable a truer romance to develop.

* * *

There was no such identity as the 'single woman' in the Victorian era. With feminine character expressed primarily through the domestic roles of wife and mother, unmarried women were either framed as eligible brides or redundant spinsters. The cultural construction of the 'superfluous' or 'odd' woman served to undermine independent female agency. As marriage declined in popularity, unmarried women were regarded as a danger to the balance of society and increasingly pathologized by medical narratives of ovarian insanity, old maid's mania and inversion. As well as being a danger to the fabric of society, unmarried women were also frequently represented as being *in* danger themselves without husbands to protect them from sexual exploitation, demeaning labour conditions and poverty.

Despite these fears, by the turn of the century more and more women were living their lives independently from husbands and supporting themselves financially – among them many actresses and writers like Robins, Hamilton, Craig and St. John. In 1909, at the decidedly spinsterly age of 37, Cicely Hamilton wrote, 'I suppose that in the recent history of woman nothing is more striking than the enormous improvement that has taken place in the social position of the spinster' (MT, p. 249). Hamilton reflected that, in contrast, 'nothing like the same improvement has taken place in recent years in the position of the average married woman' (MT, p. 250). Middle-class spinsters' growing determination to be economically independent, in combination with the nation's demographic 'crisis' of unmarried women, necessitated a move from the spinster's traditionally unpaid labour as housekeeper, companion or charity worker into expanding paid public fields such as nursing, typing or teaching. Newly employed in the professions opening up to middle-class women, these twentieth-century spinsters were transitional figures of female empowerment in the prewar years, both as workers and consumers in the public sphere. Women who had once been stigmatized as 'surplus' or 'odd' re-appropriated the term 'spinster' and fashioned unmarried life as a positive choice, rather than the ultimate failure, paving the way for younger women to shape themselves in the more active, confident moulds of the New Woman, the modern woman and the suffragist. Less encumbered by family responsibilities, unmarried women like Christabel Pankhurst rose to the forefront of the women's movement, forming the core membership of organizations like the Women's Social and Political Union, and became tremendously influential in matters of national politics, economy, law and other formerly masculine domains.

In theatre, depictions of spinsters are seldom empowering. Barker's spinster characters are progressive in his contextualization of their social circumstances rather than in his characterizations of the women themselves. For Shaw unmarried women are wasted mothers like Lesbia, unsexed aberrations like Vivie, or sexually available Szczepanowskas. Sowerby depicts the humiliations of spinsterhood and the perils of sexual agency for the daughter of a wealthy family as a no-win situation. Without independent means or a father or husband to provide and protect for them, Williams's unmarried sisters Margaret and Violet are sexually exploited, a horror only marriage can save them from. In addition to being vulnerable to sexual exploitation, Lyttelton's unmarried sisters Theodosia and Phoebe are abused as sweated labourers – Phoebe is literally worked to death. Hamilton's unmarried romantic heroines see the world and potential suitors almost entirely in economic terms, though they do not 'fall' morally; Diana refuses the rich Sir Jabez and Georgiana makes an honest confession to Adam. Frances is one of Hamilton's most romantic characters, the character most like herself, sacrificing material comforts for art and independence. Frances and some of the characters in Hamilton's *Pageant of Great Women* hint at the possibilities of same-sex primary relationships (whether sexually active or more familial partnerships) which women like Craig and St. John and Robins and Wilberforce were modelling in real life. In theatre, spinsters are often passive symbols of eroded human potential whose plights are used to indict society, but who seldom voice the criticisms and concerns of 'real life' unmarried women activists, except in the explicitly suffrage drama of 1907–14 (the subject of Chapter 5).

CHAPTER 4

Motherhood: The Double Bind

Motherhood was not Elizabeth Robins's goal in life. The considerable surviving evidence signposts that choosing a career over motherhood was a deliberate path. Robins's biographers John and Gates conjecture that she may have been pregnant in her early twenties and had a miscarriage or an abortion that could have contributed to her husband George Parks's suicide.[1] Thomas Postlewait (1986, pp. 118–19) speculates that Robins may have been pregnant by Archer ten years later in 1895, explaining a year of marked inactivity from the theatre despite having the production rights to *Little Eyolf*, which she postponed until 1896 on the grounds of nervous exhaustion. Postlewait hazards that if she did have a child, it must have been placed in adoption, but Robins's biographer John doesn't estimate the evidence to be convincing (1995, p. 79).

Whatever the truth of her private life, as an artist Robins had a decidedly unconventional relationship with the subject of motherhood. Her breakthrough role was Hedda Gabler, a pregnant character who shoots herself. Her play *Alan's Wife* (1893) is the story of a mother who kills her baby, then hangs for infanticide. In her New Woman novel *George Mandeville's Husband* (1894), a successful female author ('George Mandeville' – her male nom de plume) neglects the care of her frail daughter in favour of her career and her daughter dies. Her successful novel *The Open Question*[2] (1898) explored the desire for romance without procreation in the story of Val and Ethan who make and keep a suicide pact not to bring a child into the world, instead sailing out to a shared death at sea when Val becomes pregnant.[3] Robins's best known play *Votes for Women!* (1907) is the story of a woman who, having survived an abortion that nearly kills her, goes on to find a powerful calling as a feminist speaker and social reformer.

In her Edwardian writing onwards, as well as in her work for campaigns and causes, Robins endorsed a feminism focused on improving the welfare of society at large, including children, a commitment broader than the nuclear family and a project which did not exclude non-parents or non-heteronormative households like her own.[4] Compared to male contemporaries like Shaw who focused on women's biological role as propagators of the race, Robins did not agree that gestating and birthing babies was necessarily the highest contribution a woman could make to society. Eschewing the customary reverence on the subject, Robins wrote of women, 'I would hesitate to say her greatest service is the same as that which the female of the species (whether animal or vegetable) renders blindly to propagation' (1940, p. 173). Robins also cast doubt on the inherent good of individual procreation by highlighting a socialist concern with feeding and educating the world's existing population. She extolled the qualities of caring, compassion and altruism traditionally associated with motherhood, but argued that these qualities should be incorporated into public life, not reserved for private families. All too aware, however, of the challenges facing women striving to contribute to public life, she noted that, 'To say "a public man" is to convey the idea of one arrived at eminence, usually at office; at honours, if not honour. To say "a public woman" is, or was recently, to say a woman of the streets' (1924, p. 76). Her articulation of a socialist motherhood, caring for the welfare of all children instead of exclusively for one's own, is at the heart of her suffrage play *Votes for Women!* The attempt to negotiate non-exclusive links between feminism and motherhood presented one of the greatest challenges for women in Robins's generation, whether they themselves were mothers or not.

HIGHEST CALLING OR PRIMITIVE INSTINCT?

Questions of motherhood have always been ideological battlegrounds between patriarchy and feminism, never more so than at the turn of the twentieth century. Nineteenth-century evangelism had seen a reconstruction of female sexuality from the temptress Magdalene to the Blessed Mother or Madonna. In Victorian separate spheres rhetoric motherhood was venerated as the highest calling and supreme fulfilment of a woman's life. This fulfilment was conditional on patriarchal law, however, because if a woman was unmarried, pregnancy was regarded as shameful, possibly worse than death. By the end of the century, evangelical Victorian depictions of the Madonna were rivalled by new 'scientific truths' from the male worlds of medical and evolutionary sciences where pregnancy and childbirth were fast becoming characterized as lower animal functions that kept women from attaining the higher evolutionary development of (white) men. Even the womanly characteristics so admired in Victorian art and literature – intuition, tenderness and self-sacrifice – were described by Darwin in *The Descent of Man and Selection in Relation to Sex* as 'characteristic of the lower races, and therefore of a past and lower state of civilisation' (1859/1901, pp. 857–58).

In this scientific discourse European women were frequently compared, in stature, brain size and evolutionary development, to males and females of the 'lower races'. Using pelvimetry, the influential sexologist Havelock Ellis hypothesized that white women had a significant evolutionary advantage over women of other races: they had developed wider pelvises in order give birth to distinctively large-brained white male babies.[5] Whereas scientists were keen to emphasize the disparity between the average brain size of European males and females, they claimed that in non-Europeans male and female brain sizes were the same, stressing the global superiority of white males and by implication the need for their governance at home and throughout the British Empire. In the face of degradation at the hands of science, feminists appropriated evangelical discourse to defend womanhood from the dehumanizing gaze of medical science[6] and to serve their political agendas. Over time feminists attempted to combine evangelism with science by linking concepts of feminine morality with theories of evolution, advancing women as the agents of evolutionary progression in which the entire race would be elevated to higher standards of morality and sexual purity. Thus, in the Preface to *Getting Married*, Shaw predicted that 'the political emancipation of women is likely to lead to a comparatively stringent enforcement by law of sexual morality' adding the caveat, '(that is why so many of us dread it)' (1908/1986a, p. 69).

Motherhood was commonly lauded as women's principal contribution to the state, braving bodily pain and risking death in order to replenish the British population. Amidst paradoxes between romantic-spiritual and animalistic-scientific representations of motherhood, feminists began to broadly question the patriarchal agenda behind male depictions of mothers. 'Men,' Cicely Hamilton wrote, 'are capable of being both reverent and ribald on the subject of maternity; I have never met a woman who was either' (MT, p. 208). Frances Power Cobbe denounced mainstream culture's exaltation of The Mother as a ploy to deny women self-determination and urged women to reject the notion that 'the whole meaning and reason of her existence is, that she may form a link in the chain of generations' (1869, p. 8). Some feminists, like Hamilton, began to speak out against romantic depictions of motherhood as male contrivances to entice women into becoming 'breeding-machines' (MT, p. 64) manufacturing the Sons for the Empire.

EUGENICS

Eugenics, the 'science' of improving human stock, was used by conservative and progressive thinkers alike, including dramatists, to further their diverse theories on motherhood in relation to human evolution and to the nation-state. The idea of selective human breeding can be traced back to antiquity, with Plato advocating a state-run programme of procreation to fortify the guardian class in *The Republic*. The Victorian eugenics movement was founded by Francis Galton (Charles Darwin's cousin) who coined the term 'eugenics', meaning 'good in birth', in 1883. Galton's goal was to improve the human race through positively encouraging breeding in the 'fittest' members of society while negatively discouraging or preventing breeding among the 'weak' – accelerating nature's process of selection. Defining the fittest and the weakest members of society was, of course, revealing of class, race and gender prejudices, with the working classes generally described as 'undesirable' along with 'the feebleminded', a popular but vague Victorian term which could mean anything from criminally insane to alcoholic, uneducated or poor. The fittest, of course, were the (white) upper and middle classes. Eugenic theories were considerably energized in 1900 by a rediscovery of Mendel's laws on biological inheritance, which privileged 'nature' to the virtual exclusion of 'nurture' as a causative factor of behaviour and ability. Social and economic conditions such as poverty, illiteracy and prostitution were cast simplistically in Mendelian terms as genetic traits that would be inherited rather than behaviours rooted in social conditions thus eliminating the need to address or reform those social conditions.

A sense of panic among the upper and middle classes about being out-peopled by undesirables became a rationale for the advocacy of state-regulated eugenic policies to prevent an apocalyptic 'race suicide' (Sprague, 1915, p. 158). Proponents of eugenics attempted to quell social anxieties over a rise in the working-class population, frequently characterized in terms of degeneration and atavism, by proposing a form of race control in which the fittest members of society (upper- and middle-class people like themselves) would become the genetic guardians of British stock. The increasing popularity of evolutionary theory meant that impoverished material living and working conditions could now be dismissed as the result of biological degeneracy, leading to arguments against state support and private philanthropy aimed at helping the poor or infirm as unnaturally perpetuating withered stock.[7] As I touched on in the Introduction, race had a broader meaning to Victorians than it does today, as anthropologists classified races by environmental elements like languages and cultures as well as by inherited physical traits like skin tone, conflating heredity and culture. When nineteenth-century authors speak of 'the race' in terms of British nationalism and the need to replenish the population, we can infer they are speaking of the white majority, but it does not always follow that they are thinking in terms of ethnicity.[8] The slippage between race and culture[9] in the era means that notions of perpetuating 'the race' aren't exclusive to racial types. The dramatists considered here are much more explicit about class differences in terms of racial 'fitness' than they are about geographic or ethnic origins. In *The Idea of Race in Science,* Nancy Stepan makes a case that unlike in Germany or America, 'Eugenics in Britain was never extreme in its racialism' (1982, p. 111), a restraint she attributes in part to the fact that at this time the country did not have large numbers of immigrants in its major cities (p. 126).[10]

Eugenic theory regarded motherhood not only as the greatest means to a woman's self-actualization and fulfilment, but also as a national duty, one worth the sacrifice of individual (i.e. women's) civic rights. Pro- and anti-feminists attempted to harness eugenic theories in support of both conservative and progressive causes, sometimes strange blends of both. In his book *Woman and Womanhood,* for example, the pro-suffrage physician Caleb Saleeby lauded feminists as the best of the British female stock, but argued that in their fight for rights and freedoms they had overlooked the urgency of their true vocation: motherhood. Saleeby, who claimed that he was 'much more feminist than the feminists' (1911, p. 8) in his recognition of the centrality of motherhood, urged the leaders of the women's movement to embrace a 'Eugenic Feminism', warning that feminist leaders who deprived 'the blood of the future of its due contribution from the best women of the present' were 'leading not only one sex but the race as a whole to ruin' (p. 5). While male[11] eugenicists used arguments about women's duty to the health of the race to dissuade them from pursuing the feminist aims of education, employment and independence at the expense of motherhood, some feminists in turn began using elements of eugenic theory to sharpen their critiques of male licentiousness and its degenerate influence on the race. In her book *The Bar of Isis*[12] Frances Swiney shifted the focus from women back to men as the transmitters of

STDs into the nuclear family, describing profligate men and their issue as branded by enfeebled frames, diseased tissues, weak will, idiocy, insanity and criminality (1907, pp. 38–39). Swiney declared that women had been martyrs to men's 'organised and systemic sexual wrong-doing' (p. 38) and proposed that the only way to protect future generations was to challenge the double standard. Though many feminists preferred not to conceptualize themselves in terms of their duty to the race, in general feminist criticism of eugenics was subdued, largely because the centrality of the mother in eugenic discourse served to shift what had been considered 'women's issues' into the larger debates of race and nation.

Man and Superman

The most famous expression of eugenic theory in the drama of this period is Shaw's *Man and Superman*, first published in 1903 and first staged in 1905 at the Royal Court Theatre by Harley Granville Barker, who also played the philosopher protagonist John Tanner. (Tanner was consciously styled on Shaw with Barker donning a red Shavian beard for the role, fuelling a genetic rumour that Shaw and Barker were father and son.) An avid supporter of eugenic theory, Shaw foretold that humankind would, by necessity, have to progress to a fitter state in order to cope with the demands of democracy or face ruin at the hands of Yahoos. In the Preface to *Man and Superman* Shaw argues that 'the only fundamental and possible Socialism is the socialization of the selective breeding of Man' (1946a, p. 245) and suggests establishing a State Department of Evolution. Shaw derived his theories on the desired improvement of the race from the writings of authors such as Thomas Carlyle, Samuel Butler, Henri Bergson and Havelock Ellis as well as New Malthusian and eugenics tracts. The idea of the *Übermensch* comes from Nietzsche, who uses the concept more metaphorically, where Shaw presents his eugenic vision of the Superman literally in biological terms. Shaw draws specifically from Schopenhauer's 'Metaphysics of the Love of the Sexes' and Nietzsche's *Thus Spoke Zarathustra* in crafting his vision of progressive evolution in the play. Schopenhauer's grim theory of man's inexorable World Will[13] along with his unromantic notion of love and sexual attraction (as a manifestation of the instinctive determination of the race) becomes a comedic dance in Shaw's play, replete with farcical embellishments.

For all its lengthy discussions of eugenic philosophy, the plot of *Man and Superman* is a traditional romantic comedy with a gender reversal showing the woman as the active hunter and the man as her mark, ending with an engagement. Shaw's female protagonist, Ann Whitefield, selects the unsuspecting John Tanner as the father of her future children, stalks her prey, and takes him down. In the second act Shaw energizes the romantic pursuit by liberating it from the conventional drawing room setting and having his hero take flight across Europe in the first dramatic car chase. The third act is a surreal symposium set in hell in which Tanner and Ann, freed from Edwardian convention by their transfiguration into Don Juan and Ana, speak freely about sex and procreation and Ann reveals her true purpose: '[*Crying to the universe*] A father! a father for the Superman!' (p. 173).[14] This act, the most challenging in style and content, was omitted from the 1905 Court production (the play wasn't performed in its entirety until 1915). In the final act Shaw delivers the conventional comic resolution of marriage with an engagement scene between Tanner and Ann in the romantic garden of a villa in Granada, a cultivated Eden.

Unlike the Biblical Eve, derived from Adam's rib, Shaw's heroine Ann Whitefield represents a primal, gynocentric Everywoman who has created the (dispensable) male sex as a means to producing greater genetic variation and more advanced life forms than would be possible through single-sex reproduction.[15] Shaw's philosopher protagonist John Tanner habitually speaks of women using atavistic animal imagery, much to the dismay of the artist Octavius who has a more poetic, if clichéd, view of women. Failing to recognize that he is Ann's prey, Tanner repeatedly warns Octavius in terms of impending animal danger, likening Ann to a strangling boa constrictor (p. 49), a devouring lioness (p. 60), a mate-killing spider and a drone-killing queen bee (p. 92). Tanner's primordial interpretation of the female sex is a uterocentric essentialism in which the female is allied with the forces of Nature, and thus more powerful than Man (which, in spite of Shaw's socialism, belies women's material position in society). Tanner dismisses women's grievances on the subject of the sexual double standard by arguing 'how can so feeble and transient a folly as man's selfish pleasure enslave a woman as the whole purpose of Nature embodied in a woman can enslave a man?' (p. 61). Following Darwin, Tanner claims that since Woman has spared Man the labour of gestation, she has enabled him to evolve to become the dominant sex. While Woman exhausts her energies creating Man, Man creates civilization, 'without consulting her, taking her domestic labor for granted as the foundation of it' (p. 148). Woman's part in the creation of the Man is an animal function, whereas Man shapes superhuman evolution through his higher social development. Equating Woman with Nature and Man with Civilization, each ruthlessly set on the fulfilment of their contradictory purposes (hers to replenish, his to evolve), Tanner/Shaw asserts that of 'all human struggles there is none so treacherous and remorseless as the struggle between the artist man and the mother woman' (p. 62). Where New Women novelists like Elizabeth Robins[16] and Mona Caird[17] explored struggles between 'the artist woman' and 'the father man', for Shaw artists are male and parents are mothers.

Only once in this extremely long work (comprising the Preface,[18] the play and the 'Revolutionist's Handbook') does Shaw/Tanner mention the possibility that artistic genius might manifest itself in a woman. When he does, he imagines it as an appalling prospect: 'George Sand becomes a mother to gain experience for the novelist and to develop her, and gobbles up men of genius, Chopins, Mussets and the like, as mere hors d'oeuvres' (p. 20). While a woman acting as a muse to a male artist makes perfect sense to Shaw, he describes a female artist who draws from personal experience in the negative terms of using her children and cannibalizing her lovers. Significantly, the artist Octavius has a sister, Violet, who prior to 'the fulfilment of her highest purpose and greatest function – to increase, multiply, and replenish the earth' (p. 64) has been wasting herself on 'sillinesses' (p. 64). These 'sillinesses' are artistic pursuits, 'making bad water color sketches' and 'practising Grieg and Brahms'[19] (p. 64). Beatrice Ethel Kidd's review of the first published edition of *Man and Superman* shows that these issues rankled Edwardian feminists as much as they have continued to irk successive generations of feminists, who often look to Shaw for feminist prototypes, but do not always like what they find.[20] Kidd's criticisms warrant quoting at length:

> [T]he Superwoman is not admitted at all, even as an ideal. Woman, so far as he has observed her, has no other object in life than to entrap men … We ask, amazed, where is the writer's sometimes almost uncanny perspicacity, that he has failed to observe the modern woman's increasing independence of marriage, and the fact that she, too, is apt to regard it as something of a hindrance to *her* 'dreams, follies, ideals, heroisms, and the like?' Can it be that Mr. Bernard Shaw is ignorant of women? … The fact is, women are quite as anxious for superhumanity as men, and are probably nearer its attainment; and if marriage be a hindrance to the man, what must it be to them? […] Instead of vanishing into the void, according to Mr. Shaw's tableau, crying to the Universe, 'A father! A father for the Superman!' She is more likely to emerge into the broad light of day demanding (with

a little gentle assistance to the supposed 'prey,' who is making himself ridiculous by his frantic efforts to get out of her way) 'Room – room for the Superwoman!'.

(Quoted in Gainor, 1991, pp. 208–09)

Despite criticisms from some feminists, others found qualities to admire in Shaw's Ann Whitefield. Lillah McCarthy, who originated the role, said 'She was a "new woman" and she made a new woman of me' (1933, p. 63), suggesting that she interpreted Ann as a self-determined modern woman, liberated from the conventions of 'ladylike' behaviour, not simply a tool of nature. For McCarthy, Ann was 'earthy' (p. 63) and 'a real woman' (p. 63) who was insistent rather than submissive, modelling a bolder, more honest form of self-expression in contrast to the conventionally passive female characters she compared to mannequins (p. 63). Famously identified with the character, McCarthy reflected in her memoirs that many women confided to her that 'Ann brought them to life and that they re-modelled themselves upon Ann's pattern' including Emmeline Pankhurst who apparently told McCarthy that Ann 'had strengthened her purpose and fortified her courage' (p. 64). (As a purity feminist, Pankhurst's appreciation of Ann was no doubt helped by the Court production's omission of the third act.) For McCarthy, Shaw's Ann 'set the leading lady – and with her all the ladies of the theatre – free' (p. 64), contributing to women's emancipation on stage and off. Ann also led McCarthy into a romance with the leading man, her future husband Harley Granville Barker (Fig. 4.1).

While Shaw represents female sexuality as dynamic and vital, his Everywoman's greatest purpose is, as Kidd points out, to produce a Super *Man*, not a correspondingly Super Woman. The woman's part in evolution does not evolve. Shaw's positive contribution to feminism in *Man and Superman* lies in discarding stereotypes of 'angelic' or 'fallen' women, and debunking the notion that women's sexuality and desire for maternity could be regulated solely by the patriarchal legal construction of marriage, something New Woman novelists like Caird had been pointing out for years.[21] Kirsten Shepherd-Barr observes that, 'For all the thousands of words [Shaw] expends in trying to distinguish his theory form Darwin's, it seems to boil down to a single concept – agency' (2015, p. 140). Ann's agency distinguishes Shaw's pro-active human mother from Darwin's,[22] but as Shepherd-Barr points out, Shaw wasn't the first to recognize female agency in human evolution; Eliza Burt Gamble who published *The Evolution of Woman* in 1894 'emphasized female choice as

Fig. 4.1   Lillah McCarthy as Ann Whitefield, Harley Granville Barker as a Shavian-styled John Tanner in *Man and Superman*, printed by permission of the V&A

a key feature of sexual selection' (quoted in Shepherd-Barr 2015, p. 96). While he delights in depicting women as predatory animals and marriage as irrelevant to the Life Force, Shaw ends his comedy conventionally with an engagement that will legitimize Ann's progeny. If measured by the Pankhurst's WSPU standard of 'deeds not words', Shaw's characters, for all their talk, are more conformist than radical.

Alan's Wife

Ten years prior to the publication of *Man and Superman*, Elizabeth Robins and Florence Bell anonymously authored a much darker play, *Alan's Wife*, which has been read as endorsing eugenic values by casting a sympathetic light on the young mother protagonist (played by Robins) who kills her genetically imperfect baby. Unlike *Man and Superman*, however, it is possible to read this play in ways that aren't necessarily in keeping with eugenic theories. Elin Diamond and Catherine Wiley have persuasively interpreted it as a work more focused on destroying the Victorian angel-mother than about the moral dilemma of culling imperfect offspring.[23] *Alan's Wife* was adapted by Robins and Bell from a Swedish story by Elin Ameen titled *Befriad*, meaning 'released' or 'set free' – a title that fore-grounded the idea of euthanasia and one which Robins and Bell decided not to keep. In adapting the story they transposed it to England against the express advice of William Archer, the sole confidant of their secret collaboration, who thought that English audiences would show greater tolerance for infanticide if it happened abroad. Instead, Robins and Bell set their adaptation in a factory village in the industrial North, a world Bell had extensive first-hand knowledge of.[24]

An important contextual point in relation to the violence in *Alan's Wife* is that infanticide was a well-documented occurrence in England in this era, frequently reported in newspapers and tried in the courts. Annie Besant, a birth control advocate whom Elizabeth Robins admired and whose biography she undertook, reported a widespread knowledge of infanticide among the medical profession. A Dr Lankester claimed that 'there were in London alone 16,000 women who had murdered their off-spring' (Besant, 1879, p. 25) and a Dr Attwood attested that in northern manufacturing towns like Macclesfield children were often 'put away' (p. 25). Cicely Hamilton noted that she had heard women discussing the practice of passing the death sentence for infanticide many times and was struck by the 'typically unfeminine and unmaternal' attitude of women on this point, 'since their sympathies were invariably on the side of the erring mother, and I cannot remember having heard a single woman's voice raised in defence of the right to its life of the unwanted child' (MT, p. 212). In drawing attention to infanticide, Robins and Bell[25] shone a light on an ugly truth of the life-and-death moral dilemmas faced by mothers in desperate circumstances, crises far removed from the superhu-man objectives of male philosophers like Shaw.

Alan's Wife opens on the scene of a newlywed, Jean, preparing dinner for her husband and eagerly anticipating his arrival back from the factory. As Jean performs her chores, her mother speaks openly of her regret that Jean didn't 'look higher' by choosing the middle-class minister Jamie Warren. Jean scorns the idea of 'poor little Jamie Warren' (p. 11) as a mate, derisively remembering how she was stronger and bolder, even as a child. By contrast Jean speaks ardently of Alan as 'the handsomest, and the strongest' (p. 11), 'a man who is my master' (p. 12) and, in a passage suggestive of his virility, a man who loves to feel 'the blood rushing through his veins' (p. 12). Even the bookish Jamie Warren acknowledges Alan as 'a Hercules' (p. 13). While Jean's mother's aspirations are for social mobility and material comfort, Jean choses physical attraction and strong genetic stock, anticipating a son, 'wee Alan', who will 'be just such another as his father' (p. 14). Robins and Bell depict their heroine as strikingly self-determined and sexualized in her uninhibited physical attraction to Alan and her disregard of class as a factor in marriage. The vitality of Jean and Alan's relationship is visibly manifest in her pregnancy, but the act ends in tragedy. The Herculean man is killed in a machine accident at the factory. As his shrouded corpse is carried past on a stretcher, Jean runs to it and collapses as the curtain falls.

In the second act Jean is a widow with an infant son who, far from expressing the eugenic perfection of his father, is 'sent, hideous and maimed, to stumble through this terrible world' (p. 19). Jamie Warren visits and consoles Jean that her son 'will grow up to be a scholar and a God-fearing man' (p. 19). Though she rejects his advice that she should bow to the will of God in her misfortune, the minister's visit awakens Jean's hope that the baby might be made 'straight and fair and happy' (p. 25) in heaven. Alone with the infant, Jean talks in turns to herself, to the baby and to God, articulating the mental process leading up to the infanticide. In the scene, Robins's acting tour de force and the climax of the play, Jean reacts with horror to visions of the future, whispers wildly with fear, and blanches at the realization of what she must do. Speaking to the baby, she says, 'I seem to see you in some far-off time, your face distorted like your body, but with bitterness and loathing, saying "Mother, how *could* you be so cruel as to let me live and suffer?"' (p. 21). Moving in a sort of trance, Jean performs a baptism to ensure that the baby's soul will be saved. Looking into the cradle she falters momentarily and turns away with a sob, then, in a moment of realistic acting detail, twice struggles to find the right page in the Bible before closing the book, falling to her knees and appealing directly to God, 'Have pity on us, Lord – show us the way!' (p. 21). She lets the Bible fall to the floor as she dips her hand in water and baptizes the baby 'Alan'. She looks anxiously over her shoulder to the door and the window before blowing out the candles one by one and clutching the eider quilt with which she will suffocate him. The curtain falls on the image of Jean moving 'steadily towards the cradle with a long wailing cry' (p. 21).

The final act takes place in prison where Jean receives the news that she has been sentenced to death for the murder of her baby. The emotional turmoil of this scene is played out by Jean's distraught mother, who implores Jean to offer an explanation or repentance that will soften the ruling. Jean is already removed, 'strangely hardened' (p. 23) and throughout the scene she remains hauntingly silent as her mother and Jamie Warren discuss her situation. Robins and Bell note 'Jean's sentences are given as stage directions of what she is silently to convey, but she does not speak until nearly the end of the Act' (p. 23).[26] This authorial/acting technique drew on Robins's early training in the body language of melodrama, fused with the psychological realism of her Ibsen work, and entrusts Robins as performer to communicate beyond language. The stage direction 'silent' is given 11 times in the scene with variations on Jean's physicality and the sentiments she conveys wordlessly: '(silent – stares vacantly into space) I can tell him nothing'; '(silent – smiles strangely) I don't want mercy'; '(silent – puts out her hand to her mother) Poor mother!'; and '(silent) I shall not die unforgiven' (pp. 23–24). In the final moments of the play, Jean says the unsayable, rejecting mercy with the affirmation: 'I've had courage just once in my life – just once in my life I've been strong and kind – and it was the night I killed my child!' (p. 25). She embraces her execution at the hands of the law as a welcome euthanasia. Ending the play with Jean's release (rather than the baby's) may have been one of the reasons Robins and Bell went against Archer's advice to keep the story set in Sweden – Sweden did not have capital punishment, but in this English version of the story both Church and State are links in the chain of tragedy.

Performed by the Independent Theatre Society at Terry's Theatre in 1893, the piece provoked outrage, a reception Robins and Bell had anticipated, concealing their identities so completely that even their producer J.T. Grein apparently remained ignorant of the play's true authorship. In his preface to the published version of *Alan's Wife*, Grein compared the play's tragic power and modern realism to Ibsen's *Ghosts*.[27] The *Athenaeum* review summarized the plot of *Alan's Wife* directly in relation to *A Doll's House*, comparing Nora, who leaves her children because she finds out that her husband is weak and contemptible, to Jean, 'who has married her husband for his Viking stature and beauty' and who slays their child 'when she finds him puny and deformed' (6 May 1893). The *Athenaeum* concluded that the story was 'shudderingly nude, and its truth of detail is revolting', suggesting an issue with realism as well as the plot. The *Era*, while condemning Jean as 'a monster' and 'an ignorant, cruel, and presumptuous person', had high praise for Robins's acting, noting that she 'rose to a fine height of tragic expression in the child murder scene, and thrilled her audience by the intensity and poignancy of her acting' (6 May 1893). Out of the scores of reviews of *Alan's Wife* she collected and pasted into her scrapbook, Robins circled just one word, perhaps isolating what was for her, as author and actress, Jean's key quality (Fig. 4.2).

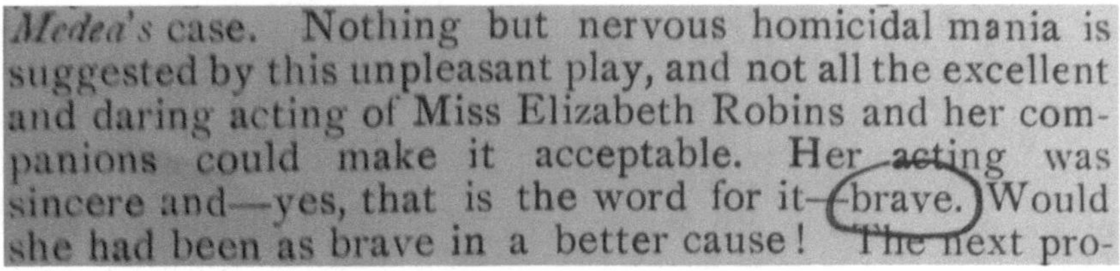

Medea's case. Nothing but nervous homicidal mania is suggested by this unpleasant play, and not all the excellent and daring acting of Miss Elizabeth Robins and her companions could make it acceptable. Her acting was sincere and—yes, that is the word for it—brave. Would she had been as brave in a better cause! The next pro-

Fig. 4.2   *The Gentlewoman*, 6 May 1893 with Elizabeth Robins's autograph annotation, reproduced from The Fales Collection by permission of Independent Age

In the most famously hostile and visceral review of the piece, A.B. Walkley challenged the play's very right to exist, submitting that it 'ought never to have been written' and confessing that the recollection of it hung on him 'like a nightmare' (*The Speaker*, 6 May 1893). In what can be interpreted as a fascinating example of male hysteria, Walkley vividly recounted images of the mangled corpse of Alan and the corpse of the strangled baby, though neither of these were actually staged, as Archer and Robins both took pains to point out. Catherine Wiley argues that what Walkley actually saw was 'the violent but bloodless disruption of the nineteenth-century mechanics of representation keeping women captive in the role of idealized motherhood' (1990, p. 432), a disruption so horrific that it triggered his hallucination.[28]

In his lengthy introduction to the published version of *Alan's Wife*, Archer seems to assure (male) critics that he would have handled Act II very differently. In an act of stunning hubris, Archer first claims to be 'in great measure responsible for the existence of the play'[29] (1893a, p. ix) before going on to rewrite it in detail according to his own plan, a practice often used by male critics when reviewing female playwrights' work. In Archer's version, Act II is a clinical dialogue between Jean and a doctor during which 'the audience was to have felt the resolution to end the crippled life growing gradually in her mind' (p. xiii). On the doctor's departure, Archer cuts Robins's long virtuosic acting monologue down to 'a few words – a very few almost incoherent words' after which she would have 'done the deed' on stage, 'seen but vaguely by the audience' (p. xiii). Archer's Act III is 'a mere conversation' (p. xiii) between the woman and the doctor, set dispassionately several years in the future in a capital-punishment-less Swedish jail. Gone is Jean/Robins's brave farewell to life, which Grein admired as 'so affecting that old men, as we saw, cried, while women melted in tears' (1893, p. viii). Though Archer kept the secret of their authorship, calling Robins and Bell 'he' throughout his introduction, part of Archer's project in fronting their script with his version was to save the play from what he saw as the excesses of female melodrama, making it into a more rational study of the question of euthanasia – a more eugenic version.[30] Naturally, Robins and Bell were irritated by Archer's overbearing introduction which they thought smothered the published play (Gates, 1994, p. 66).

If you accept, as I do, Diamond and Wiley's reading of *Alan's Wife* as a play that is more about killing the angel-mother than about killing the baby, then Archer's alternative version misses the point of the female authors' project entirely. In his version, the question of euthanasia for the eugenically imperfect child is the moral crux of the play, ushered in and seen out clinically by a man of science instead of a man of God, while the female protagonist is imprisoned for life as the price for setting her child free. Though he worked intimately with Robins on *Hedda Gabler*, a play in which the female protagonist chooses death over life and motherhood with a mediocre scholarly husband (much like Jamie Warren), it doesn't seem to occur to Archer that in Robins and Bell's adaptation the female protagonist is the one who is 'released'. Perhaps Archer's (mis)reading of the play stems from what Diamond identifies as its 'vehemently un-Ibsenite' structure, rejecting 'the process whereby the past remembered produces or explains a hysteria, its necessary confession, and its cure' (1997, p. 35). Where Shaw uses eugenics to naturalize women as mothers and men as the creators and keepers of civilization, Robins and Bell use it to justify infanticide and trouble the desirability of middle-class marriage. *Alan's Wife* received only two private performances; *Man and Superman* was a popular success and is now part of the canon.

UNWED MOTHERS

Three years after the success of *Man and Superman*, St. John Hankin took a risk by making an unmarried upper-class mother the protagonist of his play *The Last of the De Mullins* (discussed in Chapter 2). Hankin's character Janet De Mullin is arguably the most positive personification of a single independent working mother in the drama of the period. Her lack of repentance and pride in her son, however, presented significant moral challenges to audiences when the play was first produced. Like Shaw's

Tanner, Janet refuses to acknowledge the indivisibility of the institutions of marriage and motherhood, and provocatively claims, 'I believe it's how *all* wholesome women feel if they would only acknowledge it' (p. 86). Janet counters patriarchal social convention with a more universal glorification of motherhood:

> Whatever happens, even if Johnny should come to hate me for what I did, I shall always be glad to have been his mother. At least I shall have lived. These poor women who go through life listless and dull, who have never felt the joys and the pains a mother feels, how they would envy me if they knew! If they knew! To know that a child is your very own, is a part of you. That you have faced sickness and death itself for it. That it is yours and nothing can take it from you because no one can understand its wants as you do. To feel its soft breath on your cheek, to soothe it when it is fretful and still it when it cries, that is motherhood and that is glorious! (p. 86)

As in Shaw's plays, the universal forces of life and evolution are emphasized above the ethics of any particular social code, but Hankin's heroine Janet is more iconoclastic than Ann Whitefield or Lesbia Grantham in her disregard for marriage as a necessary precursor to motherhood. Janet De Mullin wasn't by any means the first unwed mother on the stage in this era, but she is uniquely focused on her happy present instead of shamed by her past. Critics expressed disbelief at Janet's refusal to act ashamed of herself. In *The Times Literary Supplement* Walkley questioned whether Hankin might have meant Janet as a bad joke, remarking:

> She is allowed to do all the talking, to win all the victories, to ride the high horse round the stage and over the prostrate bodies, not only of the De Mullins, but of the sex that cannot be mothers ('louts of men'), and of modern society at large.
>
> (10 December 1908)

The *Pall Mall Gazette* also asked, 'Is it all a joke, or is it not?' and noted with satisfaction, 'The applause at the finish was scanty; there was no call for the author; and it was pleasant to get into the wholesome open-air again' (8 December 1908).

Harley Granville Barker was in New York when *The Last of the De Mullins* debuted in 1908 with his wife Lillah McCarthy in the lead role. Shaw wrote to Barker with his thoughts on the opening night, and the 'scanty' applause.

In the third act Lillah appealed with extraordinary gusto to every unmarried woman of twenty eight in the house to go straight out and procure a baby at once without the slightest regard to law or convention. As Lillah regards this a most obvious and reasonable doctrine, she had no idea of the effect she was producing on the audience. At the end of the Act the majority were simply afraid to applaud: the thing had gone quite beyond mere play-acting for them, and although they were interested, they felt – quite rightly – that to clap such sentiments would be to vote for them. Consequently, though there were curtain calls, they were forced by a partly friendly, partly assenting minority. Anything like a hit in the ordinary uproarious way is quite out of the question.

(HRC: Shaw Box 37, Folder 2, 7 December 1908)

Sos Eltis observes that theatre was 'a particularly sensitive and charged forum for engaging with sexual issues' in a time when there was a 'significant difference between public utterance and private views' (2013a, p. 7). While the *Pall Mall Gazette* took the scant applause as a straightforward audience rejection of the play and its morals, Shaw saw a more complex dilemma for theatregoers who, though perhaps sympathetic, were 'simply afraid to applaud'. Hankin's play may have failed because it didn't allow for slippage between public utterance and private views either on the part of his character Janet, who refuses to act repentant in public, or on the part of the audience who have to decide at the end of the play whether or not to publicly 'vote for' motherhood outside of marriage.

In *The Madras House,* Harley Granville Barker splits the difference between repentance and pride in his depiction of Miss Yates, an employee of the Roberts & Huxtable drapery establishment who becomes pregnant. Though she admits 'I started by crying my eyes out' (1994, p. 57), she moves from the conventional shame of a fallen woman towards the pride of motherhood, explaining to her employer, Philip, 'I am really proud and happy about it now sir … I am not pretending' (p. 57). In the final act, Philip's 60-something father, Constantine Madras, is revealed as the father of Miss Yates's baby. Constantine is a convert to Mohammedanism who abandoned Philip's mother some years earlier to settle in the Middle East with several wives. He regards women's stature in the world almost exclusively in terms of their 'their perpetual use', motherhood, and asserts that 'the world's interest is best served by keeping them strictly to it' (p. 100). The conventional men, Major Thomas and Mr Huxtable, express moral distaste for Constantine's lifestyle, which is both polygamous and philandering. Constantine, in turn, critiques the British social codes that condemn unmarried middle-class women to childlessness while working-class women 'are worked at market rates until they can't give you children' and exclaims, 'For such treatment of potential motherhood, my prophet condemns a man to Hell' (p. 106). Although Miss Yates's pregnancy is still an affront to Edwardian standards, her admission that she cried her eyes out invites audience sympathy and her lower-class status makes her 'fall' less remarkable. Barker's most provocative comment lies in the juxtaposition between Miss Yates's vitality and the other women in the play, especially the six withering Huxtable spinsters (discussed in Chapter 3) and Philip's wife Jessica, described as 'the Galatea of the middle class' (p. 60) who, in a reversal of the Pygmalion myth, is ossifying from flesh to stone. Miss Yates is the first woman to deny Constantine by refusing financial support for their child. Miss Yates's child and Philip's daughter are both disinherited from Constantine's legacy at their parents' insistence, a break from patriarchy in both the 'legitimate' and 'illegitimate' family.

Critical reactions to *The Madras House* were generally more favourable than to *The Last of the De Mullins*, although *Sketch* called it a 'Polygamy for the People Play' (16 March 1910). While *The Athenaeum* ventured that Barker had 'gone "off the rails" in this play', the reviewer found much to praise in his survey of the relations of modern men and women, noting 'Mr. Barker sketches in these various types of womanhood with a vivacity and an insight that are undeniable' (11 February 1911). Max Beerbohm also remarked on Barker's depiction of a broad composite rather than a single character in his notice for the *Saturday Review*, noting the 'unifying principle of the play is that the theme throughout is the present and future of woman – woman regarded from various standpoints, moral, aesthetic, economic, and so on' (19 March 1910). The mosaic composition of *The Madras House* enabled Barker to present an unwed mother in a positive light without making her story the narrative centre of the four-act piece, freeing the audience to clap for the play without 'voting for' a particular moral stance at the end.

In his one-act play *The Magnanimous Lover* (1912) St. John Ervine poses questions that are uniquely aimed at the Church rather than at the unwed mother. Ervine's Northern Irish protagonist Maggie has managed to become a strong and independent single parent despite the humiliation and taunting she and her son have received in their small religious community. When, after a religious conversion, the father of her child 'magnanimously' returns from England ten years later to marry her and legitimize their son, she rejects his notion that it is in his power to 'save' her and accuses him of hypocrisy:

You're not thinking of me, nor the wrong you did. It's yourself you're thinking of. You're afraid of God, and you want to use me to buy Him off. You can well call yourself a God-fearing man, Henry. I'm nothing to you. The child you're father of is nothing to you. You're just frightened out of your wits for fear you should go to hell for all you're saved. I won't marry you. I'm as good as you are for all I'm not saved. (p. 15)

Maggie's parents push hard for the marriage as a chance for Maggie to redeem the family, but Maggie refuses to acknowledge a fundamental difference between married and unmarried mothers, saying to her own mother, 'You've only been to the minister, and I haven't. There's not much difference between us' (p. 18). Ervine leaves little room for sympathy for his profligate-turned-Christian character Henry, who repeatedly refers to Maggie as a whore and his son as a bastard. Instead, he gives the last word and the moral high ground to Maggie, who concludes, in defiance of Church and patriarchy, 'I'm not needing to marry, but if I do, I'll marry to save my own soul, and not Harry Hindle's' (p. 19).

Voluntary Motherhood

Female writers were less keen than their male counterparts to dramatize single motherhood, a model which placed all the labour and financial obligation of parenting on women. Openly embracing single motherhood as a progressive path was widely regarded as dangerous to the credibility of the feminist movement. Too close a focus on motherhood also ran the risk of naturalizing the essentialist notions of womanhood and the 'woman's sphere' that many feminists were working to deconstruct. Critics were also more likely to assume autobiographical links between female authors and their main characters, making women writers even more wary of the subject. Feminist writers were, however, increasingly interested in exploring notions of *voluntary* motherhood – the radical notion that even married women might not always want to become mothers and should have the right to choose. Many feminists began to reject equating childlessness with a lack of womanhood. Cicely Hamilton claimed, 'Women have been trained to be unintelligent breeding-machines until they have become unintelligent breeding-machines' (MT, p. 64), arguing that motherhood was not always a higher calling, but sometimes 'an involuntary consequence of a compulsory trade' (MT, p. 213). Appropriating the language of industrial capitalism for feminist ends, the term 'breeding-machine' stripped motherhood of the evangelical sentiments associated with it in Victorian separate spheres rhetoric.

By thinking and speaking less as angels and more as labour organizers, feminists began to seek to control the means of production of the Empire's most valuable resource of all – the population. One of feminism's first tasks was to assert that motherhood was not the entirety of a woman's existence. Even for women who did marry and have children, full-time motherhood was an occupation which might consume less than a third of their lifetimes. For women who chose a career over motherhood, motherhood was framed as a vocation with its own very real set of drawbacks. Hamilton wrote, 'we hear a very great deal about the beauty and sanctity of motherhood; we might, for a change, hear something about the degradation thereof – which has been very real' (MT, p. 62). Feminists argued that, like any other calling, motherhood was not a vocation suited to all women.

Another crucial step towards women taking more control over reproduction was to discard Victorian prudishness around sex education. While some feminists lauded notions of female purity in an effort to assert their cultural and evolutionary centrality, others were intent on exploding the idea of purity, especially where innocence was confused with ignorance. Young women were generally uneducated about the design and functions of their reproductive organs, encouraged to regard sex as base, and often vague as to the mechanics of conception, perpetuating a hostile pattern between the sexes with man as the taker and woman as the taken. Female medical pioneers like Elizabeth Blackwell and Marie Stopes stressed that better sex education for both boys and girls was needed in order to break the cycle of ignorance on the fundamental questions of sex and reproduction. In her hugely influential book *Married Love*, Stopes, founder of the first birth control clinic in Britain, despaired of the Victorian conflation of innocence and ignorance, protesting: 'there is a lack of knowledge so abysmal and so universal that its mists and shadowy darkness have affected even the few who lead us, and who are prosecuting research in these subjects' (1931, pp. 10–11). Sex within marriage was still the only socially accepted channel for women's sexuality, widely regarded as something to be endured rather than enjoyed by women whose role was to accommodate husbands' sexual needs and perpetuate the race. Any attempts to define an independent female sexuality, therefore, struggled with the taboo of defiling the sanctity of motherhood. Though purity feminists like Christabel Pankhurst used this conservative view to their own ends, other feminists, like her sister Sylvia,[31] rejected this dichotomy and created lives for themselves outside the traditional path of marriage and motherhood.

Today 'birth control' almost always refers to some form of contraceptive, but the term had a broader meaning to Victorians and Edwardians. To middle-class women 'birth control' was generally more likely to mean abstinence, from sex or even from marriage. Contraceptives, known as 'preventive checks', 'artificial checks' or 'Malthusian appliances',[32] were available, but not readily so. Quinine pessaries were developed in the 1880s and spermicidal jellies and powders also became available at the turn of the century, but these products were expensive and awkward to obtain. Abstaining by marrying late in life was recommended by Malthus,[33] though birth control advocate Annie Besant strongly objected that this would lead to an increase in prostitution (1879, p. 27). Abstinence within marriage is thought to have been the most widespread and frequently used method of birth control up until WWI (Szreter, 1996, p. 399). Despite underground networks and a limited range of products coming onto the market, many women, especially middle-class women, were ignorant of birth control techniques. It is telling that doctors, although they refused to provide women with advice on birth control, had the smallest families in Britain (Thompson, 1998, pp. 77–78). In 1877 Besant was put on trial for publishing Dr Charles Knowlton's book on contraceptive advice, *Fruits of Philosophy*[34] and though she narrowly avoided a prison sentence, she lost custody of her daughter as a result of the trial. The publicity of the Bradlaugh-Besant trial brought so much attention to the book that sales soared to the extent that the trial has been retrospectively credited with popularizing contraception and reversing British population growth. Besant went on to publish her own tract on birth control, *The Law of the Population* (1879), in which she argued that birth control was neither unnatural nor immoral because it was the rational outcome of nature's highest product, the human brain: 'Production of offspring recklessly, carelessly, lustfully, this is irrational nature, and every brute can here outdo us; production of offspring with forethought, earnestness, providence, this is rational nature, where man stands alone' (p. 37). In 1886, English physician Henry Allbutt published *The Wife's Handbook*, in which he mentioned a new contraceptive possibility, the 'Dutch cap'[35] (a diaphragm). Although his book was a great success, selling 390,000 copies, he was struck off the medical register as a result of its publication. Though open discussion of birth control remained more or less taboo until after WWI, the notion of 'choice' was one of first-wave feminism's earliest battles in the struggle to help women to envision and lead more self-determined lives, though for them 'choice' might refer to spinsterhood or abstinence rather than contraception or abortion.

While many regarded contraception as crucial to feminist aims, allow-ing women to take control of reproduction and along with it many other aspects of their lives, many feminists publicly spurned it, fearing that it would perpetuate the sexual subjugation of women. Men were also divided, as some feared that eliminating the threat of unwanted pregnancy would unleash new possibilities of extra-marital sex for women. Doctors warned that contraceptives deprived women of fluids vital to health, resulting in nervous disorders such as loss of memory, neurasthenia, depression and/or madness. The government attacked contraception as a threat to the family and by extension the Empire, arguing that if contraceptives were easy to obtain, women might refuse to marry and have children. By 1875, however, a decline in the birth rate, especially among middle-class married couples, suggests that people were using contraceptives more widely and this trend continued: until the 1880s the average number of children per family was six; by 1914 it was less than three. Neo-Malthusians[36] theorized that the Women's Movement would never have evolved to the extent it did without the significant decline in the birth rate in Britain at the turn of the century.

Abortion was a widely used form of birth restriction, especially among working-class women. Abortifacients were cheaper and less complicated to obtain than contraceptives and working-class women, who often had more freedom of movement than upper- and middle-class women, were able to pass on techniques or recipes to each other under the radar. Advertisements for herbs or medicines for this purpose relied on women reading between the lines in their promises to 'remove obstructions' or 'restore vitality' to 'exhausted' women, emphasizing that the products could be used without a husband's knowledge (Steinbach, 2004, p. 123). Though the practice was not unknown or even uncommon at the turn of the century, abortion wasn't the widely discussed topic of pro- or anti-feminist platforms that it became later in the twentieth century or the wedge issue that it remains in some countries today.

Contraception and abortion are addressed sparingly in the drama of this period, licensed for public performance only after passing through the hands of the censor. In *Man and Superman*, which makes a rare direct reference to the topic, contraception is denounced as a perversion and deg-radation of the Life Force into sheer voluptuousness[37] though Shaw's hero John Tanner allows that the popularization of contraception might have a beneficial influence on human evolution by enabling pleasure-seeking degenerates to gradually 'weed themselves out of the race' (p. 225).

Waste (1907) by Harley Granville Barker and *Votes for Women!* (1907) by Elizabeth Robins are two notable Edwardian plays in which abortion is central to the plot. One was censored, one was not.

Barker's play is a tragedy about a rising political star who has an affair with a married woman, resulting in her death through an illegal abortion which ruins his career and leads him to take his own life. Just a few months prior to the scheduled premier of *Waste*, Barker successfully produced and directed Robins's play *Votes for Women!* (discussed in Chapter 5) as part of the final Vedrenne-Barker Court Theatre season. Robins's play, which also centres on an abortion plot involving a prominent politician, was granted a licence by the censor, encouraging Barker to believe that his play would also be licensed, though references to abortion in *Votes for Women!* are less explicit and shrouded by time. In Robins's play, the female protagonist shows deep remorse for the death of her child, who is terminated at the urging of its father. The passage of time and the redemption of traditional womanly traits in the heroine, who becomes mother to all since she cannot be mother to the lost child, helped *Votes for Women!* obtain a public licence where *Waste*, whose crisis is immediate and explicit and whose characters show no contrition, was denied.[38] Despite the marked differences between the two plays, Barker was shocked when the Savoy run of *Waste*, which had already been fully rehearsed and announced as the centrepiece of the new season, had to be cancelled.[39] It was a serious financial blow to his new enterprise.[40] *Waste* was relegated to two private subscription performances by the Stage Society,[41] thwarting Barker as an author and financially jeopardizing him as a producer. The play was not performed publicly until 1936, by which time Barker had substantially rewritten it. For discussion here, I use Barker's original Edwardian text (1907/1987c).

Barker wrote much of this distinctly unromantic play in 1906 while on honeymoon with Lillah McCarthy. In sharp contrast to the 'Life Force' affirming comedy *Man and Superman*, which Barker was so thoroughly steeped in, Barker's play is a tragedy in which the woman encourages sexual attention, but rejects procreation. In the first act, Barker's female protagonist, Amy O'Connell, a married woman living apart from her husband, strikes discord amidst the wives and spinster sisters of Conservative political oligarchs at a country weekend house party through her blatant disinterest in politics and openly flirtatious manner. Barker's male protagonist, Henry Trebell, is introduced as a political genius who is being courted for the incoming Tory cabinet, based on his radical bill to disestablish the

Church of England and fund a grand new national scheme for education. Amy admits to designs on Trebell, but when they are left alone she seems to crave romantic attention more than sexual consummation in her desire to bring him 'within arms' length' (p. 176). Although she is coquettish, she seems unsure of how far to let things go. In the hiatus of Amy's uncertainty, Trebell's sexual desire becomes the driving force in the scene as he speaks to her 'low but commandingly' (p. 177) and she instinctively moves towards him, resulting in the most titillating seduction scene in Edwardian drama.

When Amy next appears in Act II at Trebell's office, he is refreshed after a Tuscan holiday while she has aged; she is pale, there is pain in her eyes and her voice is unnaturally steady. She delivers the news of her pregnancy '*swiftly and sharply as one speaks of disaster*' (p. 188). Trebell is quickly transformed by the news into '*a sceptic who has seen a vision*' (p. 188). In a reaction to the news that is both abstract and political, he bows to the Life Force as a greater purpose, but is concerned to avoid a political scandal. By contrast, Amy's response is personal and visceral as she rails at the physical curse of being a woman, 'worse off than an animal', and speaks of lying through the night 'simply shaking with bodily fear' (p. 189). Unsympathetic, Trebell quashes her plea for romantic affection:

> TREBELL: (*quite inexorable*) Wouldn't any other woman have served the purpose … and is it less of a purpose because we didn't know we had it? Does my unworthiness then … if you like to call it so … make you unworthy now? I must make you see that it doesn't.
> AMY: (*petulantly hammering at her ideé fixe*) But you didn't love me … and you don't love me.
> TREBELL: (*keeping his patience*) No … only within the last five minutes have I really taken the smallest interest in you. And now I believe I'm half jealous. Can you understand that? You've been talking a lot of nonsense about your emotions and your immortal soul. Don't you see it's only now that you've become a person of some importance to the world … and why? (p. 190)

Alienated by Trebell, Amy asserts her right to agency, stating, 'There's no child because I haven't chosen there shall be and there shan't be because I don't choose' (p. 191). Trebell's callous, if honest, remarks on the circumstances of conception and Amy's assertion of her right to choose not to become a mother are remarkable for the era, making Barker's characters particularly distasteful to the censor G.A. Redford as well as to critics who attended the private performances. The review in *The Times* concluded that the ban on *Waste* was to the public good, judging that the subject matter of the play, 'together with the sincere realism with which it is treated, makes it, in our judgment, wholly unfit for performance' (27 November 1907). Barker stands out among his contemporaries in giving this familiar subject a distinctively unsentimental treatment. In Trebell, Barker depicts a very different kind of man, one who succumbs to a sexual urge but is not a profligate. Although he is politically ambitious, he is also honest to the point of brutality, breaking the mould of hypocrisy associated with the double standard. Perhaps most unexpectedly, Trebell is a man who is spiritually transformed by the prospect of fatherhood, in sharp contrast to Amy who says she would 'sooner kill myself' (p. 190) than have the child.

Amy is unique in her explicit rejection of motherhood. As if to highlight the blasphemy of her plan to seek an abortion, her conversation with Trebell is cut short by the arrival of Lord Cantelupe, the representative of the Church. In their final whispered exchange, Amy swiftly asks Trebell to give her the name of a doctor, but he declines. Amy rebukes men: 'what unpractical sentimental children you men are! You and your consciences ... you and your laws. You drive us to distraction and sometimes to death by your stupidities' (p. 192). The rebuke is prophetic as well as bitter; Amy dies from a backstreet abortion. The audience learns of her death from Trebell's doctor, Wedgecroft, who reveals that he knew but withheld the names of several doctors capable of safely performing an abortion. Significantly, Wedgecroft tells the rising cabinet that if only Amy had named Trebell as the father, he would have helped, depicting a patriarchal conspiracy of silence existing to help men, but certainly not women, in trouble.

The Conservative Party fears that Amy's husband, Justin O'Connell, will avenge himself by bringing about Trebell's political downfall, but O'Connell unexpectedly allies himself to Trebell, cursing Amy's 'unnaturalness' in pitting the notion of her 'freedom' against their expectations of fatherhood, rendering her 'a worthless woman' (p. 210) in his eyes. In Trebell's discussion with the rising cabinet, he shocks his colleagues by suggesting that he reveal the facts of Amy's death 'soberly and seriously' to the House of Commons, offering it as an opportunity to break from the conventional hypocrisy of the double standard. Rather than expressing the expected personal remorse over the affair, Trebell holds the mirror up to his colleagues and, in a comment that may have been the real reason the play was banned, says 'You know we're an adulterous and sterile generation' (p. 211). After he has been cut from the rising cabinet, ending hopes for his Education Bill, Trebell speaks of his work in terms of fertility and infertility. He reasons that he might still be effective outside the cabinet, but suddenly feels 'that the work would be barren' and questions 'what is it in your thoughts and actions which makes them bear fruit?' (p. 234). Pain at the loss of his child is prominent as Trebell says to his sister Frances, 'that's the mystery no one need believe till he has dipped in it. The man bears the child in his soul as the woman carries it in her body' (p. 235).[42] There is a complex blurring between the hero as the father of a dead child and the father of a dead political reform, which layers moral questions of procreation with moral questions of state provision for children's futures.

Although William Archer questioned the artistic justification for Trebell's suicide, he pronounced *Waste* 'our greatest modern tragedy' (1923, p. 360). In the end the tragedy isn't so much the waste of any of the individual lives as the waste of the potential political work left undone, as Trebell's secretary Kent expresses in the final lines, 'Look at the work undone ... think of it! Who is to do it! Oh ... the waste ...!' (p. 239). In this ending Barker inverts the usual formula of a fallen woman play in which society condemns individual sinners to their punishments; in *Waste* the fates of individuals expose the hypocrisy of society and the entire nation suffers as a result. Barker portrays Trebell's honesty as a tragic flaw within the context of Edwardian politics. In linking personal tragedy to the moral corruption of society, Barker anticipates the socialist plays of J.B. Priestley by half a century.

LEVERAGING MATERNAL POWER

Rutherford and Son (1912) by Githa Sowerby dramatizes a rare shift in dynastic power from a domineering patriarch to a selfless mother. The play is set in the oppressive home of John Rutherford, an ageing self-made northern industrialist who bullies his three grown children. The eldest son John, groomed to be the heir, is a disappointment; instead of marrying into the upper class and becoming a gentleman, John turns his back on the family business and goes to London where he marries a working-class girl. In London, his wife Mary supports him and their son until the child's health becomes a worry and Mary forces John to swallow his pride and ask his father to take their family in. Rutherford is openly hostile to John and treats Mary as 'a stranger in the house' (p. 143). Though Mary finds life in the Rutherford house 'like a prison' (p. 145), devoid of even a 'scrap of love' (p. 145), she endures it for the sake of her child's welfare. By the end of the play Rutherford has alienated all three of his children and is left without an heir. Alone with her tyrannical father-in-law and her infant son, Mary strikes a bargain: if Rutherford will support her and her son, giving her complete control of her son's upbringing and education for ten years, she will hand the boy over to him. Rutherford, who hasn't bothered to speak to his daughter-in-law before this, reflects, 'You think me a hard man. So I am. But I'm wondering if I could ha' stood up as you're standing and done what you've done' (p. 189). Mary answers as a mother, 'I love my child. That makes me hard' (p. 189). The play closes with the mother cutting the industrial capitalist off with a gesture and a 'Hush!' (p. 189) at the sound of her son waking, suggesting that the Rutherford of 'Rutherford and Son' who rules the house is now Mary Rutherford. The reviewer for the suffrage paper *The Vote* viewed Sowerby's portrayal of a selfless mother prevailing among selfish men as powerfully feminist: 'No play has ever been written that in the truest, strongest sense was so really a "Suffrage" play, although the word is never uttered and the thought never enters the minds of the people portrayed' (20 July 1912). Admittedly, it is no surprise that a reviewer for *The Vote* interpreted the piece as pro-suffrage, but with the altruism associated with motherhood often evoked as a rationale for extending women's influence into public life, this wasn't such a far stretch.

Produced in the same year, Jess Dorynne's one-act *The Surprise of His Life* shows suffrage ideas impacting decisions about motherhood and marriage. Dorynne makes a direct link between an unmarried pregnant woman's plight and the suffrage movement as a conduit of female empowerment. In the play, a pregnant girl's father offers the baby's father, Alf, a position in the family grocery business in exchange for marrying his daughter – an offer made more to save his own reputation than out of care for his daughter Emily. Alf, who threw Emily over as soon as he found out she was pregnant, appreciates her father's offer as a 'soft berth' (p. 11) and in turn throws over his new lover, Sally, to take advantage of this attractive business offer. Emily, however, is not keen on the deal struck between the two men. The suggestion that Alf can make her an 'honest woman' strikes her as deeply ironic, since she now regards him as a liar and a coward. Though she admits she went down on her knees to Alf, begging him to marry her when she found out she was pregnant, his disdain and his quick attachment to another woman has killed her love for him. Emily's narrative of Alf's abandonment centres on a government bill, one that proposes state subsidy for the single mothers of illegitimate children:

> A month ago I told yer wot 'ad 'appened, an' yer behaved like a blaggard. You *larfed* when I arsted yer to marry me as quick as possible like yer promised faithful ter. I went on me knees ter yer; I told yer me farver'd turn me out er doors. You didn't see 'ow there was any call ter marry me, yer said. A wife an' fam'ly was a burden on a young man, yer said, an' Lloyd George was abringin' in a bill to maintain mothers of illegitimate children, which *yer* thort very sensible of 'im. It took so much moral responsibility orf you young fellers! While I wos breakin' me 'eart an' beggin' yer ter save me from shime, yer wos a-larfin' about that bill. (p. 15)

Where Shaw's unmarried character Lesbia advocates for such a government programme as good for single women and good for the country, in Dorynne's play, the potential bill is presented as a man-made mechanism for letting men off the hook. Despite her protests and regardless of politics, Emily's father insists on the marriage, but Emily's Aunt Eliza intervenes. Eliza offers testament of a marriage made in similar circumstances as a cautionary tale; she was mocked and beaten by a husband who 'never ceased to fling it in me face that 'e 'ad made me an honest woman' (p. 16) and reckons that the river (i.e. suicide) might have been better than marriage. Ignoring the domestic abuse, Emily's father attributes Eliza's outburst to the corrupting influence of the suffrage movement – 'This all comes from that blarsted Mrs Wilson, with 'er meetin's an' darned tork of Female Rights an' Votes fer Wimmen, an' all that blarsted rot' (p. 17). Emboldened by the speeches she has heard from the Association of Self Supporters, Emily chooses legal and financial independence over the conventions of Church and state:

> I don't care nothin' about no votes, nor yet about no polerticks [...] But goin' to 'er an' the meetin's 'as taught me sure wot I felt before – ter respect meself as a woman, an' ter insist that I shall be so respected. (p. 17)

The play ends on a note of female solidarity as Emily leaves her father's house to set up house with Aunt Eliza. In a final turn of the screw, Emily's mother suddenly takes courage and stands up to her husband, asserting that Alf wasn't good enough for Emily. Dorynne's final image hints at the potential for patriarchal evolution as Mr Jenkins stares at his wife 'as if a new view of life were vaguely dawning upon his indignant and bewildered mind' (p. 20). The portrayal of a selfish patriarchy in contrast to a more generous female solidarity was significantly heightened by the intertextual fact that Dorynne herself was abandoned while pregnant by Edward Gordon Craig and her play was produced by his sister Edith Craig and her women-run company the Pioneer Players.

J.K. Jerome's play *The Master of Mrs. Chilvers* (1911) provides a more ambiguous take on the relationship between politics and motherhood. The play begins in the Russell Square drawing room of Geoffrey Chilvers, MP and President of the Men's League for the Extension of the Franchise to Women and his wife Annys Chilvers, Honourable Secretary of the Women's Parliamentary Franchise League (WPLF). Women from the WPFL discuss a loophole in the law that allows women to stand as candidates in local elections despite not being able to vote. Seizing on this, the WPFL committee resolves to bring forward a woman candidate to contest the next by-election and determines that the beautiful and charming Annys is their best chance as 'our candidate must be a woman popular with men' (p. 17). By comic coincidence, Geoffrey and Annys are pitted against each other in the contest for the East Poplar seat, and though his wife assures him that she expects and in fact hopes he will win, over the next two acts Geoffrey's support for women in politics is tested to the limit.

In her campaign, Annys aligns herself with traditional selfless womanly/motherly qualities, assuring voters that she is entering politics 'to give, not to get' (p. 23) and affirming 'It is the mother instinct that makes us politicians' (p. 86). While Annys offers these maternal qualities to the public sphere for social benefit, Geoffrey, alarmed by feminists who call motherhood a 'burden' (p. 76), worries that his wife may no longer want to bear his children. His friend St. Herbert assures him that feminists are a 'handful of cranks' and that motherhood has always been 'the one supreme desire' for 'normal' women (p. 76). Geoffrey is less certain about the essential nature of women, asking 'Is there not danger of her *preferring* political ambition, the excitement of public life, to what has come to be regarded as the "drudgery" of turning four walls into a home, of peopling the silence with the voices of children?' (p. 77). In the climax of Act III, Annys wins the seat and while she receives rounds of applause and choruses of 'for she's the jolly good fellow', Geoffrey slinks out of the town hall through a side door. In the final act, Annys returns home from the WPLF celebrations, dropped off by a doctor. Sitting in an armchair, she 'feebly stretches out her arms' (p. 165) to Geoffrey and reveals that she has just discovered she is pregnant. Harmony is restored to the warring household as it becomes clear that Annys will concede her seat to Geoffrey and become a mother instead of a politician.

Though it's challenging to read the story of a woman who wins a seat in parliament and gives it up to have a baby as a progressive narrative, Jerome offers a feminist-compatible through-line to Annys who assures her husband that becoming a mother is going to make her want the vote more than ever. Seeing Lena Ashwell, a prominent member of the Actresses' Franchise League, in the role of Annys would have signalled to pro-suffrage audience members that the play was on their side. Annys closes with the line, 'You will let me help you make the world better for our child – and for all the children – and for all the mothers – and for all the dear, kind men: you will, won't you?' (p. 167) which doesn't foreclose on her future involvement in politics, but is posed as a permission-seeking question to her husband rather than a direct statement of political intention. Ashwell's inflection here may have helped with an interpretation of Annys as more canny than submissive – a woman who knows how to achieve her political aims while keeping peace with her husband. In closing Geoffrey admits that he regarded the WPLF as 'strange voices' that were calling her 'away from life and motherhood' (p. 167) and exalts in the restoration of traditional family values:

> God has laughed at my fears. He has sent you back to me with His command. We will fashion His world together, we two lovers, Man and Woman, joined together in all things. It is His will. His chains are the children's hands. (p. 167)

No doubt some in the audience heard the emphasis on 'lovers' and 'children' while others heard 'command' and 'chains'.

* * *

While Shaw, Barker and Hankin were progressive in advocating for a freer or more pro-active sexuality for women that recognized female desire, they were also products of their time in their conformity, as writers of female characters, to a principally 'uterine' theory of female sexuality in which reproduction was central. All three of these men had childless or child-free marriages, so they were not modelling this uterine female sexuality from their own experiences. Shaw's Ann Whitefield's Life-Force drive to be a vessel for the superman has the ruthless single focus of a mate-killing spider or a drone-killing queen bee. Barker allows that female sexuality may not be entirely motivated by conscious hopes of maternity, but his female characters who engage in sex outside marriage become pregnant and are either punished (Amy) or rewarded (Miss Yates), depending on their willingness to become mothers. Hankin's character, Janet, is likewise rewarded with a child, whose birth supplants any but maternal passions, in line with conservative medical explanations of female sexuality. Jerome's Annys Chilvers is more progressive than her husband in her politics, but instead of becoming an MP she becomes a mother. Twentieth-century feminists would denounce this uterine moral and medical model as a, if not the, chief operator of women's sexual oppression in its denial of women's pleasure divorced from reproductive functions.

Female authors like Cicely Hamilton are more cautious on the subject of motherhood in their writing for the theatre than in their novels, books and articles. Theories of motherhood well-drawn in Hamilton's political writings are absent from her plays. While she freely used the term 'breeding-machine' and personally voiced the opinion that to 'stunt one's brain in order that one may bear a son does not seem to me a process essentially sacred or noble in itself' (MT, p. 63), Hamilton didn't put these words into the mouths of female characters in her plays. In her dramatic works Hamilton shirks the subject of motherhood altogether: her characters are not mothers, do not discuss becoming mothers and do not even have mothers. In most New Woman plays by female authors like Hamilton, Baker, Irish, Hatton and Young the female protagonists, whether they are either single or married, are not mothers. In plays like Lyttelton's *Warp and Woof,* Robins's *My Little Sister* and Williams's *The Street,* the female characters who make self-sacrificing choices for the sake of others are older sisters rather than mothers. Female dramatists' reluctance to represent the same issues in their dramatic work that they wrote of freely in their political essays mirrors the defensive partitioning practised by feminists more generally. Powell notes that when female authors do write about motherhood, many of them 'avoid the polarized choice between being a "good" or "bad" mother' and instead 'devise morally ambiguous scenarios in which this patriarchal version of maternity is tested and found wanting' (1997, p. 136) as in Robins's and Bell's *Alan's Wife,* Leighton's *Thyrza Fleming* or Blanche Crackenthorpe's *The Turn of the Wheel* (1901).[43] The relationship between feminism and motherhood was (and still is) one of the toughest issues for women to negotiate without either discarding the fundamental importance of the role or being defined or limited by it. The most challenging dramatic example of leveraging maternal power for socio-political good is found in Elizabeth Robins's *Votes for Women!,* a function the protagonist's name, *Levering,* makes explicit. In Robins's narrative it is not the presence of a child, but rather the death or absence of a child, that opens the way for a woman to turn her maternal instincts to the welfare of children at large through the suffrage campaign, the subject of the next chapter.

CHAPTER 5

Votes for Women

By the height of the suffrage campaign Elizabeth Robins was working full time as a writer and increasingly involved in feminist networks. Her play *Votes for Women!* (1907) was the first suffrage play staged in London, and its success opened the floodgates for a wave of suffrage theatre. In 1908 Robins became a founding member of the Actresses' Franchise League (AFL) as well as president of the Women Writers' Suffrage League (WWSL) founded in the same year by Cicely Hamilton and Bessie Hatton. Along with over a thousand actresses and playwrights, including Lena Ashwell, Gertrude Kingston, Lillah McCarthy, Edith Craig, Christopher St. John, Kitty Marion and Sybil Thorndike, Robins threw her energies into the suffrage campaign. These talented, impassioned artist/activists harnessed their professional skills to refashion the male-dominated world of theatre into a powerful forum for critiquing gender-based social injustice and promoting feminist ideas. As well bringing feminism to the theatre, these women brought theatrical know-how into the streets, consciously shaping the public image of the women's movement.

Robins's private correspondence between 1907 and the outbreak of WWI in 1914 vividly illustrates the conflicting pressures of art circles and political networks, a push-pull of artistic merit vs political efficacy value systems that Robins and many other feminist artists found themselves caught between. Many of Robins's oldest and best friends from the art world were uncomfortable with her increasing ties to the militant 'suffragette' WSPU and her friendship with its famous and controversial leaders Emmeline and Christabel Pankhurst. In 1908, William Archer allowed what started as a birthday letter to become an argument imploring Robins to eschew militancy and stick to art: 'There are heaps of people who can throw stones and make stump speeches, but not so many people who can write "The Convert". After all, the pen is mightier than the stone'.[1] Though Robins did not personally advocate or take part in civil disobedience,[2] her refusal to condemn militant acts and her association with suffrage political prisoners was contentious. Despite varying degrees of disapproval from Archer and other notable literati such as John Galsworthy, Henry James and Florence Bell, Robins continued to serve on the leadership of the militant WSPU.[3] She stuck to the pen, but sometimes used the pen to defend the stones.[4]

Robins was strongly pressured by her political friends as well. The Pankhursts recognized Robins's value to the cause and courted her fervently. Robins was an attractive celebrity, with a virtuosic skill for addressing large audiences and an actress's flair for powerful, emotive delivery. The Pankhursts knew, from their early links with the labour movement, that words from the mouths of East End labouring women would not carry the same influence as speeches delivered by a glamorous figure like Robins. Not only was she charismatic, photogenic and a splendid orator, Robins was a talented writer who could author her own speeches. Her fame as a former actress and bestselling novelist meant that she had unique access to publishers and newspaper editors. Robins also moved in the powerful social circles the suffrage leaders sought to penetrate. Among others, she was close personal friends with the liberal cabinet minister Edward Grey who served as Foreign Secretary from 1905 to 1916 (she often used his fishing cottage as a writing retreat). The Pankhursts relentlessly pressured Robins to lend not just her talents but also her personal networks to the cause, sometimes asking for more than she was prepared to give.[5]

Rather than giving herself solely to the suffrage campaign as the Pankhursts wished, or devoting herself entirely to creative work as many of her oldest friends like Archer and Bell advised, Robins continued to divide her energy between art and politics. As part of her contribution to the suffrage cause, Robins eventually established her Sussex farmhouse as a convalescence centre for women recovering from prison sentences and hunger strikes, aided by her domestic partner Octavia Wilberforce, who was training as a doctor. Thus, while Robins devoted most days to the artistic labour of writing novels or plays, during the years from 1907 to 1914 her personal life was increasingly spent among feminist activists. It suited her. With a passion that equalled her early years as an Ibsen actress 'who wouldn't for a kingdom be anything else' (Robins, 1928, p. 31), she wrote, 'I cannot myself imagine anything more glorious than to be a woman living in these times – a woman able to take active part in this great work' (WS, p. 86).

THE SUFFRAGE MOVEMENT

The British suffrage movement is often associated with dramatic images of Edwardian ladies in crinoline smashing windows on Oxford Street, chaining themselves to railings and being dragged to prison by police officers. Its roots, however, were far deeper and wider than the media-grabbing militant phase of 1905–WWI. The women's suffrage movement arose gradually over many decades, emerging in the latter half of the nineteenth century and formalizing as a national campaign in 1866 before gaining enormous momentum in the prewar years. Milestones along the way included publications such as Mary Wollstonecraft's *A Vindication of the Rights of Woman* (1792), William Thompson and Anna Wheeler's *Appeal of One Half of the Human Race, Women, Against the Pretentions of the Other Half, Men, to Retain them in Political, and Thence in Civil and Domestic Slavery* (1825), Harriet Taylor Mill's 'The Enfranchisement of Women' (1851) and John Stuart Mill's *The Subjection of Women*[6] (1869). In 1866 John Stuart Mill and Henry Fawcett presented a petition to the House of Commons to extend voting rights to all female and male householders; it was defeated 196 to 73. The first women's suffrage societies were founded in London, Edinburgh and Manchester in 1866 in the wake of this parliamentary defeat.

A year later in 1867 when the House of Commons considered The Second Reform Act, a new bill to enfranchise large sections of working-class men, Mill proposed to replace the word 'man' with the gender-neutral word 'person'. Mill's amendment was defeated, but so was an alternative proposition to clarify the bill by changing 'man' (often claimed to be a universal term) to 'male'. The allegedly universal 'man' or 'mankind' included women for taxation but excluded them from representation. The Representation of the People Act 1867, which enfranchised part of the urban male working class in England and Wales, and the consecutive Representation of the People Act of 1884, which extended voting qualifications to working-class men in the countryside, gave the majority of British men the vote for the first time.[7] This left women more specifically discriminated against at the end of the nineteenth century than they had been at the beginning, with gender now the principal grounds for exclusion. In his writing on evolution Darwin had described women as arrested or underdeveloped men, stunted by the burden of pregnancy, labour and motherhood. Darwin's increasing influence gave fuel to arguments that women should not vote because they were so unlike men as to justify classification as a separate species. Anti-suffrage essentialists like

Almroth Wright[8] compared the notion of votes for women to votes for monkeys, votes for horses and votes for dogs. George Bernard Shaw parodies this stance in his play *Press Cuttings* (1909) when the Minister of War answers the cry, 'Votes for Women!' with the sneering rejoinder 'Votes for children! Votes for babies! Votes for monkeys!' (1986b, p. 227).

Despite fierce opposition, by the end of the nineteenth century advocates of women's suffrage were increasing exponentially. In 1897 a collection of suffrage societies from around England amalgamated into The National Union of Women's Suffrage Societies (NUWSS), led by Millicent Garrett Fawcett. The Women's Social and Political Union (WSPU) was founded in Manchester in 1903 by Emmeline Pankhurst and her daughters Christabel and Sylvia. While Garrett Fawcett and the NUWSS had faith that suffrage would eventually come about through rational persuasion, the Pankhursts and members of the WSPU grew increasingly impatient for change and more cynical about the sincerity of promised help from male politicians. The WSPU adopted the slogan 'deeds, not words' to underscore a more combative stance than the NUWSS, a stance which soon developed into militancy and attracted thousands of supporters, particularly younger women.

On 13 October 1905 WSPU members Christabel Pankhurst and Annie Kenney[9] staged the first militant protest, interrupting the Foreign Secretary Edward Grey at a Liberal meeting in Manchester with the direct question, 'Will the Liberal Government give women the vote?' Pankhurst and Kenney were forcibly removed and arrested for disorderly behaviour.[10] Given a choice of paying fines or serving prison time, the pair chose prison, initiating a pattern of incarceration which would stretch over the next nine years and see more than a thousand women imprisoned in the name of the cause. Members of the NUWSS objected that the notoriety gained by Pankhurst's and Kenney's actions hurt rather than helped the cause. Over the years the split between the militant and non-militant groups would continue to stress and fracture the movement. Despite their differences, however, both the NUWSS and the WSPU understood that suffragists needed to capture the attention of the public at large if they were to force Members of Parliament to act.

SUFFRAGE THEATRE

As the movement came to rely more on spectacle and public events, women from the world of theatre became key players in staging suffrage, drawing on their many transferable professional skills such as producing, stage management, directing, design, elocution, memorization, public speaking, writing, costume and disguise.[11] As Katherine Cockin points out, a great deal more was involved in the use of 'performance – scripted, site-specific, partially improvised, rewritings and parodies [...] than simply the use of drama as a vehicle for the political ideas of "the suffragettes"' (2017, p. 99). In 1911 Edith Craig formed the Pioneer Players, a women-led group devoted to progressive causes including but not limited to suffrage. In 1913 Inez Bensusan started the Woman's Theatre with the aim of furthering women's careers as theatre artists as well as promoting more progressive representations of women on the stage. Actresses, dramatists and producers like Robins, Hamilton, St. John, Hatton, Bensusan, Ashwell, Kingston, Marion and Craig not only wrote plays for the theatre, shaping the message, but also performed at national public rallies and directed theatrical marches through city streets, personifying the modern woman.

The Actresses' Franchise League grew to nearly a thousand members by 1914 and, as noted by Claire Hirshfield, 'represented the glamorous face of the movement, the beauty and popularity of its members helping to offset the widespread stereotype of the suffragette as mannish, unsexed and physically unattractive' (1985, p. 130). Generally, actresses did not participate in violent acts of civil disobedience. In practical terms, the prison sentences militant acts often resulted in would have derailed their careers, making it impossible for theatres to hire them. On a more tactical level, actresses were too valuable as celebrities to want them in prison when they could draw crowds to public events and drive home messages with their sensational public speaking skills. In addition to specifically suffrage-focused theatre organizations, other theatre groups with wider feminist aims contributed to the movement.

Cicely Hamilton reflected that the suffrage movement was the first political agitation in Britain to partner with the arts on a major scale.[12] Whether theatre artists saw their politics as secondary to their art or vice versa, the movement was decidedly more interested in political results than artistic masterpieces. Sylvia Pankhurst, a painter who designed many of the logos, posters and banners that gave the SWPU a coherent visual identity, noted that 'the creation of a Michelangelo would have ranked low in the eyes of the WSPU members beside a term served in Holloway' (1931/1988, p. 284). In addition to political organizations like the NUWSS and the WSPU, artists and actresses joined other groups according to their particular talents, including the AFL, the WWSL, the Suffrage Atelier, the Artists' Suffrage League and the Ladies' Ecclesiastical Embroidery Society. Some of these groups did attempt to set certain artistic standards – the

WWSL, for example, invited only women who had already published work to become members. Artists within the suffrage movement shared a common political goal, if not a broader political agenda. Sylvia Pankhurst, for example, saw women's enfranchisement within the wider social context of the new society promised by the young Labour Party, while Cicely Hamilton saw it as one task within a broader feminist economic agenda. In an address to the WWSL, Robins looked to issues of representation as a central concern, declaring it the business and privilege 'of men and women writers to correct the false ideas about women that many writers of the past have fostered' (WS, p. 110).

Votes for Women!

The most direct marriage of art and politics in Elizabeth Robins's career was Harley Granville Barker's Court Theatre production[13] of her play *Votes for Women!* The play was political not only in terms of the propagandist content signalled by the title, but also on a financial level. Robins judiciously advertised that she would split her percentage of the box office returns between the older, more stately NUWSS and the young, more radical WSPU, fast becoming known as the 'suffragettes' and associated with of acts of civil disobedience.[14] The play combines the kind of fallen woman story made popular by Pinero, Jones and Wilde in the 1890s with the politics of the women's movement at the inception of the militant phase of the campaign. Robins attended eight suffrage rallies between July and October 1906, taking copious notes on the platform speeches which she drew from extensively in writing the second act, a suffrage rally in Trafalgar Square, the site of her own conversion to the cause (Fig. 5.1).[15]

When Robins began writing the play in the autumn of 1906, the militant phase of the campaign had not yet gained full momentum. This changed on 23 October when WSPU members disrupted proceedings in parliament, resulting in the imprisonment of ten women; the publicity brought the WSPU more funds and new members than any previous militant action. By the end of 1907 militant tactics were in full swing, marking a radical change in the nature of the suffrage campaign and public reactions to it. Written in this transitional moment, Robins's play addresses a complex array of feminist issues including the double standard, female economic dependence, abortion, suffrage and reactions to feminist civil disobedience.

Fig. 5.1   Flora Drummond[16] addressing a crowd in Trafalgar Square, 1908, printed by permission of the Museum of London

Robins's heroine Vida Levering is a cultured, attractive woman in her early thirties who has returned from ten years abroad and now moves in fashionable society despite whispers of a mysterious past. While weekending at a fashionable country house, Vida unexpectedly encounters her past seducer, the Conservative politician Geoffrey Stonor, who is now on the brink of attaining a cabinet seat and engaged to a young heiress. Geoffrey's fiancée, Jean Dumbarton, unexpectedly becomes captivated by Vida and impulsively follows her to London. The second act, for which the play was most celebrated, depicts a suffrage rally in Trafalgar Square where Jean witnesses Vida's first political speech and becomes a convert. (Conversion was a major theme of suffrage literature and theatre; *The Convert* was the name of the novelized version of the story Robins published in the same year.) The third act returns to a drawing room setting to play out the political and romantic triangle between Vida, Geoffrey and Jean and determine whether Jean's future will be with the rising Conservative politician Geoffrey or the emerging feminist crusader Vida.

In the first two acts the ingénue Jean serves as a moral compass, guiding audience responses to Vida and Geoffrey's actions, past and present. Early on, a society woman discourages Jean from associating with Vida by heavily implying that she had an abortion. Far from shunning Vida for her past, Jean regards her as extraordinary for having survived it. Meanwhile, Geoffrey is shown in a poor light when Jean realizes that he is pledging support to the suffrage campaign as a political strategy but doesn't intend to back the cause once he is in office. At the end of the first act, Jean lies about a telegram so that she can attend Vida's suffrage rally in London. During the rally Jean deduces that Geoffrey is Vida's past seducer and becomes more disillusioned with him and more enthralled by her. She follows Vida into the crowd at the end of the act to ask to work with her, allying herself with Vida and her politics rather than Geoffrey and his. In the final act Jean demands that Geoffrey make amends by marrying Vida. Unlike the fallen woman Gladys Lessingham (a part Robins played years earlier) who was offered the same solution by her seducer's younger fiancé and took it, Vida has moved on. She confides to Lady John, 'For me he's simply one of the far-back links in a chain of evidence' (p. 197), rewriting the fallen woman's established script. Dismissing Jean's proposed solution to her own past, Vida looks instead to Jean's future and sees two possibilities: Jean could renounce marriage and motherhood and become 'the new Joan of Arc'[17] (p. 204) of the women's movement; or she could help the cause through her influence on a powerful male politician. In language that is more pecuniary than sisterly Vida determines to 'coin' the younger woman's sympathy for her 'into gold for a greater cause' (p. 197). Jean becomes a 'Ransom' (p. 203) Vida relinquishes to Geoffrey in exchange for his political support.

Like many real and fictional first-wave feminists, Vida Levering is an evangelical figure, proselytizing feminist ideas to people of diverse classes and experiences. Vida's feminist ministry is carried out largely through parable, using private suffering to identify social ills. As well as drawing from her own personal experiences, Vida gains first-hand knowledge of key social issues through pilgrimages into the underworld disguised as a pauper.[18] The character's evangelical quality was emphasized in the first draft by the name Christian Levering, which was changed at the direct request of Emmeline Pankhurst who thought it too suggestive of her prominent daughter. In a letter to Robins she wrote, 'people might connect the imaginary with the real and say that Christian's story is Christabel's' (19 November 1906. HRC: Robins Box 2, Folder 2). In what reads more like a royal command than a request, Pankhurst says, 'We should not like this to happen should we?' (ibid.). Because Robins's heroine is a woman with a past, Pankhurst also requested that Robins alter the script to make her a sympathizer with the WSPU, but not an actual member.[19]

Robins introduces suffrage within the context of a fashionable house party. The guests voice disapproval of militant tactics as they discuss an episode based on the real events of 25 April 1906 when 12 WSPU members interrupted MPs, shouting from the Ladies' Gallery[20] to protest a suffrage resolution being 'talked out' (filibustered) without a vote. The house party guests argue that the suffragettes have made their cause impossible to support: 'the work of forty years destroyed in five minutes!' (p. 161). Vida amiably counters condemnation of militant interruptions from the Ladies' Gallery by pointing out the women's media victory, remarking, 'It does rather look to the outsider as if the well-behaved women had worked for forty years and made less impression on the world than those fiery young women made in five minutes' (p. 163). Throughout the play Vida's most impressive trait is her charismatic ability to interact with people of different social backgrounds and political opinions, a trait she shares with her author, Robins, who enjoyed unique social mobility. Robins had a wide span of friends in the aristocracy, the government and the suffrage movement, and often attended weekend house parties like the one depicted in the play's opening act, making her a sort of 'double agent'. Her biographer Angela V. John notes that rather than 'jettison her society friends whom she had known rather longer than the suffragettes, she played a delicate balancing act with all the tensions, charges of duplicity, hypocrisy and irony this could engender' (1995, p. 154).[21]

The suffrage rally marks a turning point for Vida who crosses over from her own privileged world, with its private philanthropy, to becoming a public platform speaker. Initially, Vida 'stumbles and stops' (p. 180) as she delivers her first platform speech 'with a visible effort' (p. 181), giving her account of a police court hearing during which she witnessed a half-starved boy tried for stealing milk. Through the tale of the boy's conviction, Vida depicts an unreasonably harsh masculine system of justice in need of a balancing feminine element of mercy and compassion. Vida's expedition to the police courts evokes the militant suffrage tactic of encouraging the visible, vocal presence of women in courtrooms. The Pankhursts encouraged followers to attend police courts to discourage the mistreatment of women by police and to influence sentencing, believing the presence of women in the courtroom would subdue sentencing against children and young women and encourage harsher sentencing for violent male crimes against women (Fig. 5.2).[22]

Hitting her stride as a speaker midway through her speech, Vida relays a more graphic case from the police court, the story of a working-class girl tried for murder after being abandoned by an employer and arrested for leaving the body of their dead baby at his doorstep. The teenage orphan mother is imprisoned while the married middle-class father goes free. Unlike a man who is entitled to justice as decreed by a jury of his peers, 'A woman,' Vida points out, 'is arrested by a man, brought before a man judge, tried by a jury of men, and by a man she's hanged! Where in all this,' she asks, 'were *her* "peers"?' (p. 184). Both of these police court parables are well received by the on-stage Trafalgar Square crowd. The most powerful effect of the scene, however, lies not so much in what Vida says as in her relationship to the on-stage audience, in other words the

Fig. 5.2 The Act II Trafalgar Square scene from *Votes for Women!* (*Sketch*, 15 May 1907), image provided by British Newspaper Archive and printed by permission of the Mary Evans Picture Library

parable of Vida herself. She begins the scene haltingly but by the end, as police threaten the crowd and speakers, Vida turns 'with a sudden gleam in her lit eyes' and silences the chaos, 'holding the people by the sudden concentration of passion in her face' (pp. 185–86), dramatizing her cross-over from private to public figure. For Penny Farfan this is where Robins's character Vida moves from the 'retrograde and problematically elitist phi-losophy of individualism' characteristic of Ibsen protagonists to a more collective 'grass-roots feminism' (2004, p. 24). Robins's depiction of the suffrage movement in this play is defined by an image of universal moth-erhood, articulated by the working woman who declares, 'We don't only want better things for our own children. We want better things for all. *Every* child is our child' (p. 171).

Although a theatrical performance is managed to a much greater degree than a political rally, Robins's writing and Barker's direction of the crowd dialogue[23] created a struggle for control in this scene which made the vul-nerability of the speakers immediate and threatening, especially in the case of the novice Vida. Robins cleverly employed the theatre building itself as a safe space for the propagation of political views, while retaining the electric charge of mob opposition, breaking the fourth wall to create a pioneer-ing immersive theatre experience for the audience who could potentially become 'converts'. As well as offering them a conversion opportunity, Robins's play offered men the possibility of feeling protectively towards, and therefore allied with, the female speakers as protagonists against a hostile (male) crowd. The reviewer for the *Evening News* confessed, 'For my part, I felt like climbing over the footlights and inviting the dirty, drink sodden ruffians who interrupted [Vida] to come outside one by one and have their heads punched into rice-puddings!' (10 April 1907). Robins and Barker's stage crowd was less hostile than many real crowds; suffrage speaker Mary Richardson recounted that 'The sex filth which elderly men in particular seemed determined to inflict on us was the most hateful part of my daily experience' (1953, p. 12). In addition to heckling, suffrage plat-form speakers were frequently pelted with missiles ranging from pepper, tomatoes, fish and rotten eggs to live mice. So, while the stage audience was hyper-real in one sense, in another it was sanitized or stylized to func-tion as somewhere between verisimilitude and a Greek Chorus.[24]

Harley Granville Barker's suggestion to alter the title of Robins's play from 'A Friend to Women' to 'Votes for Women!' was good from the point of view of ticket sales and topicality, but Robins's original title, as well as the title of the novelized version of the piece, *The Convert*, are more indicative of the play's broader feminist themes, which are not exclusively suffragist. In her final confrontation with Geoffrey, Vida draws the connection between personal experience and political agency, asking, 'What general significance has my secret pain? Does it "join on" to anything?' and answering:

> And I find it does. I'm no longer merely a woman who has stumbled on the way. I'm one (*she controls with difficulty the shake in her voice*) who has got up bruised and bleeding, wiped the dust from her hands and the tears from her face, and said to herself not merely, 'Here's one luckless woman! but – here is a stone of stumbling to many. Let's see if it can't be moved out of other women's way.'. (p. 207)

Robins represents female suffrage as part of an overall programme of social reform, not the ultimate goal of the women's movement or even its most important element, which is the shared experiences and emerging voices of women themselves. Considered within the wider context of feminist issues Robins examines within the piece, the suffrage movement can be read as the setting rather than the subject of the play.

Newspaper critics, suffragists and fellow writers like Shaw, Archer and Barker agreed that the suffrage rally was by far the most engaging and effective part of the play. In *Play-Making*, Archer pronounced it 'one of the most admirable and enthralling scenes I ever saw on any stage' (1912/1960, p. 14). The reviewer for the *Illustrated London News* called it 'the best stage managed and the most original scene we have had in the theatre for many a day', but disputed the scene's realism; 'there were never such speeches in Trafalgar Square' (13 April 1907). Women who frequently attended suffrage rallies, however, found them convincing. In a letter to Robins, Amber Reeves wrote, 'Of course the second act was glorious. It was impossible not to believe that one was in Trafalgar Square jumping with excitement in the crowd' (n.d., 1907. HRC: Robins Box 1, Folder 6). The drawing room scenes of Acts I and III were part of established Edwardian theatre conventions, set in private domestic space, whereas the realistic staging of the suffrage rally with 40 actors and a stage orientation that put the audience in a public crowd was revolutionary. It is not surprising, then, that the second act received critical attention almost to the exclusion of the others. In the *Saturday Review*, Max Beerbohm wished that the second act could be 'extended at each end that there would be no time for performing the first act and the third' (13 April 1907). While the play was still in development, Shaw and

Barker had both suggested cutting it down to feature the second act[25] and Henry James sent Robins 49 pages of critical notes on the first third of the first act alone,[26] but Robins largely rejected their advice. Without the first and third acts, without revealing the process of transformation, the second act might have simply been a novel spectacle peopled with stock characters. As Barbara Green has argued, 'Spectacle opens autobiography, the singular speech-act of an individual woman, to collectivity, group-action, and intersubjectivity' (1997, p. 8). As a convert to feminism herself and as a connoisseur of stage craft, Robins understood the significance of retaining Vida's story and refashioning the woman with a (private) past into a woman with a (public) future. The second act offered an exciting and new agitprop intervention into the bourgeois space of theatre, but Robins's feminist message necessitated the contextual frame of the personal story of 'the convert', making the first and third acts essential. The reviewer for *The Manchester Guardian* appreciated Robins's fusion, calling it 'a play of definite political advocacy', and noting 'It is remarkable how effective an instrument the theatre can be made in such ingenious hands' (10 April 1907).

In a note thanking Robins for the cheque received by the NUWSS for a percentage of box office receipts, Millicent Garrett Fawcett dissents with theatre critics, stating 'the whole kernel of the thing is in the third act'. Fawcett and her sister Elizabeth Garrett Anderson speculated that 'the novelty of treating the Sex relationship from its fundamental and most serious human side rather than from the conventional stage point of view is what makes people say that the third act is the weak point in the play' (5 May 1907. HRC: Robins Box 1, Folder 3). I find it fascinating that Garrett Fawcett, the leader of the NUWSS, believed that Robins's feminist reworking of stage conventions of fallen women plays was the real reason behind (male) critics' lack of interest in the third act. Where Pinero had provided sexual scintillation in his fallen woman plays, with a New Woman who ends up in plunging décolletage despite her earnest desire to write feminist essays, Robins's heroine sticks to her sober feminist ministry. What's more, she denies the central importance of her past lover, saying, 'You don't seriously believe a woman with anything else to think about, comes to the end of ten years still *absorbed* by a memory of that sort' (p. 196). Beerbohm lamented that Robins was 'not "out for" fun' and remarked that it was strange 'that Miss Robins, one of the cleverest of her sex, evidently takes Miss Levering quite seriously, presenting her not as the butt of a satirical comedy, but as the triumphant preacher in a didactic play!' (*Saturday Review,* 13 April 1907). Garrett Fawcett's observation acknowledges the Vida narrative as more radical in theatrical terms than it is usually given credit for when Acts I and III are dismissed as melodramatic bookends to a spectacular suffrage rally scene. Though *Votes for Women!* succeeded on many levels, its sold-out run cut short only by the end of the Vedrenne-Barker lease of the Court theatre, after *Votes!* suffrage theatre writers and producers generally stuck to one-acts which often promised more 'fun' to audiences.

SUFFRAGE ONE-ACTS

With the exception of the full-length *Votes for Women!,* suffrage plays have a sketch-like quality and style that makes them less literary, more agitprop than other Edwardian problem plays on the woman question. Suffrage plays assume that their audiences are already versed in arguments for women's enfranchisement and so often employ concise satirical strategies to undermine the opposition rather than repeating pro-suffrage arguments. Just as cartoon caricature had been an effective weapon against New Women and later suffragists, portraying them in various unflattering guises such as 'the shrieking sisterhood', suffrage theatre provided a quick, impressionistic means to strike back at opponents with the very weapon which had proved so difficult for feminists to wield: humour.

Opposition groups are frequently characterized as having little sense of humour; jokes aren't as funny to their targets. Colluding in jokes with dominant groups averts the potential danger of becoming the butt of them, and is thus a powerful tool in maintaining cultural hegemonies. Defending themselves from the onslaught of cartoons and jokes aimed at them was a daily trial for suffragists. Feminists responded to satirical attacks by adopting martyrs as their icons, especially the exploited labourer, the widow and the saint. While these images appealed to the need for dignity, purity and womanliness, they were also rather austere and solemn. Pro-suffrage playwrights like Cicely Hamilton and George Bernard Shaw contributed hugely to the cause by tapping into the power of humour as an offensive weapon, strategically crafting comedy as a means to spotlight and lampoon contradictions in dominant ideology and winning mainstream support through the promise of pleasure via laughter. Where anti-suffrage humour had been personal in its attacks, often aimed at discrediting individuals, suffragist humour, for the most part, rose above name-calling to tilt its lance at the much larger target of patriarchal logic.

How the Vote Was Won

How the Vote Was Won (1909) is a classic example of Cicely Hamilton's speciality as a feminist writer with a knack for popular appeal, undermining conservative arguments by taking them to their logical conclusions. The play, authored in collaboration with Christopher St. John and directed by Edith Craig, was one of the most popular and frequently performed suffrage sketches. The piece dramatizes the consequences of a literal interpretation of separate spheres ideology when women go on strike against all forms of labour outside a home provided by their nearest male relative: 'Every man, either in a public capacity or a private one, will find himself face to face with the appalling problem of maintaining millions of women in idleness' (p. 24). The central character is a staunchly anti-suffragist middle-class clerk, Horace Cole, whose initial reaction to the 'Suffragette strike' is cavalier: 'Who cares if they do strike? They're no use to anyone' (p. 26). His attitude changes, however, as more and more female relations appear claiming their right to financial dependence on him. When he realizes that women at large are on strike, not simply a small group of rowdy suffragettes, Horace begins to ask questions:

> *HORACE:* But why can't you support yourself? You've done it for years.
> *AGATHA:* Yes – ever since I was eighteen. Now I am going to give up work, until my work is recognised. Either my place is in the home – the home provided for me by some dear father, brother, husband, cousin, or uncle – or I am a self-supporting member of the State, who ought not to be shut out from the rights of citizenship. (p. 27)

When Horace's niece Molly, a successful novelist, arrives and demands to be supported, he is bewildered; she makes more money than he does. 'Ah, yes;' says Molly, 'but you never *liked* my writing for money, did you? You called me "sexless" once because I said that as long as I could support myself I didn't feel an irresistible temptation to marry' (p. 28). By the arrival of the fourth female dependent, all pretence of manly chivalry has evaporated and Horace proclaims: 'I don't care a damn where any of you go' (p. 29).

While Horace is faced with the personal dilemma of how to get rid of female dependents at home, the nation scrambles to replace women in the workplace. The black sheep of the family, music hall actress Maudie Spark, arrives with her luggage and reports that the theatres are dark, businesses can't open and households are in disarray. Seeing that the standing of women bears directly on his own financial position converts Horace to the cause. 'If this rotten Government think we're going to maintain millions of women in idleness', he says, 'this Government have reckoned without the men' (p. 32). As he disappears into the night to join the army of men who are forming a procession to the town hall, he exclaims, with his chauvinism still perfectly intact, 'When you want a thing done, get a man to do it! Votes for Women!' (p. 33).

How the Vote Was Won is a fantasy of female solidarity in line with early trade unionism. Hamilton shows that the plight of women is not unlike that of the worker in relation to the capitalist; individually women are paupers, but on a national level they wield enormous economic power. As Sheila Stowell has pointed out, Hamilton's 'strike' is purely economic, avoiding all issues of physical sex: 'Women here do not deny sexual favours; on the model of striking trade unions, an increasingly familiar phenomenon for the Edwardians, they simply withhold their labour' (1992b, p. 58). Though the backbone of Hamilton's work is her feminist economic critique, the success of this play lies primarily in its use of humour to diffuse an atmosphere of out-and-out sex antagonism and to draw the audience into the suffrage camp through their laughter at and even sympathy for the men. The women are represented not so much as aggressors as amusingly literal in their proposal to live by the separate spheres guidelines laid out for them. They behave perfectly rationally while the men exhibit the emotional excess of hysteria. Through its humour, the play invites potential converts to laugh at Horace and by so doing relax or reject their own former 'separate spheres' logic.

Channelling comedy's unique power to undermine the logic of the status quo while providing 'fun' for audiences proved a successful tactic for suffrage writers, and one they returned to in many of their plays. In Beatrice Harraden's sketch *Lady Geraldine's Speech* (1909) the title character comes to her old friend Alice Romney to ask her to ghostwrite a suitable speech for an anti-suffrage meeting. While waiting in the drawing room for Alice to pen the speech for her, Lady Geraldine meets four of Alice's accomplished women friends: a famous pianist, an eminent artist, a professor of literature, and a typist and shorthand writer who also sells the newspaper *Votes for Women*. The pro-suffrage friends initially assume that Lady Geraldine is one of them, but when she outs herself as an 'anti', they rise above their political differences with charm and wit. The artist offers to paint her portrait, exclaiming with excitement, 'I've never seen a real Anti-Suffragist before' (p. 98) while the literature professor jokes, 'Oh, and to think I shan't be able to go and heckle you!' (p. 98). The sketch ends on an upbeat note with Lady Geraldine throwing the just completed anti-suffrage speech into the fire and asking for the typist's last copy of *Votes for Women*, saying 'Do you know what I'm going to do next? I'm going home to think' (p. 98).

Gertrude Jennings's *A Woman's Influence*, first performed in 1909 and published by the Actresses' Franchise League in 1913, also works to undermine anti-suffrage women. In it, the heroine, Margaret, an earnest young wife, tries in vain to convince her husband Herbert to take a stand on improving women's labour conditions and pay in their town's Hill Rise Factories, but her fact-based and moral arguments fall on deaf ears. Mrs Perry, an anti-suffrage flirt, who is content to wield power indirectly through feminine influence over men, wagers a sovereign that she can succeed where Margaret has failed. Her performance of sham tears, flirtation and flattery indeed succeeds and Herbert agrees to take up the matter of factory conditions with their local MP. Herbert is horrified when Margaret reveals that Mrs Perry tricked him into action on a bet. Margaret makes a final attempt to convince Herbert that intelligent partnership between men and women is preferable to forcing women to act through flirtatious subterfuge, arguing that men should give women 'the use of our intelligence, so that we could realize that we are reasonable creatures, fit to be heard equally with man, not parasites' (pp. 136–37). The play ends on a note of cooperation between men and women, a favourite suffrage theme.

In Evelyn Glover's skit *Miss Appleyard's Awakening* (1911) the anti-suffragist campaigner Mrs Crabtree undermines the logic of her own position that women shouldn't participate in politics by collecting signatures door to door for the unfortunately initialled ASS (Anti-Suffrage Society). She ends up unwittingly converting Miss Appleyard, an 'anti', into a suffrage supporter. In *A Chat with Mrs Chicky* (1912), also by Glover, Mrs Holbrook, a middle-class anti-suffragist, is made ridiculous by her inability to supply her charwoman Mrs Chicky with a logical reason for signing an anti-suffrage petition. Mrs Holbrook argues, for example, that only men should be enfranchised because only men serve in the military. Mrs Chicky's questions, however, force Mrs Holbrook to concede that most soldiers and sailors cannot vote because they do not have fixed addresses. Mrs Holbrook's refusal to understand most of Mrs Chicky's comments and questions is shown to be more a product of class condescension than politics. This class contempt, Glover suggests, is at the root of many of the hypocrisies of the status quo. Mrs Chicky expresses appreciation for suffragists as the only members of the middle classes whose rhetoric does not contradict her working-class experience: 'she didn't waste no time, I say, jorin' to women like that about the splendid way their int'rests are perfected already! *She knew*' (p. 113).

Mary Cholmondeley's *Votes for Men* (1909) turns the tables by depicting a future Britain (2109) in which men have already been disenfranchised for a hundred years, following the election of a radical feminist government in 2009 led by Mary the Manhater. The Prime Minister, Eugenia, patiently explains to her husband who watches a parade of the Men's Reinfranchisement League from their window, 'it is merely hysteria to combat the basic fact that the sex which controls the birth-rate must by nature rule the nation which it creates' (p. 204). In this new matriarchal version of separate spheres, men have their place as defenders of the nation – soldiers, sailors and policemen, roles which also make them expendable and ensure their subordination, while women control the means of reproduction and rule the country. Though the skit contains humorous reversals, with men marching in the streets chanting 'Votes for Men' and chaining themselves to the women's airplanes in protest, there are also ominous eugenic overtones as the symbolically named Eugenia attempts to bring in a bill that will make motherhood, three children per woman, compulsory for all women[27] whether they are married or not. The dystopian systems of oppression at work in Cholmondeley's twenty-second-century matriarchy mirror repressive patriarchal systems of the Edwardian present, suggesting that gender equality is essential in creating a society that is more just (and more pleasant) than one dominated exclusively by one sex.

In Netta Syrett's *Might is Right* (1909) a Secret Suffrage Society (SSS) successfully conspires to kidnap the prime minister with the help of Bobby Bins, a well-known variety actress. During his house arrest at the hands of the SSS, the PM, clad in a flowered dressing gown, is guarded by pistol brandishing women who try to extort a promise to support an equal franchise Bill as the price of his release. In the romantic comedy resolution, the eligible bachelor PM becomes a convert through falling in love with Miss Tracy, the President of the SSS who willingly trades her hand in marriage for his pledge to support the cause. Syrett makes it clear that 'it's no sacrifice' (p. 28) for Miss Tracy, who reciprocates the PM's romantic feelings but doesn't let sentiment keep her from getting him to sign 'the marriage contract' (p. 28), a pro-suffrage press release, before she allows him to take her in his arms.

Many similarly witty short propaganda plays were produced by writers in the WWSL. Apart from the invaluable contribution of adding humour to the feminist arsenal, suffrage theatre was a tremendously important nexus for feminist artists and audiences. Edith Craig enthused, 'One play is worth a hundred speeches!' (quoted in Cockin, 2017, p. 100). Suffrage plays also made interventions into the conventions of female characters' physical placing within stage space. Centre stage was the universally accepted domain of the male protagonist, with female characters normally contained to more domestic on-stage spaces: sides, background, balconies and beds. Nancy Reinhardt observes that if a female character 'defies convention and invades the male central stage area, she is often exaggerated or distorted as "an angel or a monster"' (1981, p. 43). Suffrage theatre negotiated theatrical conventions to its own advantage by sometimes using centre stage to make monsters of anti-suffrage female characters or angels of pro-suffrage characters. In many of the short sketches pro-suffrage characters are naturalized into the domestic areas of the stage – Mrs Chicky, for example, performs domestic tasks to the sides – while anti-suffrage characters monopolize centre stage, appearing as 'monsters' of self-importance. Vida Levering's address to the crowd in Trafalgar Square positions her centre stage, surrounded by a hostile crowd, inviting associations with religious martyrs like Joan of Arc. Conversion was a major theme of suffrage plays and stage positioning could be used to invite parallels between feminists and disciples, hunger strikers and religious martyrs.

Though a critical mass of the women involved in the suffrage movement and suffrage theatre were middle class, prompting criticism that the more accurate slogan for the campaign would have been 'Votes for Ladies', working-class women frequently appeared in suffrage plays voicing their complaints against the patriarchy with down-to-earth logic and humour. These plays were intended to have cross-class appeal and demonstrate the need for all classes of women to have a voice and a vote, making the testimony of characters like Robins's Ernestine Blunt and Glover's Mrs Chicky essential in revealing the hypocrisies of separate spheres rhetoric. Similar lessons are also learnt through the dramaturgy of role reversals, such as the journey of a privileged character like Vida Levering into the underworld or a gender role reversal as seen in L.S. Phibb's *Jim's Leg* (1911) when an injured working-class man is schooled in the demanding labour of running a household when he and his wife have to trade places. In Joan Dugdale's *10 Clowning Street* (1913) the Prime Minister sends his daughters out as test cases for a newly proposed government scheme of National Service for unmarried woman over the age of 21. Isabella becomes a parlour-maid, Judith works at the Snowdrop Laundry and Enid works in a haberdashery shop. All three daughters return from their experiences having become ardent suffrage supporters and Judith challenges her father's authority to pass laws on women's working conditions, asserting 'You know nothing about it, so you have no right to legislate for it' (p. 182).

Many male dramatists and actors also wrote pro-suffrage plays, among them H.V. Esmond (*Her Vote*, 1910), H.M. Paull (*An Anti-Suffragist* or *The Other Side*, 1910), Henry Arncliffe-Sennett (*An Englishwoman's Home*, 1911), Graham Moffat (*The Maid and the Magistrate*, 1912) and Arthur M. Heathcote (*A Junction*, 1913). George Bernard Shaw described his one-act suffrage play *Press Cuttings* (1909) as 'a topical sketch compiled from the editorial and correspondence columns of daily papers during the Women's War of 1909' (1986b, p. 223). The action is set in a Shavian projection of 1912, where suffragists hold the entire capital at their mercy: telephones are tapped, the streets are impassable and martial law has been called in as a last-ditch effort to restore order. The play opens in the war office of General Mitchener.[28] A loud cry of 'Votes for Women!' from the street below sends the general clutching for his pistol, but the 'suffragist' turns out to be Prime Minister Balsquith,[29] whose safe passage from Downing Street to the War Office can only be procured by disguise. After a lengthy debate, during which the threat of suffragists is compared to the threat of a German invasion, the prime minister agrees to receive Anti-Suffraget League president, Lady Fanshawe, and secretary, Mrs Banger. Lady Fanshawe is the siren, 'beautiful and romantic', a compulsive flirt who describes herself as 'one of those women who are accustomed to rule the world through men' (p. 259). She objects that the suffrage movement is 'essentially a dowdy movement' (p. 259) that 'would degrade women from being rulers to being voters' (p. 259). The foil to Lady Fanshawe, Mrs Banger, is described as 'a man in petticoats' (p. 258) and possesses a sword, a Napoleonic revolver and a booming baritone voice. When asked by the incredulous Mitchener if her sex was never suspected during her military career, she replies tersely: 'I had a comrade – a gentleman ranker – whom they called Fanny. They never called me Fanny' (p. 254). Mrs Banger's objection to female suffrage is that it pales in significance against the much more urgent matter of female military service: 'Give me a well-mounted regiment of women with sabres, opposed to a regiment of men with votes. We shall see which will go down before the other' (p. 254). In creating Mrs Banger, Shaw takes the stereotype of the masculine feminist (used by the popular press against the women's movement) and mischievously places her in the conservative camp where she destabilizes gender not only through her manly bravado but in her patronizing treatment of Mitchener, whom she warns not to cry and beg.

The most ideologically challenging aspect of the play is its inversion of stereotypes. The anti-suffragists are power-crazed and violent; the most powerful men in Britain exhibit 'hysterical' behaviour; and the suffragettes are spoken of dismissively as gentle, pretty, sheep-like creatures, disrupting binaries of 'manly' and 'womanly', 'suffragette' and 'anti' and 'militant' and 'non-militant'. In the end, the traditionalist, Mitchener, champions 'the dowdies' (suffragists) and becomes engaged to his charwoman. While Shaw was pro-suffrage, as an ambitious playwright gaining popularity he was also very good at exploiting women's issues to his own advantage, leading some female suffragists, including Elizabeth Robins, to regard his feminism as specious. When Annie Horniman produced the piece in 1909, the reviewer for the *Common Cause* noted that Shaw's humour struck an uneasy chord with audiences:

> When one remembers that women are at the present moment being tortured in prison by a Government whose only remedy for disorder is repression, one can scarcely laugh very heartily at 'Shoot em down!' or if the laugh is loud, it is bitter too.
>
> (30 September 1909)

Shaw's prediction that violence would escalate considerably by 1912, however, was proved correct.

Though not specifically a suffrage play, J.M. Barrie's *What Every Woman Knows* (1908) is a more serious attempt on the part of a male dramatist to illustrate women's capacity for politics and expose the hypocrisy of men who rely on, yet deny, women's talents. It was also a hit with audiences. Produced by the impresario Charles Frohman the play ran for 384 performances at the Duke of York's Theatre and transferred to Broadway. A comedy in minor key, the play is a sympathetic portrait of a plain but brilliant woman, Maggie Wylie. Throughout the play men refer to Maggie as 'queer' (p. 36) and off-putting. Her male relatives are all too aware that her intelligence isn't a selling point in the marriage market, noting 'Men are nervous of remarkable women. It's an instinct, and all the remarkable women know it, and spend half their lives in concealing that they are remarkable' (p. 34). Teetering on spinsterhood, Maggie is bartered in marriage by her father who agrees to pay for the education of John Shand, a starving student six years her junior, if he will marry Maggie after he takes his degree. After they are married, Maggie brings John to political prominence, engineering political connections and ghost writing speeches without him noticing that she is the driving force in his career. When he is elected to parliament John exclaims with no irony, 'I've done it Maggie, and not a soul to help me – I've done it alone!' at which Maggie laughs and claps her hands 'hysterically' (p. 7), perhaps in joy, perhaps in frustration. As an MP, John feels that he should have a more beautiful and charming society wife and becomes infatuated with Lady Sybil Lazenby (played by Lillah McCarthy). Maggie agrees to bow out if John finds that Lady Sybil can be of greater help to his career than she can. John quickly discovers that a clever partner is better than a pretty muse and the play ends on his line, 'it nearly makes me laugh Maggie, to think that you may have been helping me all the time – and neither of us knew it' (p. 21). The irony of the line invites the audience to laugh at the male politician as still not having grasped 'what every woman knows', i.e. that women have been making significant contributions to male careers and by extension to civic life all along.

CONTROLLING THE IMAGE – MARCHES

Suffragists had a complicated relationship with essentialism. They rejected the essentialist separate spheres notion that by definition of their gender women lacked the innate qualities to succeed in the 'masculine' domains of higher education, careers and politics. However, they also capitalized on essentialist ideals of women as the morally superior sex as a rationale for extending their influence into the public realm. The tone of pro-suffrage arguments were, thus, frequently sober and often evangelical. Anti-suffragists suffered no such conflict in their wholehearted subscription to essentialism and drew heavily on traditional notions of womanliness to discredit suffragists as unnatural horrors. A plethora of cartoons depicting 'unsexed' suffragettes appeared, intended to illustrate the incompatibility of public ambition with true womanhood. In these cartoons, suffragists are drawn as dowdy scolds, cross-dressing termagants, shrewish old maids, or as weapon-wielding viragos or abuse-hurling furies. While anti-suffragists had a vast arsenal of ready-made negative female stereotypes, suffragists struggled to craft empowering images for their campaign that were still compatible with conventional ideas of femininity. One of the most successful counter-representational series was published in 1910 by the women's suffrage paper *The Vote*. Designed to refute stereotypes of feminists as frumpy, mannish or aggressive, the postcard series depicted (married) suffragists at home engaged in traditional womanly tasks. Some of the photographs featured were 'Mrs Snow Makes Pastry', 'Mrs Despard knits a Comforter', 'Mrs How-Martyn Makes Jam' and, the winner of *The Vote*'s prize for best image, 'Mrs John Russell Tending her Invalid Mother'. In the end, however, the most effective means to reshape perceptions of suffragists as unnatural was for women themselves to come out in public *en masse* to support the cause.

Taking to the streets took tremendous courage for suffragists on their first public march, the 'Mud March' of 9 February 1907. Many feared hostile crowds, some disliked the idea of public exhibition, and others worried that they might lose their jobs or their reputations if their pictures got into the papers. Suffragist Ray (Rachel) Strachey recalled women's reluctance, noting that 'In that year the vast majority of women still felt that there was something very dreadful in walking in a procession through the streets' (1928, p. 306). The NUWSS had no idea how many women might make the march from Hyde Park Corner to an assembly in the Exeter Hall but, despite fear and uncertainty, 3,000 women turned out to brave both the public and the winter weather and muddy streets that gave the march its name. The women in the procession, described by the press as 'well mannered and well bannered', carried colourful, hand-sewn and embroidered signs, bearing slogans such as 'Gentle but Resolute'. Strachey reflected on the success of the first march as a test case, 'Crowds watched and wondered; and it was not so dreadful after all [...] the idea of a public demonstration of faith in the Cause took root' (1928, p. 306). Peaceful public marches became the events that both militant and non-militant groups could rally around, events which drew more and more on the skills of actresses and artists as they increased in scale and spectacle.

Women were quickly learning to capitalize on the fact that spectacle sold papers; the Mud March gave the suffrage issue more publicity in one week than it had enjoyed in previous decades. As the marches grew, they went a long way towards countering the negative stereotypes of feminists propagated by the opposition. Instead of the anticipated parade of wizened old maids, mannish freaks and violent hysterics, the public eye-witnessed thousands of ordinary, smartly dressed women with pretty banners. *The Graphic*, which produced a spread sheet of illustrations of various 'types' of women who took part in the Mud March, predictably included 'The Military Type' and 'The Masculine Type', but also introduced the 'Sweet Girl Graduates', noted 'Peaceful Persuasion', and described some of the suffragists as 'Attending to the Inner Woman' (16 February 1907). The correspondent for *The Tribune* was, first and foremost, impressed by the class and geographic diversity of the group of women, noting, 'Not one class of women alone was represented in this great procession of voteless citizens' (10 February 1907) which included Cambridge students alongside mill workers from Lancashire and London society women.

Suffragists and their banners were carefully controlled and stream-lined, in some cases literally cast and costumed, into four recurrent 'types': the working woman, the modern woman, the militant woman and the womanly woman (Tickner, 1987, p. 173). The working woman was rep-resented as a noble, long-suffering 'peasant', often a widow supporting children on starvation wages; the modern woman wore university robes or a professional costume; the militant woman was most often represented in the image of Joan of Arc; and the womanly woman borrowed from 'the pictoral vocabulary of Pre-Raphaelitism and art nouveau' (Tickner, p. 220). The sight of female labourers marching alongside 'sweet girl grad-uates' (*Morning Leader,* 14 June 1907) was particularly powerful. Female labourers were walking testaments to the contradictions inherent in ideas of the 'weaker sex' and 'separate spheres' while the university and profes-sional women gave living proof of what women could and would become. Actresses became central to the public image and growing popularity of the cause. Claire Hirshfield notes that newspapers 'which regularly denounced suffragettes as "cranks", invariably gushed over actresses as "charming franchisettes"' while crowds 'which pelted suffrage processions with stones often paused to applaud those marching under the banner of the AFL' (1985, p. 130).

By 1907 women's suffrage had become a mainstream issue with celeb-rity advocates. Prior to the high visibility of the campaign, MPs could pledge support to women's suffrage and then simply delay bringing bills before the House from year to year. Prime Ministers Balfour and Asquith both stated during their administrations that they would grant the vote to women if and when they became convinced that British women really wanted it; the marches were a means for thousands of women to demon-strate that they did. Recognizing the power of mass demonstrations, Emmeline Pethick-Lawrence[30] wrote, 'Petitions go into parliamentary

Fig. 5.3 Indian Suffragists on the Women's Coronation Procession, 17 June 1911, printed by permission of the Museum of London

waste-paper-baskets. They cannot put a procession of fifteen thousand women into waste-paper-baskets' (*Votes for Women,* 15 July 1910). Beyond their function as a powerful tool of propaganda, the marches were a locus of solidarity, inspiration and galvanization among the women who, in greater numbers and with great confidence, participated in them. They also provided an opportunity for members of the public, who were coming round in favour of the suffragists, to express support. By 1911, the Women's Coronation Procession was seven miles long including women from New Zealand, Australia, Canada, South Africa, India and the Crown Colonies and Protectorates (Fig. 5.3).

A Pageant of Great Women

Drawing on the spectacular appeal of suffrage marches and heightening the theatrical possibilities by introducing a series of extraordinary characters and costumes, Cicely Hamilton's *A Pageant of Great Women* (1909) is the most 'interdisciplinary' suffrage text, incorporating literature, history, politics and drama. The piece was conceived and produced with extensive collaborative input from Edith Craig, as Hamilton freely acknowledged.[31] First produced at the Scala Theatre in London on 10 November 1909, the pageant featured dozens of women from history and literature and three allegorical characters: Woman, Prejudice and Justice. Woman pleads her case to Justice (originally played by Lillah McCarthy) with the great women bearing witnesses for the defence, arguing against the prosecutor, Prejudice. Craig appeared as the artist Rosa Bonheur, and top of the list for star value, Craig's mother Ellen Terry played England's first famous actress, Nance Oldfield. Among the notable roles were: 'The Learned Women' Hypatia, Jane Austen, George Sand and Madame Curie; 'The Artists' Sappho, Margaret Van Eyck and Angelica Kauffmann; 'The Saintly Women' St. Hilda and Catherine of Siena; 'The Heroic Women' Flora Macdonald, Kate Barlass and Grace Darling; 'The Rulers' Queens Victoria, Elizabeth and Isabella and Catherine the Great; and 'The Warriors' Joan of Arc, Boadicea, Hannah Snell and Florence Nightingale. By the end of the courtroom-style pageant, Woman convinces Justice that women are worthy of full citizenship by virtue of their genius and bravery through the ages. The script was flexible enough to be staged with between 40 and 90 women in cities and towns across the country with participants playing favourite characters from this feminist canon. Joan of Arc was so popular with militants that Hamilton noted that fierce competition to play 'Joan' sometimes caused 'real unpleasantness' (Adlard, 1949, p. 42), disrupting sisterly solidarity.

Unlike the one-act suffrage comedies, this production created an exciting and spectacular event that non-actresses could participate in, an experience which was inspiring and sometimes profound for the hundreds of women who took part. Although this was a tremendously popular suffrage piece and the most widely performed, the premise of proving worthiness based on extraordinary individuals was somewhat incongruous with claims that suffrage was a basic human rights issue, especially for suffragists with links to the Labour movement. In this respect, it is ironic that Hamilton was the writer commissioned to undertake the script for the pageant, as one of her personal qualms with the militant suffrage movement was its tendency to promote the cult of personality. On the whole, the *Pageant* was perhaps staged less as a vehicle for delivering a political argument than as a means of inspiring women through a celebration of women's achievements and potential; to this end it was hugely successful.

As the campaign mass-produced more posters, papers and pamphlets, the dominant image of the movement became the martyr, Joan of Arc (beatified in 1909, but not yet canonized). As an allegorical character, she had several obvious points of appeal to women who wanted to present a strong, but distinctly feminine, image. In the words of Christabel Pankhurst, Joan of Arc represented to the suffrage movement 'the loveliness of simplicity, purity, courage and militancy' (*The Suffragette*, 9 May 1913). Joan of Arc also embodied wrongful persecution. The suffragists needed to capitalize on martyrdom and the ill-uses of women in the past to demonstrate the need for political change while presenting a strong, empowering image for the future to prove that the public sphere would benefit from their involvement. At once a religious martyr and a military hero, the use of Joan as a suffrage icon broke from domestic rhetoric and framed women's mission within the public sphere.

From 1907 to the summer of 1910 the suffrage movement went from strength to strength. Suffrage theatre boomed in the wake of Robins's *Votes for Women!* with a proliferation of suffrage one-acts which could be performed in theatres, but could also easy transfer to town hall meetings and regional amateur venues. Marches and rallies which empowered

Fig. 5.4   The Suffragette Marjorie Annan Bryce representing Joan of Arc, 1911, printed by permission of the Museum of London

women to embody and voice their political opinions in public grew exponentially from 3,000 participants in the 1907 'Mud March' to 300,000–500,000 at the 'Women's Sunday' 1908 Hyde Park rally with 20 platforms for over 80 speakers. A plethora of women's political organizations like the NUWSS and the WSPU as well as specialist organizations such as the AFL and the WWSL vastly increased their memberships and their coffers, as converts, volunteers and donations flooded in. By 1910 the prospects for women's suffrage looked so promising that Emmeline Pankhurst called a truce on militant activity for several months in anticipation of the government passing the Conciliation Bill which would give women the vote on the same terms as men. The WSPU organized a magnificent march on 18 June, led proudly by 617 women who had served prison sentences. Suffrage societies lobbied diligently and peacefully for the Bill, collecting resolutions in its favour from 182 city, town and urban district councils. It looked like this was their moment.

BLACK FRIDAY AND BEYOND

The Conciliation Bill made it to a second reading, but was killed by Prime Minister Asquith. Mrs Pankhurst immediately called off the truce. On 18 November 1910 the WSPU sent a deputation of some 300 hundred women[32] to parliament and up to 200 were assaulted by police as they attempted to enter the building. One hundred and twenty women were arrested during the violent chaos that ensued. Because of the brutal treatment women received at the hands of the police, with at least one woman alleged to have died from injuries she sustained,[33] this date became known among suffragists as 'Black Friday'. The event was a public relations disaster for the government, who made things worse for themselves by attempting to gag the press. When the *Daily Mirror* published a photograph of suffragette Ada Wright cowering on the ground with her hands protecting her face, police officers looming over her, the government intervened to stop sales of the paper and ordered the editor to destroy the negatives. The Home Secretary Winston Churchill blocked a government inquiry into police violence against the women.

Suffragists and their supporters were appalled by the physical and often sexual abuse they were subject to. Women were pushed and battered, dragged by their hair, flung into the crowd and taunted with lewd jeers. Women's clothing and undergarments were ripped, their breasts deliberately attacked and their skirts pulled up to humiliate them. Henry Noel

Brailsford and Dr Jessie Murray collected depositions from 135 women involved. Nearly all of them describe the use of unnecessary violence; 45 women detailed acts of deliberate torture like twisting arms and thumbs to the breaking point and 29 women described acts of sexual indecency. One woman described how several police officers and members of the crowd had sexually assaulted her by grabbing and pummelling her breasts, resulting in severe bruising, and further degraded her by lifting her skirt and entreating other men to do the same (Lee, 2008, p. 347). Another woman testified 'The policemen who tried to move me on did so by pushing his knees in between me from behind, with the deliberate intention of attacking my sex' (p. 348). Dr Murray noted that the language reportedly used by police during these assaults proved that they were consciously sexual (p. 348). This blatant sexual aggression, intended to intimidate women from demonstrating publicly by tacitly equating the women who did with 'public women' (prostitutes) did not deter suffragists. The press sided with the unarmed women, increasing public sympathy and support for the women's cause and galvanizing the ever-growing number of suffragists in their determination to prevail against sexual tyranny. To purity feminists like Christabel Pankhurst, this public exhibition of male sexual aggression against women served as a vivid exposure of the real gender dynamics beneath the veneer of the supposedly benevolent patriarchy.[34]

A Second Conciliation Bill failed a year later in November 1911, provoking one of the most notorious and best remembered acts of militant protest. On 21 November suffragettes throughout London astonished police and the public by smashing windows in government offices and West End shops. As Sylvia Pankhurst recounted, all across London in fashionable shopping streets and in Whitehall, 'well-dressed women suddenly produced strong hammers[35] from their innocent looking bags and parcels, and fell to smashing shop windows' (1931/1988, p. 374). Emmeline Pankhurst, who personally broke windows at 10 Downing Street, was arrested and given a nine-month sentence for incitement to riot. Within a few hours 217 women had been arrested. WSPU militants defended their actions, arguing that, denied government representation, women were, by definition, 'outlaws'. Many suffrage supporters disagreed with violence[36] and increasingly regarded the Pankhursts as extremist fanatics. Others were wary of Emmeline and Christabel as bourgeoisie and politically conservative outside their interest in women's suffrage. Cicely Hamilton distrusted the autocratic leadership of the Pankhursts and their split with

the Labour Party, and later reflected that elements of the militant movement foreshowed the rise of fascist cult leaders (1935, p. 68). For a
supposedly 'outlaw' organization, Hamilton noted that the WSPU exer-
cised pseudo-military punctiliousness in their dress codes so that 'the outfit
of a militant setting forth to smash windows would probably include a
picture hat' (1935, p. 75).

While the WSPU orchestrated the violent events of March 1912 and
many other militant protests, some of the most extreme actions were taken
by individuals without the endorsement or foreknowledge of any suffrage society. The most haunting act of protest in the campaign was Emily
Wilding Davison's fatal run onto the Epsom race track where she was
trampled by the king's horse at the Derby Day race of May 1913. The act
was eye-witnessed by thousands of horrified onlookers as well as captured
on film and publicized worldwide. Generally seen as an act of self-sacrifice,
literally dying for the cause, Wilding Davison became the movement's
martyr.[37] In one respect this type of personal act played into the hands of
the ready-made stereotypes of 'viragos' and 'hysterics', which anti-suffrage
papers seized on. *The Daily Mirror*, for example, published a catalogue of
variations on the hysteric titled 'The Suffragette Face: New Type Evolved
by Militancy'. The new types, represented by unflattering photographs,
were captioned with phrases such as: 'ecstasy on arrest', 'dishevelled after
fighting' and 'screaming with impotent rage' (25 May 1914).

Nothing attracted publicity like women going to prison. Inciting
arrest to heighten their martyr status, suffrage prisoners and hunger strikers weren't simply frail feminine figures in the hands of male officials;
they were strong-willed provocateurs. The government refused to recognize militant suffrage action as political protest, classifying suffragettes
as common criminals and thus denying their right to representation and
often tolerating their abuse at the hands of police officers, prison staff and
doctors. Like their heroine Joan of Arc, the women were captured by a
hostile government, imprisoned and tortured – in their case by forcible
feeding. Forcible feeding, a procedure that involved penetration of the
mouth, nostrils or anus with a long rubber tube pushed into the stomach,
was described by Dr Forbes Ross as 'an act of brutality beyond common
endurance' (S. Pankhurst, 1931, p. 310). Performed on women who were
violently held or strapped down, it left many with lifelong physical injuries
(from accidents like feeding tubes being inserted into the trachea) as well
as the trauma of intense personal violation. Kitty Marion,[38] one of the few

actresses to engage in militant acts and undergo forcible feeding, lost her ability to perform on stage through injury to her throat and voice. In her unpublished memoir, she recounts her first ordeal:

> Not knowing the procedure of forcible feeding and thinking it was done through the mouth, I clenched my teeth when they had me in position and helpless. Then suddenly I felt something penetrate my right nostril which seemed to cause my head to burst and eyes to bulge. Choking and retching as the tube was forced down to the stomach and the liquid food poured in, most of which I vomited back when the tube was withdrawn. I must have lost consciousness for I found myself on the floor.
>
> (Quoted in Cockroft and Croft, 2010, p. 86)

Surviving prison and hunger striking became a symbol of honour and strength as well as martyrdom. Many women wore arrows stitched to their clothing to indicate the number of sentences served. Prison gates became popular as a symbol for banners in marches and demonstrations. Suffrage supporters who had not served gaol terms frequently expressed guilt for remaining 'on the outside'. In a letter to Robins, her WWSL colleague Evelyn Sharp wrote, 'I do feel ashamed to be outside prison. Under this government it is the only decent place for a self-respecting woman to be' (1913. HRC: Robins Box 2, Folder 4).

Prior to the devastating disappointment of the failed Conciliation Bill in the autumn of 1910 and the resulting violence of Black Friday, the mood in the suffrage campaign had been purposeful and optimistic. Campaigning for the vote brought women a new sense of freedom, excitement and solidarity. Dramatic one-acts produced before Black Friday are often comedic and confident, lampooning anti-suffrage conservatives and anticipating a victory that is only a matter of time. After Black Friday, the mood changed. Though supporters still wrote comedies, suffrage plays produced in the final years of the campaign are often focused on painful social issues like coverture, child labour, single motherhood, sexual compromise and gender barriers in education and employment. Margaret Nevinson's *In the Workhouse* (1911) deals with one of the most extreme consequences of coverture through the narrative of a respectable middle-aged matron, Mrs Cleaver, who is compelled by law to follow her drunken husband into the workhouse, a sort of prison/labour camp for the poor. Despite the fact that she is capable of working and supporting her children, her petition for release is denied, since under coverture she is not her own person in the law. Her children are also condemned to the workhouse since they fall entirely under the custody and control of their father. In contrast, Penelope Law, an unmarried mother, can come and go from the workhouse, retaining her own legal rights and rights over her children as a single woman. A young unwed mother, Lily, begins the play fervently hoping her baby's father will marry her, but after comparing the situations of the married and unmarried women, she decides to remain single. In her introduction to the International Suffrage Shop publication of the play, Nevinson warns, 'The shrewd and self-supporting younger generation hesitate before they accept wedlock on the present terms and endure the wrongs they have seen their mothers suffer' (p. 22). By dramatizing the abject destitution of the workhouse, a grim reality she was personally familiar with from her work as a Poor Law Guardian, Nevinson underscores the evils of existing marriage laws as destructive to the health and well-being of women and children.

Gertrude Vaughan's allegorical play *The Woman with the Pack* (1912), staged with help from Edith Craig, uses a combination of visionary tableaux interspersed with gritty realistic scenes to contrast present struggles with projected victories. The dual structure, which the *World* described as 'a delightful blend of stern fact and impressive fantasy' (quoted in Vaughan, p. 13), features a symbolic Woman and a real woman, Philippa Tempest. Philippa is an updated New Woman, a young Oxford student, prevented by gender from obtaining her degree as a lawyer, and worried about having to promise 'to obey' if she marries her fiancé, Hugh. Like Sarah Grand in *The Heavenly Twins*, Vaughan gives her heroine a twin brother as a way of contrasting the similarities in their abilities and inequities in their opportunities. In a unique act of brotherly solidarity Philippa's brother Dick refuses to take his law degree until Philippa can take hers. The Woman with the pack appears as a vision carrying a cross, a child and a lantern, patiently treading a path to emancipation. Holding her hand over Philippa's head, the Woman induces a vision that Philippa describes for the audience: 'women of the future, not slaves in thought, not weighed down by fear of the unknown, women free and strong and happy, with all the gates thrown open so that they may work unfettered' (p. 55). This future vision is contrasted with a scene of present misery as Philippa searches for her friend Fanchette in a destitute tenement and learns that she has been forced into prostitution. In the tenement she observes sweated child labourers in rags, one of whom is blind from malnourishment, making matchboxes with their mother. When their drunken father threatens his wife with violence, Philippa intervenes, but he asserts that it is his right by law to beat his wife (p. 59). From the street outside, Philippa hears newspaper boys shouting suffragette headlines and determines to join the crusade, proclaiming, 'I won't hesitate any longer! I see it all now. It's for this that women are fighting. This is why they go to prison!' (p. 71). She rushes out to join a march of women to Westminster.

The play closes on an exultant tableau of Philippa, now champion of the cause, dressed as Joan of Arc, holding a great banner as a chorus of children joyously sing and dance around her. In her notes on staging Vaughan is careful to specify that Philippa must not be associated with the stereotypic 'shrieking sisterhood', stressing that she 'must be played with great restraint. She must not be aggressive; even in her most revolutionary speeches she never loses her charm' (p. 92). The final tableau is less centred on women's rights for their own sakes than on the need for women to step in and act as protectors of vulnerable children. Former child labourers symbolically lay down their matchboxes and take up tambourines and cymbals to perform what the *Standard* called a 'Dance of the Innocents', circling around Philippa/Joan 'as though she were the Goddess of Joy' (Vaughan, 1912, p. 13). Though Philippa is at the centre of the final image, the presence of the children, along with Vaughan's insistence on the actress's feminine charm, invites conservative approval of the selflessness of motherhood.

Vera Wentworth's solemn play *An Allegory* was staged by prisoners in Holloway in March 1912, directed by Mrs. Pethick-Lawrence (Croft, 2009, p. 225). The central character, Woman, is depicted travelling the road to the City of Freedom in tattered garments with bleeding, dusty feet. She wears chains with an *'expression of pain and resignation'* (p. 3) and struggles behind while Man, *'tall and strong'* walks *'with firm step and uplifted head'* (p. 3). Woman encounters Fear and Prejudice, who both block her path, but with some help from Courage she overcomes them and breaks free of her chains. Continuing her journey, she meets an extravagantly dressed and coiffured Slave Woman, who is content to be shackled almost from head to foot with jewelled chains and derides her efforts to reach the City of Freedom. Rising above the Slave Woman's mocking laughter, Woman earnestly declares:

> All women's chains are not jewelled, sister. Some are chains of iron, which drag upon their limbs until they die, because they cannot bear their constant weight. I am in haste to reach my journey's end, that I may help them. (p. 11)

Like *The Woman with the Pack,* the play ends on the image of the progressive feminist woman as altruist rather than solipsist.

Another allegorical feminist play, Margaret Macnamara's *The Baby in the Ring* (1918) centres on child welfare and blends moments of social realism with elements of fantasy. A mother's baby is stolen by ten pixies who, in their indecision about whether or not to keep it, hear arguments from various advocates about what would be best for the child. 'Mother' argues that her baby should be returned to her. 'Matron' who is an agent for the new Institution of Applied Eugenics lays claim to the baby, arguing that her institution can provide superior resources: abundant food, first-class education, thorough discipline and the best medical attention. 'England' intervenes to help settle the baby's future and pointedly asks the Matron 'how much love?' (p. 41) her institution will provide. The Matron relinquishes her claim to the baby and instead decides to organize a School for Mothers as a more impactful strategy for improving society. England makes a rallying cry to mothers, telling them their love lacks strength without courage, and urging them to political action: 'Venture out of doors! Band yourselves together, "for home and country!" Rich mothers, stand by the poor!' (p. 44). One of the pixies concludes by remarking, 'There ought to be a School for Fathers, I should think' (p. 45) opening a rare window of critical questioning on the role of fatherhood.

* * *

Macnamara's play is rare in having been written after the outbreak of WWI, after which the suffrage campaign and suffrage theatre both ground to a virtual halt. After the war, parliament passed the Representation of the People Act 1918 abolishing property qualifications for men over 21 and franchising women over 30 who owned property or were graduates voting in a university constituency, opening voting to over eight million women. Ten years later, the Representation of the People (Equal Franchise) Act of 1928 gave British women electoral equality with men. Throughout the long campaigns, the issue of female suffrage was regarded by the majority of its supporters as one means, perhaps the most symbolically significant, of repairing the injustices and double standards inherent in the laws, practices, customs and attitudes of the established order as younger women at the turn of the century looked to new opportunities. It was not an isolated battle, but a field upon which many battles were fought. Unlike the more socially sensitive subjects of prostitution, conjugal rights, birth control, sexually transmitted diseases, sex education, the age of consent and abortion – all of which were of vital concern to early feminists – female suffrage was a debate which could be spoken of in polite society, making it a convergence point.

No theatre production could equal the drama of the hand-to-hand combat publicly fought between militant suffragettes and the politicians, police officers and prison guards of the British government. The most striking and original art to come out of the suffrage movement could be said to have come directly from the women themselves in the form of what we might call performance art[39] (though some have also called it terrorism). In *Spectacular Confessions* (1997) Barbara Green broadens the understanding of the performative nature of suffrage activism by treating hunger strikes, autobiographical texts and acts of civil disobedience alongside theatre performances. From the first women's march through London until the outbreak of war, women experimented with various performative protest techniques which included marching, chaining themselves to railings and carriages, breaking windows and addressing the Houses of Parliament from river launches. Suffrage drama contained to theatre buildings was, thus, frequently overshadowed by the urgent, daily public theatre of the movement itself. Sometimes even in theatres the drama didn't issue from the stage. During a performance of Henry Arthur Jones's *The Silver King*, attended by King George V, *The Suffragette* reported that 'the dramatic thrills of the play were as nothing compared to those roused by the living drama enacted before the eyes of that vast audience' as women stood and appealed directly to the king one by one before being dragged away. *The Suffragette* reporter ventured that 'no more moving and dramatic a scene has ever been witnessed on the stage' than the woman who managed to climb across the footlights and, with arms outstretched to the king, ask, 'why do you permit this torture of women fighting for their rights?' (29 May 1914). In even more sensational example of real-life drama within a theatre, in Dublin three suffragettes attempted to set fire to The Theatre Royal, protesting a visit from Prime Minister Asquith in 1912.

While often upstaged by suffrage civil disobedience, Suffrage theatre was invaluable in converting curious but undecided audience members to feminist ideologies and politically activating sympathizers. Edith Craig was convinced of the efficacy of her work as a theatre producer and director, asserting:

> I do think plays have done such a lot for the Suffrage. They got hold of nice frivolous people who would die sooner than go in cold blood to meetings. But they see the plays, and get interested, and then we can rope them in for meetings.
> (quoted in Carlson, 2000, p. 201)

The theatrical skills of women from the AFL and the WWSL were some of the most valuable assets in the suffrage movement for communicating its messages and shaping its public image. Suffrage drama also provided supporters with helpful models of how to present feminist arguments with dignity, eloquence and tactical comedy and helped feminists in its audiences anticipate what arguments to expect from the opposition and learn how to counter them. As carefully nonpartisan societies (not affiliated with the older NUWSS or the more radical WSPU) these arts-based suffrage organizations, particularly the Actresses' Franchise League, were powerful sites of coalition in an increasingly stressed and fractured movement. As self-supporting middle-class women at the heart of the nation's social, political and cultural life, artist-activists like Elizabeth Robins, Cicely Hamilton, Lena Ashwell and Lillah McCarthy became symbols of modern womanhood through the overlapping roles they enacted on stage and in the women's movement. In playing more varied and more nuanced parts than their melodramatic forerunners who were either 'too good or all bad' (Tilghman, 2011, p. 345) actresses in this generation embodied the complexity and the range of what modern women could be and do, on stage and off. The women's movement, in turn, inspired a new generation of artists to reimagine representations of women. The 'woman question' was a mainspring of realism as it developed in British theatre, from Pinero's fallen woman dramas to Robins's influential Ibsen productions with their complex female protagonists; from Hamilton's economically challenged romantic heroines to Hankin and Barker's unwed mothers; and from Lyttelton and Baker's working women to Robins's full-circle portrayal of a fallen woman turned suffrage leader. The political urgency of their work also spurred feminist writers to innovations in form, from political theatre,[40] agitprop, satire and journalistic theatre[41] to pageant and fantasy to early modernism, diversifying theatre practice in the wake of their political goals.

Cicely Hamilton, who was by temperament less zealous than many of her feminist contemporaries, captured the incredible fervour and excitement of this era in her happy observation, 'To no man, I think, can the world be quite as wonderful as it is to the woman now alive who has fought free' (MT, p. 33). Noting that old traditions and values had fallen away and new ones were not yet firmly set, Hamilton wrote of women, 'The world to her is in the experimental stage' (ibid.). Robins also recognized the immense formative possibilities of this transitional moment in women's history. Addressing the Women Writers' Suffrage League in

1911, she declared, 'you are in that position for which Chaucer has been so envied by his brother-poets, when they say he found the English language with the dew upon it' (WS, p. 236). Speaking specifically to her fellow women writers, Robins focused on representations of women (in both fiction and nonfiction), summoning her peers with the challenge, 'there she stands – the Real Girl! – waiting for you to do her justice' (WS, p. 236). Although Hamilton predicted that future generations of women would not treasure their freedoms as highly as women of her own, entering 'by right of birth upon what she attains by right of conquest' (MT, p. 33), Hamilton's voice and the voices of Robins and their peers still ring with possibility, inviting feminists today to engage with their past in the creation of a more equitable present and future. The greatest tribute we can give to our feminist forerunners is to acknowledge that gender equality around the globe is still very much in what Hamilton called the experimental stage and to keep passing the torch.

ENDNOTES

INTRODUCTION

1. William Archer, 'Ibsen and English Criticism' in the *Fortnightly Review* (1 July 1889), reprinted in Egan (1972, pp. 115–23).
2. Robins began her acting career in the United States, where she played with various American companies, including touring extensively with the matinee idol James O'Neill, who was later immortalized as James Tyrone by his son Eugene O'Neill in *A Long Day's Journey into Night*. She also toured with the renowned tragedian Edwin Booth (whose brother John Wilkes Booth assassinated President Lincoln).
3. Robins's friends Virginia and Leonard Woolf published *Ibsen & the Actress* through the Hogarth Press on the centenary of Ibsen's birth in 1928.
4. See Thomas F. Van Laan's 'Ibsen and Nietzsche' (2006) pp. 270–300 for detailed overview of links between Nietzsche's theories and Ibsen's protagonists.
5. See Bratton, 'Reading the Intertheatrical' (2000, p. 15) and *New Readings in Theatre History* (2003, pp. 37–38).
6. Florence Bell was born in 1851, Oscar Wilde in 1854, A.W. Pinero in 1855, William Archer, Dorothy Leighton and George Bernard Shaw in 1856, Margaret Nevinson in 1858, J.K. Jerome in 1859, J.M. Barrie and Annie Horniman in 1860, Gertrude Kingston and Elizabeth Robins in 1862, Clotilde Graves in 1863, Beatrice Harraden in 1864, Janet Achurch, Stella (Mrs Patrick) Campbell, Bessie Hatton, Edith Lyttleton and Netta Syrett in 1865, John Galsworthy in 1867, Edith Craig and St. John Hankin in 1869, Inez Bensusan and Christopher St. John in 1871, Lena Ashwell and Cicely Hamilton in 1872, Margaret Macnamara in 1874, Lillah McCarthy in 1875, Elizabeth Baker and Githa Sowerby in 1876, Harley Granville Barker in 1877 and Stanley Houghton in 1881.
7. Many women took leadership roles in the British anti-slavery movement, including Elizabeth Heyrick, Lucy Townsend, Anne Knight, Sophia Sturge and Jane Smeal. Women cemented the movement together through grass-roots

activism, from door-to-door canvassing to petitioning parliament and organizing and observing boycotts of sugar from plantations using slave labour. By 1831 there were 73 women's organizations across Britain campaigning against slavery. When slavery in the colonies was abolished in 1833, many women who had been prominent in the anti-slavery movement became active advocates of universal suffrage for men and women.

8. The Langham Place group was a feminist activist network named for the London address (19 Langham Place) of the offices of The *English Woman's Journal* (1858–64), a periodical edited, staffed and published by women, devoted to issues of gender equity in relation to British laws, education and employment. The group's work on the *Journal* helped to establish a political community of feminist readers (male and female). Education reformer Emily Davies was an influential member of the group, as were the sisters Elizabeth Garrett Anderson, the first woman in Britain to qualify as a doctor and surgeon, and Millicent Garrett Fawcett, who became the leader of the National Union of Women's Suffrage Societies. Bessie Rayner Parkes, Barbara Leigh Smith (later Bodichon), Emily Faithfull, Jessie Boucherett, Matilda Hays, Helen Blackburn and Lady Theodosia Monson were also prominent members.

9. While second-wave feminists are often criticized for being too caught up in middle-class white women's problems, many were deeply involved in the politics of other movements, advocating for Black, Chicanx, Indigenous, Asian and LGBTQ rights and protesting military invasions such as the Vietnam War and nuclear proliferation, most famously at the Greenham Common Women's Peace Camp in Berkshire, England.

10. Robins wrote the introduction to the Bath Classics edition of *Uncle Tom's Cabin* in 1909 (John, 1995, p. 225) during the suffrage years. After suffrage was granted she attempted a more sustained series of works highlighting issues of racial injustice, including in the introduction to *Ancilla's Share* (1924). See John, 1995, pp. 223–29 for an overview of some of Robins's publications on race.

11. See Anne McClintock's 1995 study *Imperial Leather: Race, Gender and Sexuality in the Colonial Contest* (especially pp. 43–53) for an analysis of a triangulated analogy among racial, class and gender degeneration in the late-Victorian era.

12. Women's suffrage was legislated in two phases: in 1918 voting rights were granted to women over the age of 30 who were householders, the wives of householders, occupiers of property with an annual rent of £5, and/or graduates of British universities (about 8.4 million women). In 1928 suffrage was extended to all women over the age of 21, granting women the vote on the same terms as men.

13. The abolition of slavery led to a steady decrease in black immigration during the nineteenth century, as did restrictions on African immigration in the

mid-century. Most of the black population of Britain were either soldiers or seamen, so the group was disproportionately male. Ethnicity-based demographics are not precise in this era, but from the information available, Black British comprised less than a thousandth of a per cent of the total population of the UK. Between 1800 and WWII the number of Irish immigrants outnumbered African immigrants by roughly 150 to 1, Jewish immigrants outnumbered African immigrants by 22 to 1; thus these groups were more frequently characterized as 'the other' than Asian, South Asian or African immigrants. See McCord (1991, pp. 433–36).

14. See Teresa Zackodnik's 'Ida B. Wells and "American Atrocities" in Britain' (2005) for an examination of Wells's lectures and their reception during her 1893 and 1894 anti-lynching tours of Great Britain.

15. Jad Adams, author of Oxford University Press's recent comparative study of suffrage campaigns in different countries, *Women and the Vote: A World History* (2014) has been interviewed about the paucity of evidence of Black British women involved in the British suffrage movement in comparison to other countries. See Radhika Sanghani, 'The Uncomfortable Truth about Racism and the Suffragettes.' *Daily Telegraph*, 6 October 2015.

16. Sophia Duleep Singh's father, Duleep Singh, was the last Maharaja of the Sikh Empire who abdicated to the British Raj and was exiled to England, where Sophia and her siblings were born and raised. In 1909 suffragists established a Tax Resistance League of which Sophia was a prominent, active member. She was taken to court for non-payment.

17. See Sumita Mukherjee's 'A Short Sketch of Indian Women's Franchise Work' (2002), and 'Herabai Tata and Sophia Duleep Singh: Suffragette Resistances for India and Britain 1910–1920' (2012).

18. Arthur Wing Pinero and Inez Bensusan were Jewish; George Bernard Shaw, Oscar Wilde, Margaret Macnamara and Clo Graves were Irish; and Edith Craig, Cicely Hamilton, Christopher St. John and Oscar Wilde were homosexual. See McClintock (1995, pp. 50–56) on atavistic 'races' within European race in this era.

19. See Chapter 1 of Bolt's *Victorian Attitudes to Race* (1971) and Lorimer's 'Race, Science and Culture: Historical Continuities and Discontinuities, 1850–1914' (1996), and 'Reconstructing Victorian Racial Discourse' (2003) for discussions on the subject.

20. Mary Higgs's *Glimpses into the Abyss* (1906), which describes living conditions in workhouses, researched in disguise as a tramp, is one of the most famous of these investigative accounts. When writing a novel about sex trafficking in 1912, Elizabeth Robins disguised herself as a Salvation Army worker to talk to prostitutes in Piccadilly in the middle of the night as part of her research. See Gates (1994, pp. 187–88) for a description of the episode.

1 THE ANGEL IN THE HOUSE AND THE FALLEN WOMAN

1. In *Women and Victorian Theatre,* Kerry Powell notes that in 'Warning her away from a part in *A Fair Bigamist,* Wilde killed her enthusiasm for a woman-centered play written by a woman playwright, a production of the kind that would become the mission of Robins's professional life' (1997, p. 150). See Powell's article 'Oscar Wilde, Elizabeth Robins, and the Theatre of the Future' (1994, pp. 220–37) for a detailed account of Wilde's contributions to and/or hindrance of Robins's early career.

2. By her own account Robins managed to get the part only because, like the character, she was a young American widow who dressed in mourning, commenting wryly 'even actors cannot believe there's such a thing as acting' (Robins, 1940, p. 193). Robins's husband of two years, George Parks, committed suicide in 1887; she wore full mourning for two years in line with the Victorian tradition for widows.

3. Robins pulled a gun on the publisher William Heinemann to try and put an end to his repeated proposals of marriage. She also pointed a gun at George Bernard Shaw when his flirting overstepped the mark, an incident that, to her annoyance, Shaw loved to recount.

4. Robins described unwanted and menacing sexual attention as quotidian for average women, not the result of an actress's beauty or allure, writing, 'What life was for the millions of infinitely better-looking young women, I don't pretend to know. I can only say: this is what it was like to the average. You were not safe even in St. Paul's Cathedral' (1940, p. 167).

5. Excepting Tennyson's *Idylls of the King, The Angel in the House* was the best-selling poem of the Victorian era.

6. The beginnings of a separate woman's sphere can be seen developing in the late eighteenth century with works such as James Fordyce's 1766 *Sermons to Young Women,* depicting women as robed in white, exerting spiritual influence over men, 'your highest glory is to conquer by benignity, and triumph by patience' (p. 233). John Gregory's sentimental work *A Father's Legacy to His Daughters* (originally published in 1774) shapes the idea of women as refining creatures who exist to soften the hearts and polish the manners of men. The influence is distinctly spiritual in nature: 'Every man who knows human nature, connects a religious taste in your sex with softness and sensibility of heart; at least we always consider the want of it as a proof of that hard and masculine spirit, which of all your faults we dislike the most' (1808, pp. 24–25).

7. See Herbert Spencer, 'Specialization and Division of Labour' (pp. 340–61) and 'A Society is an Organism' (pp. 449–62) in *A System of Synthetic Philosophy* Vol VI. (1896); and Davidoff (1983, p. 19).

8. See Sarah Ellis's book *The Women of England* (1872, p. 356) for a classic example. Ellis chastised women who sought activity beyond their proper

sphere of domestic influence as failing to recognize the magnitude of their mission.

9. Towards the end of the nineteenth century, women began to express increasing dissatisfaction with separate spheres ideology as a 'trick' or a 'cheat' that men were playing to keep the riches and pleasures of the material world for themselves. In 1869 the Liberal politician John Boyd-Kinnear linked women's growing dissatisfaction to the post-industrial economic decline in women's paid labour. He reasoned that the widespread national drop in women's employment and earnings in trades such as such as weaving, spinning and sewing had decreased women's status generally (pp. 334–35). Economically, the low status of women in the labour market enforced the low status of women's work in the home. Thus, while working-class women's wages dropped as a result of the industrial revolution and the value of middle-class women's work in the home dwindled correspondingly, middle-class men found themselves in a more prosperous, more powerful position than ever in an economic climate that increasingly valued men's work.

10. There is a wealth of feminist scholarship on separate spheres ideology. Students wishing to research this topic further might start with Elizabeth Langland's *Nobody's Angels: Middle-Class Women and Domestic Ideology in Victorian Culture* (1995); Amanda Vickery's 'Golden Age to Separate Spheres? A Review of the Categories and Chronology of English Women's History' (1993); and Janet Wolff's 'The Culture of Separate Spheres: The Role of Culture in Nineteenth-Century Public and Private Life' (1988).

11. See Dorice Elliott's *The Angel out of the House: Philanthropy and Gender in Nineteenth-Century England* (2002).

12. See Erika Diane Rappaport's *Shopping for Pleasure: Women in the Making of London's West End* (2000) for a detailed study of the impact of shopping on women's appropriation of the public sphere in this era.

13. Short for Mrs Patrick Campbell.

14. A real London apartment building that would have suggested the illicit sexual activities of wealthy men to a contemporary audience.

15. The *Illustrated Sporting and Dramatic News* commented 'one sees with astonishment young unmarried girls allowed to study openly the sordid details of the Tanqueray ménage. The moral of the piece is excellent no doubt; but it is surely one of those morals which are better enforced upon young people in private than in public' (3 June 1893).

16. The arrest was reported in 'Police' in *The Times*, 5 November 1895; Alexander's rebuttal 'The Charge Against Mr. George Alexander' was published in *The Times*, 6 November 1895.

17. By 1893 Robins was famous as an actress following the success of her performances as Hedda Gabler and Hilda Wangel, but the association limited her ability to get non-Ibsen roles. The keen intelligence Robins brought to her

Ibsen work wasn't a quality British authors and actor-managers sought in their leading ladies. Campbell, who praised Robins's performance as Hilda as 'the most intellectually comprehensive piece of work I had ever seen on the English stage' (c. 1925, p. 66) summarized the 'peculiar quality of Miss Elizabeth Robins' dramatic gift' as 'the swiftness with which she succeeded in sending thought across the footlights; emotion took a second place, personality a third' (p. 65). Though phrased as a compliment, Campbell puts her finger on a key reason why Robins's skills as an Ibsen actress weren't seen as being easily transferable to other women's roles in British theatre, which relied more heavily on personality and emotion.

18. Published under the pen name George Fleming.

19. 'As several critics have assumed that *Mrs Lessingham* must have been in some way inspired by *The Second Mrs Tanqueray*, I may mention that I read "George Fleming's" play three or four months before the production of Mr Pinero's, and that it had then, I understand, been in existence for at least a year' (TW94, p. 102).

20. This was not the first English play to draw on Hawthorne's book: there were at least three London stage adaptations of the story between 1876 and 1888, including one by Edward Aveling (published under the pen name Alec Nelson) in which Janet Achurch played Hester.

21. For a detailed account of Wilde's plays in relation to purity feminism, see Kerry Powell's *Acting Wilde: Victorian Sexuality, Theatre, and Oscar Wilde* (2009), Chapters 2 and 3.

22. The Ladies National Association for the Repeal of the Contagious Diseases Act, the first organization of its kind, was formed in 1869, led by Josephine Butler and Elizabeth Wolstenholme Elmy.

23. Butler makes this explicit in her publication, 'The Voice of One Crying in the Wilderness': 'Think of it as you will, the ordinance of medical examinations is a deed of moral shame. It is not applied to men. And why not? Because men would refuse to submit to it. But women have to submit. And why? Because they are defenseless' (1913, p. 137).

24. By using injections of nitrate silver to temporarily arrest secretions.

25. Butler compared doubting if fallen women could be 'reclaimed' to doubting that trees would regain their leaves in spring (in Jordan and Sharp, p. 121), expressing more cynicism on the subject of 'the reclaimability of profligate men' (p. 123).

26. Dr Elizabeth Blackwell expressed her professional medical opinion that prostitutes could be reformed only if caught early, before their natures had been transfigured. Unsubdued lust in both men and women, she wrote, 'injures health, produces disease, and grows into an irresistible tyrannical possession, which converts human beings into selfish, cruel and inhuman devils' (1902, p. 118).

27. Phossy jaw was a disfiguring and ultimately fatal form of bone cancer caused by working with the phosphorous used to make matches. In 1888 Annie Besant

wrote an indignant article titled 'White Slavery in London' in *The Link*, about the treatment of workers at the Bryant & May match factory in London, which triggered a strike of 1,400 of the factory women.

28. For a full account of Shaw thwarting Achurch (and female playwrights in general) see Kerry Powell's 'New Women, New Plays, and Shaw in the 1890s' (1998, p. 85) and D.A. Hadfield's 'Writing Women: Shaw and Feminism behind the Scenes' (2013, pp. 115–16).

29. See Showalter, *Sexual Anarchy: Gender and Culture at the Fin de Siècle* (1992, p. 4).

30. Interestingly, the 1975 production, staged at the height of second-wave feminism with Mia Farrow in the title role, received similar criticisms. *The Evening News* reported, 'The action begins and ends in the dark – which is where the audience remains for much of the two hours that intervene.' (19 September 1975).

31. The play received two performances by the Stage Society in January 1902 and was not published until a decade after it was written. Even then, in his book *Play-Making*, Archer questioned whether the play deserved to be published (1912/1960, p. 184).

32. This play made the name of Lena Ashwell (Mrs Dane), who went on to become a prominent actress-manager and suffrage campaigner.

33. In the prompt copy 'twelve' is crossed out, suggesting an even younger age.

34. Twelve has been crossed out, ten written in.

35. When Mrs Larne scorns Wilson's plea that she should raise Alice's baby, Nancy offers to adopt him, issuing Henry with the ultimatum that she won't marry him unless he agrees. Confusingly for Henry, no sooner has he agreed to the adoption than Nancy decides that the baby's mission is actually to *prevent* her from marrying him – instead of a wife, she will be an immaculate mother. Nancy suggests that Henry, who has stalled in his career as a painter, should paint her as the Madonna and Alice's baby as the Holy Child, enabling them to connect on the higher plane of artist and muse and recuperate his career. In the next act, while preparing for the Madonna and child *mise en scène*, Nancy exits briefly to gather a costume and while she is gone Alice emerges from a hiding place to steal her baby back. Alice is intercepted by Wilson who attempts to drag her away just as Nancy re-enters, dramatically dressed as the Madonna. The fallen woman and the 'Madonna' struggle over the child; the biological mother triumphs. Bereft of the baby, Nancy throws herself into Henry's arms as the curtain falls.

36. Though Houghton did not leave a written acknowledgement of his source material, he clearly drew from Elizabeth Gaskell's industrial novel *Mary Barton* (1848). See Thomas Recchio's 'Elizabeth Gaskell as "A Dramatic Common": Stanley Houghton's Appropriation of *Mary Barton* in *Hindle Wakes*' (2012).

37. In Britain, the same novel was published under the title '*Where are You Going to ... ?*'.

38. The concept of 'white slavery' was first connected to the migration and forced labour of Europeans (for instance Russian and Polish slaves in the Ottoman Empire) before it became associated with prostitution. The terms 'white slavery' or 'white slave trade' in reference to Victorian and Edwardian prostitution originated in the 1830s in Continental Europe, particularly France, where prostitution was state regulated, unlike in Britain. 'White slavery' was of particular concern in Britain from the 1870s onwards when pressure groups were formed to lobby for repeal of the CD Acts. The issue came to national prominence in 1885 when William T. Stead, working with purity feminist Josephine Butler, published 'The Maiden Tribute of Modern Babylon' in his newspaper, *The Pall Mall Gazette*, in July 1885, detailing his undercover purchase of a young girl. Britain's age of consent, 13 until 1885 as compared to 21 on the Continent, led to a fear that young British virgins were being abducted and trafficked to Europe as 'sex slaves'. The public's outraged reaction to Stead's account led directly to the Criminal Law Amendment Act of 1885. In *Prostitution and Victorian Society* Judith Walkowitz views the evidence of a white slave trade as thin and Stead's journalism as sensational. Stead, who died on the Titanic in 1912, was a friend and supporter of Robins. London hosted the Fifth International Congress for the Suppression of the White Slave Traffic in the year Robins's novel was published, 1913.

39. In 'The Maiden Tribute of Modern Babylon' Stead reported, 'It is easy enough to get into a brothel, it is by no means easy to get out. Apart from the dress houses, where women are practically prisoners, forbidden to cross the doorstep and chained to the house by debt, cases are constantly occurring in which girls find themselves under lock and key' (1885, p. 129).

40. The stage adaptation of *My Little Sister* has a circuitous, ill-fated history – see Katie N. Johnson's introduction to the play in *Sex for Sale: Six Progressive-Era Brothel Dramas* (2015, pp. 107–13). Initially Robins commissioned the well-known playwright, actress and fellow suffragist Cicely Hamilton to adapt the novel but, dissatisfied with the resulting script, Robins rewrote the play herself. Hamilton's adaptation adhered faithfully to the grim sacrificial ending of the novel while Robins's script ends happily with a rescue – a change she deemed necessary for getting the play produced. In a letter to the playwright J.K. Jerome, Robins explains that she tried but failed to convince Hamilton that the 'unrelieved horror of the novel would never be tolerated by an audience' (quoted in Johnson, 2015, p. 111) and so rewrote her version – apparently with Hamilton's permission. Strangely the two versions of the script ended up in competition with each other, complicating production terms until the Lord Chamberlain's office killed the matter by denying *My Little Sister* a licence a few days after Britain declared war on Germany.

41. See Joel Kaplan's 'Pineroticism and the problem play' (1992) for an account of Pinero and Campbell's artistic differences over interpreting his female leads.

Campbell's memoir, *My Life and Some Letters*, includes the actress's account of, where her interpretations and Pinero's were at odds in the rehearsal process for, *The Second Mrs Tanqueray* (c. 1925, pp. 66–90), as well as her account of their even greater differences over the part of Agnes Ebbsmith (pp. 98–100).

2 THE NEW WOMAN

1. Robins recounts that at Henry Irving's Lyceum, the young George Alexander gave 'a certain speech with such ability and power that those standing about, actors and onlookers, broke into applause. Irving listened and said drily: "Yes, you gave that very well, Mr. Alexander – we'll cut out that speech"' (1940, p. 86).
2. In 1891 Robins and Marion Lea formed a management partnership together to produce *Hedda Gabler*; in 1892 she and Lea produced Lady Florence Bell's *Karin* at the Vaudeville. In 1893 she and Bell co-authored *Alan's Wife*. In 1894 she was instrumental in getting Constance Fletcher's play *Mrs Lessingham* produced at the Garrick. Her final professional acting role was in Mrs Humphry Ward's play *Eleanor*. *Votes for Women!* was commissioned by actress manager Gertrude Kingston and during the suffrage campaign Robins was central in the Actresses' Franchise League and the Women Writers' Suffrage League.
3. In February and March of 1893 Robins co-produced *The Master Builder* at the Trafalgar Square and the Vaudeville theatres with Herbert Waring, who played Solness to Robins's Hilda. *Hedda Gabler* was revived in May and June of 1893 at the Opera Comique, co-directed by Robins and Archer with Lewis Waller as Lövborg. In May and June of the same year, Robins also co-directed *Rosmersholm*, starring as Rebecca West. She also revived and co-directed *The Master Builder* in June. In 1894 Robins toured regionally as Hedda Gabler and Hilde Wangel under the auspices of the Manchester Independent Theatre Company. In 1896 she produced and co-directed *Little Eyolf* at the Avenue Theatre, featuring Janet Achurch as Rita (later replaced by Stella Campbell) and taking the smaller role of Asta for herself. In 1897 she co-directed *John Gabriel Borkman*, playing Ella Rentheim.
4. Robins's struggle to obtain the rights for *Hedda Gabler* first brought her into contact with Archer. In her unpublished memoir 'Whither and How', Robins wrote that her work with him on the translation, clandestinely retranslated from a poor version by Edmund Gosse, involved 'an amount of secret diplomacy worthy of a major political crisis' (Robins, 1940, p. 130).
5. Katherine Newey points out that though Gosse, Archer and Shaw are largely credited with the introduction of Ibsen into English, it was women writers like Elizabeth Robins, Florence Bell, Catherine Ray, Henrietta Lord and Eleanor Marx 'who were active in making early English translations of Ibsen's plays, and

doggedly promoting Ibsen as a playwright of great importance for contemporary theatre' (2006, p. 38).

6. Performances were paid for by private subscription rather than public ticketing, a common practice in producing progressive works that avoided censorship.

7. Neither did the scripts chosen by actor-managers align well with Robins's interests – she also turned down parts she deemed vacuous.

8. As a single woman living alone and all too aware of the precarity of actresses' reputations, Robins took great care to safeguard her privacy (including destroying almost all of her correspondence with Archer), leaving her friends and biographers to speculate as to the exact details of her relationship with Archer, which may or may not have been sexual.

9. Robins took pains to keep her acting and writing careers separate, publishing her early novels – *George Mandeville's Husband* (1894), *The New Moon* (1895) and *The Open Question* (1898) – under the male pseudonym C.E. Raimond.

10. 'The New Aspect of the Woman Question' (*North American Review*, 158: pp. 270–76).

11. Women's undergarments – which, for the middle classes, had included tight laced corsets, stiff or structured crinolines, bustles and padded busts, all of which severely restricted movement – were subjects of concern and reform.

12. Also 'Bicyleus' (p. 9) and 'Biscillus' (p. 14).

13. See Conolly's introduction to the Broadview edition (2015, pp. 26–27) for multiple sources, several of them Shaw himself.

14. In *Immaturity* (1879) Harriet Russell succeeds as a businesswoman; in *The Irrational Knot* (1880) Susanna Connolly enters a free love union and has a child; in *Love Among the Artists* (1881) Letitia Cairns, a college graduate, is a suffrage supporter; Lydia Carew in *Cashel Byron's Profession* (1882) is an educated woman who manages the family estate; and Agatha Wylie embraces the personal freedom of 'unwomanly' behaviour in *An Unsocial Socialist* (1883).

15. In an article titled 'The Science of the Drama' published in *New Review*, Sidney Grundy argued against the ideas of the New Dramatists who he said 'contend that the drama ought to be the study of human nature on the stage, the analysis of character pure and simple – no "plot", there is none in nature – no "situations", they are artificial – no "pictures", they are childish – no "points", they are theatrical. They do not want a story; an episode is sufficient' (5(26), July 1895, p. 89).

16. Margaret D. Stetz has pointed out that 'British audiences were trained to anticipate that satires of the New Woman would skewer Wilde as well, and would treat him as a fellow traveller in feminist circles' (2013, p. 232).

17. 'Mr Grundy does the "new woman" cruel injustice – she can smoke half a cigarette without being sick, and she would divine by the mere light of nature, even without the aid of observation, that the gilt tip was designed for the mouth and not for the match' (TW94, p. 231).

18. *The World* (27 March 1895).
19. Originating from the Greek word for uterus, hysteria was widely patholo-gized in the nineteenth century as a particularly female neurotic condition characterized by ungovernable emotions which could cause a slew of psycho-somatic disorders from verbal outbursts to physical convulsions. The term was in such common parlance in the male-dominated world of medical practice that although Krafft-Ebing references 'hysteria' dozens of times in *Psychopathia Sexualis* he never once in this 500-page book feels the need to define it.
20. *The Sketch* published a compendium of positive and negative responses from Scott, Archer, Shaw and A.B. Walkley: Scott hailed it as 'unquestionably the masterpiece' of Pinero; Archer approved it as 'a great advance on *The Second Mrs Tanqueray*' in its examination of the institution of marriage; while Walkley found the play irritating, the Bible episode 'cheap' and complained that the 'woman's inner struggle is robbed of half its legitimate interest by the fact that the man is made so miserable a weakling' (27 March 1895).
21. Pamela's expressions of purity feminism are muddled in comparison to Grand's heroine's articulations of feminist philosophy. Evande passionately calls on women to stop debasing themselves and men by perpetuating the double standard – 'Instead of punishing them for their depravity, you encourage them in it by overlooking it' (p. 80) – and emphasizes a mother's duty to her future children not to pass on sexually transmitted diseases: 'you must know that there is no past in the matter of vice. The consequences become hereditary, and continue from generation to generation' (p. 80).
22. Sally Ledger notes that Hugh and Thyrza's friendship is radical 'in its explora-tion of the possibility of a new kind of relationship between man and woman, based on friendship and trust as well as sexual love' (2006, p. 56).
23. The Schools Inquiry Commission Report (1867–68) reprinted in Beale (1870, p. 8).
24. Davies devoted 50 years to work on the reform of women's education. In a historically pivotal move, she convinced the Taunton Commission to include an inquiry into girls' education in their 1868 report on British education. Davies trained girls to take local examinations as an inroad to higher edu-cation, and eventually co-founded and served as the first mistress of Girton College, Cambridge.
25. Fawcett was the daughter of suffragist Millicent Garrett Fawcett.
26. In 1887 Agnata Ramsay made national headlines when she stood alone in the first division of the first class of the Classics Tripos, which raised the same issue.
27. Under the pen name Alec Nelson.
28. See Bennett, 'Hygiene in the Higher Education of Women' (1888, pp. 519–30), Sprague, 'Education and Race Suicide' (1915, pp. 158–62), Maudsley, 'Sex in Mind and Education' (1874b, pp. 466–77) and Campbell, *Differences in the Nervous Organisation of Man and Woman* (1891).

29. See Clarke, *Sex in Education* (1873) and Sprague, 'Education and Race Suicide' (1915, pp. 158–62).
30. See the introduction to *Sexual Inversion,* SPSII.
31. Ellis discusses this at length in *Sexual Inversion* (SPSII) in Chapter IV, 'Sexual Inversion in Women'.
32. Ellis regarded his wife Edith as a 'congenital invert' upon whose experiences he based some of his writings.
33. In Ellis's Appendix B to *Studies in the Psychology of Sex: Sexual Inversion,* 'The School-Friendships of Girls', he writes, 'While there is an unquestionable sexual element in the "flame" relationship, this cannot be regarded as an absolute expression of real congenital perversion of the sex-instinct. The frequency of the phenomena, as well as the fact that, on leaving college to enter social life, the girl usually ceases to feel these emotions, are sufficient to show the absence of congenital abnormality' (SPSII, pp. 249–50).
34. Edith Nesbit was a prolific writer and founding member of the Fabian Society, most remembered for her children's book *The Railway Children* (1906).
35. In England, the term 'bluestocking' for an intellectual woman comes from the eighteenth-century Blue Stockings Society led by the wealthy widow Elizabeth Montague. In the Victorian era 'bluestocking' was more often used as a derogatory slur.
36. Eleanor Sidgwick's brother Arthur Balfour was a Conservative Party MP who served as prime minister from 1902 to 1905.
37. Founded in 1884, the Fabian Society is a left-wing political think tank promoting the socially democratic values of greater equality of power, wealth and opportunity through collective action, public service and active democracy. The London School of Economics and Political Science was founded in 1895 by four Fabians including Shaw.
38. Like Fanny's play, Shaw's play was presented anonymously, causing speculation over the authorship. Shaw's play, which opened at the Little Theatre at the Adelphi, was identified correctly as his work by the critics he caricatured: 'Trotter' is A.B. Walkley, 'Gunn' is Gilbert Cannan and 'Vaughan' is E.A. Baughan.
39. This figure is more than triple the number of women working in the second most common trade for women, the clothing industry, as well as nearly triple the number of men engaged in domestic work (Davis, 1991, pp. 368–69).
40. Sally Mitchell points out that the most profound change was in attitude, not in real numbers, as three-quarters of all unmarried women in England over the age of 14 had been in the labour market ever since the census began recording statistics in 1801 (1995, p. 24).
41. The ratio of female to male clerks, which was 7.8 per cent in 1891, and 18.1 per cent in 1901, rose to 32.5 per cent in 1911. Census of 1911, available at www.visionofbritain.org.uk. Accessed 21 August 2015.

42. Photograph of Lillah McCarthy as Kate and Cicely Hamilton as Lady Sims in a scene from a production of *The Twelve-Pound Look*, at the Little Theatre, 3 October 1911. V&A Theatre and Performance Archive. Museum number: S.3587-2015.

43. Until 1857 England was the only Protestant European country to retain the Catholic prohibition against all divorce. In 1910 England granted 494 divorces, compared with 8,220 in France and 83,045 in America (Harris, 1996, pp. 17–18).

44. A deserted spouse had to wait 25 years before they could apply for a divorce. A man could obtain a divorce if he could prove that his wife had been adulterous, but it was almost impossible for a woman to divorce her husband. Wives were required by law to prove their husband guilty of adultery plus one additional legal cause – desertion for two years or more, cruelty, bigamy, bestiality or adulterous sodomy. Many of the letters from women addressed to the *Daily Telegraph* in answer to 'Is Marriage a Failure?' spoke of the difficulty of obtaining a divorce as a chief cause of misery.

45. In 'Laws Concerning Women' (1854), Barbara Bodichon cites the expenses of a common divorce bill as 'between six hundred and seven hundred pounds, which makes the possibility of release from the matrimonial bond a privilege of the rich' (p. 28).

46. The solicitors representing the Crown in divorce cases.

47. Lady Colin Campbell was famous for having obtained a judicial separation from her aristocratic husband in a sensational series of court actions, making her a shrewd and perhaps wary judge of public opinion. She apparently advised Shaw that audiences would not accept the last act as written (Holroyd, 1988, p. 286). The story of Campbell's influence is widely told and accepted, but not universally regarded as the sole or chief reason for Shaw's rewrite. See L.W. Conolly's introduction to the 2015 Broadview edition of *The Philanderer*, pp. 29–31, for a summary of dissenting views.

48. Holcombe notes a 56 per cent increase in the number of shops from 295,000 in 1875 to nearly 459,592 in 1907 (1973, p. 105).

49. See Holcombe (1973, p. 103) for details on *The English Woman's Journal's* prominent campaign for saleswomen in ladies' shops.

50. Bensusan was an actress who oversaw the writing, collection and publication of suffrage plays for the Actresses' Franchise League.

51. Through personal persistence, study of government Blue Books on health care, an intense correspondence campaign and the adroit use of her powerful aristocratic family's political and social connections, Nightingale secured the first government-appointed nursing position, overseer of nursing to the British Army in the Crimean War. Her work in the Crimea earned her national respect and she was afterwards able to organize the Royal Commission to reform health care in the British Army. By 1895 the huge sum of £45,000

(a value of several million today) had been collected by subscription in honour of Nightingale to run a nurses' training institution at St Thomas's Hospital in London. The graduates would be known as 'Nightingale Nurses' and would become the most sought after in the country.

52. Margaret Leask notes that *The Earth* 'portrayed on stage for the first time the duel between the press and politics' (2012, p. 85) and that the Kingsway programme 'carried a Votes for Women advertisement promoting the Royal Albert Hall public meeting on 29 April, organised by the Women's Social and Political Union' (p. 88).

3   ODD WOMEN

1. In a letter to Florence Bell, Robins wrote 'The interest of ten years is ended […] it's as tho' in the loosening of that mind from its moorings one kept seeing swept by on the floor marred pieces of mighty work done in days of vigor – wreckage on a giant scale' (12 December 1899) in Gates (1994, p. 112). In her fraternal memoir *Raymond and I*, Robins reflected that Ibsen helped her break away from London at this time: 'Always before, he had been one of the strong bonds that held me to London. Now he was helping me to break away' (1956, p. 47).

2. See John (1995, p. 84).

3. Robins's biographers Angela John and Joanne E. Gates do not interpret Robins's long relationship with Wilberforce as a romantic partnership. Cicely Hamilton's biographer Liz Whitelaw argues that the possibility shouldn't be foreclosed on and cites Robins and Wilberforce's surviving correspondence as possible evidence of a hidden relationship, noting that they took care to excise the beginnings and endings of their letters, 'precisely the place where one would expect to find endearments' (1990, p. 114). Writing on Wilberforce, Christine Etherington-Wright interprets her close 'special friendship' with Robins as implying 'homosexual tendencies' (2009, p. 51). Whatever the terms of the Robins–Wilberforce partnership, Jane Marcus puts her finger on the point that is most central to the student of first-wave feminist history when she says of Robins, 'her capacity for intense bonds of friendship and love with other women was extraordinary' (1980, p. vii).

4. Caroline Norton found herself at the centre of two major mid-century reforms, through dealing with her own deeply troubled marriage to George Norton and her unsuccessful petition for a divorce. Caroline left her husband in 1836 primarily because of his physical violence to her. George Norton sued the Whig Prime Minister Lord Melbourne for ten thousand pounds for 'criminal conversation' (sexual relations) with his wife in a notorious case that nearly brought down the government. As a feme-covert, Caroline was not allowed to speak in court to defend her reputation. Caroline was refused a divorce and

when the couple separated she was also refused custody of and visitation rights to her three sons, one of whom died, arguably as a result of neglect, while in his father's care. The case was considered extraordinary in its day and was debated at length in newspapers, but similar situations involving less highly placed members of society were commonplace under English law.

5. St. George's Hall, London.

6. Barker's 1909 copy of *The Madras House* with autoscript revisions, HRC (p. 144).

7. Built to house the Great Exhibition of 1851, and using the recent invention of cast plate glass, the 990,000 square foot transparent construction contained the largest amount of glass ever seen in a building. Briggs describes the Crystal Palace as a symbol of the age which 'suggested at the same time both fairy tale and success story' (1965/1990, p. 45) in the human ingenuity behind the surface glitter.

8. The Men and Women's Club was a radical discussion group dedicated to progressive analyses of heterosexuality including considerations of male and female sexuality, marriage and prostitution. The group, founded by Karl Pearson, met from 1885 to 1889.

9. 'The Glorified Spinster'. *Macmillan's Magazine* 58 (1888): pp. 371–76.

10. Ibid, p. 372.

11. Feminist legal reformers like Josephine Butler were particularly concerned over the legal definition of rape as carnal knowledge by a man against the will of a woman *who was not his wife*. (The word 'rape' was not in common parlance in this era. Acts we would define as rape today could be called anything from a 'seduction' to an 'outrage' in the Victorian era. I use the commonly understood word 'rape' here for clarity about the explicit sexual violence being referred to, which Victorian language might obscure.) Marital rape could not exist under such a definition and conjugal rights were absolute. There was no humanity, women argued, in a construction of marriage that required women to relinquish all rights over their own bodies. The situation was redressed to a limited extent in 1884 when parliament repealed the law that had allowed men to have their wives jailed for refusing sex. A further blow, however, was struck against married women's legal standing in the Regina versus Clarence ruling (1889) which established that a man could not be found guilty of actual bodily harm or grievous bodily harm of his wife or unborn child even if he knowingly infected them with a sexually transmitted disease (in this case gonorrhoea) and that a wife could not refuse intercourse with her husband, even to protect herself or her baby from infection. Conjugal rights, then, were unassailable in Victorian Britain, though there was a modicum of progress in 1891 when the case of Queen versus Jackson set a new precedent that men could no longer imprison wives within the home in order to enforce a restitution of conjugal rights.

12. Mary Gaunt titled her travel book *Alone in West Africa* (1911); Etta Close called hers *A Woman Alone in Kenya, Uganda and the Belgian Congo* (1924). Ella Christine's book begins with the poem 'Down to Gehenna or up to the throne, / He travels the fastest who travels alone,' (quoted in Birkett, 1991, p. 64) and Florence Bell's stepdaughter Gertrude Bell wrote, 'I had a great desire to ride alone' (quoted in Birkett, 1991, p. 64).

13. Florence Bell's stepdaughter Gertrude Bell was a remarkable spinster traveller who also worked as a spy, political advisor and official in Greater Syria, Mesopotamia, Asia Minor and Arabia and was a key player, along with T.E. Lawrence ('Lawrence of Arabia'), in establishing the Hashemite dynasties in Jordan and Iraq. Between the wars Cicely Hamilton wrote a series of nine books based on her extensive travels. Elizabeth Robins chose the page over the stage to recount some of her own extraordinary travelling experiences including *The Magnetic North* and *Under the Southern Cross* (1907), a fictionalized account of Robins's sea voyage from San Francisco to New York via the Panama Canal. (Robins took this journey in 1888 at the end of her cross-country tour with Edwin Booth.)

14. Watson points out that Lina Szczepanowska is modelled to some extent on the French artist and writer Marie Bashkirtseff whom Shaw admired (1964, p. 159).

15. Mary Corelli was the most widely read author of the nineteenth century. In the last 20 years of her life she shared Mason Croft House (now the Shakespeare Institute) in Stratford-upon-Avon with Bertha Vyver. Their initials were proudly entwined together over the fireplace in the main hall, dating their residency as beginning prior to the increasingly homophobic atmosphere of the twentieth century.

16. Hall's 1928 novel *The Well of Loneliness* was tried for obscenity in Britain and convicted because of the line 'and that night, they were not divided', the only reference to sex between women in the book.

17. According to Martin Pugh's account of the diary of Mary Blathwayt in his book *The Pankhursts* (2001, pp. 211–12), several Women's Social and Political Union members were involved in romantic and/or sexual affairs with each other. June Purvis has disputed Pugh's reading as too speculative to be conclusive (*Times Higher Education*, 25 January 2002).

18. Local Government Act 1988 (c. 9), section 28 available at opsi.gov.uk. Accessed 26 July 2015.

19. Portraits of Hamilton and St. John in costume as Davies and Snell were included in an exhibition of portraits by Lena Connell at the Royal Photographic Society in 1910 and 1911, alongside other women in their costumes from A Pageant of Great Women. The photographs can be viewed in the online digitized version of the 1910 Suffrage Shop publication of the script, available at: https://archive.org/details/apageantgreatwo00hamigoog – Eva Balfour as Sappho (p. 29), Hamilton as Davies (p. 41) and St. John as Snell (p. 43). Accessed 14 April 2016.

4 MOTHERHOOD: THE DOUBLE BIND

1. Parks's suicide is more often and more convincingly explained by his possessive, unstable nature and his jealousy over Robins's more successful acting career – a career she refused to give up when she married him, despite his frequent urging. In an act that seemed modelled on the melodrama he struggled to get parts in, Parks wrote to Robins, 'I will not stand in your light any longer' (John, 1995, p. 39) before weighting himself with a suit of stage armour, jumping into the Charles River and drowning. See John (p. 41) and Gates (1994, p. 21) on possible pregnancy, miscarriage or quarrels over having children.

2. Despite – or perhaps because of – the dark themes of incest, joint suicide and atheism, the novel was a critical and popular success which went into its third edition within months of publication and sold roughly 50,000 copies in England and 20,000 in America. Mark Twain praised the book and Shaw called her 'the American George Eliot' (John, 1995, p. 120).

3. Robins's interest in this topic stemmed in part from the controversy of her parents' marriage. Like the characters Val and Ethan, her parents were first cousins, married at a time when many States in the US began outlawing marriage between first cousins on genetic grounds.

4. In 1907 Robins took a lease on a house in the country with the art critic Flora Simmonds and her 9-year-old ward David Scott. Robins was aware of rumours that she was David's mother (he was probably Flora's son) but didn't let that deter her from the alternative household arrangement. In 1909 Flora moved to Sweden, but Robins continued to raise David, later with Octavia Wilberforce. Robins became David's legal guardian in 1913. Contemporaries like H.G. Wells were convinced that David was Robins's secret illegitimate child, a frustrating problem encountered by other prominent actresses who didn't have biological children. In her memoir Lena Ashwell, who adopted a ward, wrote of people's reluctance to take the adoption at face value, preferring to believe that Ashwell was the biological mother: 'Without a doubt the child was mine and I was ashamed to own her! Even some who knew me well were convinced that I was concealing the facts' (1936, p. 133).

5. See Ellis: Chapter IV 'The Pelvis' and Chapter V 'The Head' in *Man and Woman: A Study of Human Secondary Sexual Characteristics* (1894/1934).

6. See Showalter, Chapter 8 in *Sexual Anarchy* (1992), and Jordanova, Chapter 5 in *Sexual Visions* (1989) for discussions of *Nature Unveiling Herself Before Science* (1899), a statue by Louis-Ernest Barrias in which 'Nature', personified as a woman, unveils her face and breasts before the male gaze of 'Science'.

7. See Bland, Chapter 6, 'Eugenics, the Politics of Selective Breeding and Feminist Appropriation' in *Banishing the Beast* (1995); and Szreter, Chapter 4, 'Class inequalities and environmentalism' in *Fertility, Class and Gender in Britain, 1860–1940* (1996) for in-depth discussions of the impact of eugenics on intellectual culture and thought.

8. See Forman's 'Race and Empire' (2006) for an overview of interconnections between race, ethnicity, empire and sexuality.

9. See Chapter 1 of Bolt's *Victorian Attitudes to Race* (1971) and Lorimer's 'Race, Science and Culture: Historical Continuities and Discontinuities, 1850–1914' (1996) and 'Reconstructing Victorian Racial Discourse' (2003) for discussions on the subject.

10. See Stepan's Chapter 5 on 'Eugenics and Race, 1900–25'. Stepan notes that London was the exception to this and some comparative studies of Jewish and Gentile schoolchildren were conducted, though she also points out that British eugenists 'were rarely anti-Semitic' (1982, p. 126).

11. The Swedish author Ellen Key wrote from a similar 'Eugenic Feminist' perspective, urging motherhood as women's national duty. Few of her works were translated into English, however, and so her British readership consisted primarily of eugenic medical writers like Saleeby, Ellis and Bloch who could read her books in German and quote her in their own books.

12. A purity feminist, Swiney used the hieroglyphic symbol as emblematic of a self-contained, self-procreative power, unpolluted by men.

13. The human will to live despite the horrendous reality of the world.

14. In Nietzsche, Zarathustra's dictum is 'Let your hope be, "May I bear the Superman"' (1969, p. 92).

15. In the same year Shaw wrote *Man and Superman*, the American biologist Lester Ward published *Pure Sociology*, advancing a 'gynaecocentric theory' of life, which posited femaleness as primal and indispensable, while maleness was simply an offshoot, developed to create greater genetic variation within a species, which had 'blossomed out in an unnatural, fantastic way, cutting loose from the real business of life and attracting a share of attention wholly disproportionate to its real importance' (1903, p. 331). Frances Swiney, a subscriber to Ward's gynaecocentric theories, predicted that men, having served their purpose of providing the species with greater variation, would disappear from the race completely, 're-absorbed into the feminine nature by a gradual and persistent transmutation of the many to the one; an integrating synthetic determination of mankind to one ideal standard of perfectibility' (1905, p. 454).

16. *George Mandeville's Husband.*

17. *The Daughters of Danaus.*

18. Written in the form of an epistle dedicatory to the critic A.B. Walkley.

19. Second-rate composers in Shaw's view.

20. In *Shaw's Daughters*, for example, J. Ellen Gainor proposes that Shaw exemplifies some of the inherent contradictions in attitudes toward women generally, but argues that 'although the surface sense or initial impact of these presentations might appear progressive and supportive, deeper analysis and more thorough investigation reveals latent prejudice, regressive values, and even hostility' (1991, p. 243). In *Theatre and Evolution from Ibsen to Beckett*, Kirsten Shepherd-Barr asks 'What should be the final verdict, then, on Shaw's

engagement with evolution?' and answers, 'The fact that we are still so divided over him – feminist or misogynist? theatrically innovative or hopelessly unplayable? backward looking or visionary? – indicates his ongoing vitality and relevance' (2015, p. 144).

21. In *The Daughters of Danaus*, Mona Caird's heroine Hadria remarks sarcastically on the supposed power of a marriage ceremony to ignite a hitherto dormant sex drive and maternal instinct: 'So we are all to be horribly shocked at the presence of an instinct to-day, and then equally shocked and indignant at its absence to-morrow; our sentiment being determined by the performance or otherwise of the ceremony we have just witnessed. It really shows a touching confidence in the swift adaptability of the woman's sentimental organisation!' (1894, p. 255).

22. Shepherd-Barr points out that despite giving many examples of female agency in the animal world, Darwin 'does not make the imaginative leap' (2015, p. 95) to recognize female human agency.

23. For Wiley, Robins/Jean is 'killing the Victorian cult of maternal idolatry along with the baby' (1990, p. 445); for Diamond 'Jean destroys not only the crippled infant, but the Victorian angel-mother' (1997, p. 36).

24. Lady Florence Bell's husband, Sir Hugh Bell, was director of the Bell Brothers steelworks at Middlesbrough, as well as serving three times as mayor of the town. Bell split her time between London and the family estate at Rounton Grange in North Yorkshire where Elizabeth Robins was a frequent house guest.

25. In *The Way the Money Goes* (1910), a play dealing with gambling addiction among working-class women in the North of England, Bell portrays what might at first glance seem like maternal callousness, but is actually the grim reality of infant mortality among the poor, where mothers commonly insure their children so as to be able to afford their burials. A woman says sympathetically to a grieving mother, 'And she wasn't insured either, was she,' to which the mother replies, 'No, she wasn't, and we had to pawn the clock to put her away' (p. 11).

26. See Joanna Townsend 'Elizabeth Robins: Hysteria, Politics and Performance' and Diamond *Unmaking Mimesis* (1997, pp. 37–39) for detailed analysis of Jean's silence.

27. Grein famously promoted the Independent Theatre's production of *Ghosts* at the Royalty Theatre in March 1891.

28. Carol Hanbery MacKay argues that, rather the hallucination being particular to this play or this scene, Robins's theatrical performances 'sought to induce in members of the audiences a dissolution of inner boundaries. At its most intense, this process might result in the experience of synaesthesia or of perceptual delusion' (2001, p. 139).

29. While he hides her authorship and claims that the play was his idea, Archer admits in his introduction that Robins was the one who found the original story, *Befriad*, in a Swedish magazine, *Ur Dagens Krönika*, and took an interest in it.

30. Powell notes that Shaw also 'rewrote' *Alan's Wife* along similar lines in a letter to Archer, 'purg[ing] it of what were to his mind the emotional excesses associated with sensational woman novelists and popular melodrama' (Powell, 1998, p. 85).

31. Sylvia Pankhurst had an ongoing affair with Keir Hardie, co-founder of the Independent Labour Party, until his death in 1915. Later Sylvia lived with the Italian revolutionary Silvio Corio, with whom she had a son. Sylvia refused, even after the birth of her son, to marry and take a man's name; her mother Emmeline never spoke to her again.

32. Thomas Malthus's 'Essay on the Principle of Population' (1798) suggested 'preventive checks' to stop the reckless over-breeding of the poor. Ironically, Malthus himself was staunchly against contraception, instead advocating deferred marriage and 'moral restraint'.

33. Thomas Robert Malthus (1766–1833) was an economist whose pessimistic works on population growth were still highly influential in the Victorian and Edwardian eras. Malthus argued that times of abundance resulted in population growth which in turn led to scarcity, resulting in hardship and suffering in the lower classes – sometimes famine – perpetuating cycles of poverty sometimes known as the 'Malthusian trap' or the 'Malthusian spectre'. These cycles, he reasoned, kept civilizations from advancing to more utopian states. He was an advocate of moral restraint in matters of sex and material consumption.

34. American Charles Knowlton was the first known English-speaking doctor to publish contraceptive advice in 1832. He received a punitive sentence of three months' hard labour, but his book became a bestseller in the US, despite vigorous government attempts to keep it from circulating.

35. Named for Aletta Jacobs, the Dutch doctor who invented it in 1883, the 'Dutch cap' was a vulcanised rubber cap with an integral circular watchspring that covered the upper vagina and cervix.

36. Like Malthus, Neo-Malthusians believed that the population needed to be kept in check in order to prevent catastrophes like destitution, famine and war. The principle difference was that Malthus, who was a clergyman, equated 'birth control' with abstinence and restraint, while Neo-Malthusians of the late nineteenth and twentieth centuries advocated for contraceptives.

37. Though Holroyd notes that Shaw used them himself on at least one occasion (1988, p. 161).

38. Dennis Kennedy has also persuasively suggested that the ban may, in fact, have had more to do with Barker's cynical representation of politics than the centrality of abortion in the play; see *Granville Barker and the Dream of Theatre* (pp. 91–98) for a detailed account of Barker and the campaign against censorship.

39. Infuriated by the censorship of *Waste* and Edward Garnett's play *The Breaking Point*, 71 prominent authors from the literary community, among them J.M. Barrie, John Galsworthy, Thomas Hardy, Henry James, Arthur Pinero and George Bernard Shaw, took up their pens in protest over the censorship

of British drama, triggering an investigation of censorship by parliamentary committee in 1909.

40. After the legendary success of the Vedrenne-Barker seasons at the Royal Court from 1904 to 1907, leasing the Savoy was an attempt to take Barker's visionary brand of theatre, featuring modern directing and new plays, out of the suburbs of Chelsea and into the commercial West End.

41. Another terrible blow for Barker came when Lena Ashwell, who had Barker's lead actor Norman McKinnel (Trebell) under contract at the Kingsway, forced him to withdraw from performances just before the opening, not wanting her actor to risk association with a banned play. Barker, who was too young and slight for the part, had to step in and play Trebell at the last minute.

42. Cary M. Mazer has pointed out that when Barker returned to revise and in some places substantially rewrite his Edwardian plays in the mid-1920s, the pre-suicide conversation between Trebell and his spinster sister Frances received the most rewriting (p. 77). In the revised passage, Trebell uses language that sounds more feminine/maternal than political to describe his feelings about his intimate connection to the aborted bill: 'I'd never given myself away before. It's a dreadful joy to do that ... to become part of a purpose bigger than your own. Another strength is added to your own ... it's a mystery.' (1919, p. 105) In a final bleak realization, Trebell explains, 'But it follows, you see, that having lost myself in the thing ... the loss of it leaves me a dead man.' (1919, p. 105)

43. In *The Turn of the Wheel* (1901) Blanche Crackenthorpe depicts an unwed mother, Isabel Broadwood, who rejects her newborn, saying, 'I don't even care enough for it to hate it. Let it live, let it die, what does it signify to me? It's not me – it's not part of me, I tell you – I've done with it' (quoted in Powell, 1997, p. 138), a sentiment so hideous to the Lord Chamberlain that the play was refused a licence, even though Isabel does experience a change of heart by the end of the play.

5   VOTES FOR WOMEN!

1. WA to ER, 5 August 1908. HRC: Robins Box 1, Folder 4.

2. Having never fully recovered from the typhoid fever that nearly killed her in 1900, Robins had serious medical reasons for avoiding incarceration, which could cause terrible health complications. In the autumn of 1907 Emmeline Pethick-Lawrence wrote to Robins imploring her to help frame the meaning of suffrage imprisonment to the wider public, saying 'you who have not to go through the bitter test, you are free to show what it really means' (n.d. 1907. HRC: Robins Box 2, Folder 3).

3. Robins was recruited to the governing Committee of the WSPU, along with Emmeline and Christabel Pankhurst, Mabel Tuke, Emmeline Pethick-Lawrence, Elizabeth Wolstenholme Elmy, Annie Kenney, Mary Neal, Mary Gawthorpe and Nellie Martel.

4. In a tract called *Why?* published by the WWSL, Robins crafted her careful, non-judgemental response to militant violence, admitting, 'I shall not deny that in the stones thrown by women some of us found very hard nuts to crack' but arguing, 'when we came to understand how little the stones meant violence and how much they meant moral indignation against the abuse of physical force, we were able to see in them the instruments not of destruction but of building' (1910, p. 70).

5. In 1908 as Emmeline Pankhurst prepared for trail and imprisonment, she wrote to Robins urging her to devote herself entirely to the WSPU, saying, 'It would be a great comfort to me during these months if I knew that you with your great gifts were giving yourself heart and soul to the cause' (23 October 1908. HRC: Robins Box 2, Folder 2). Emmeline wanted Robins to become a full-time suffrage writer and platform speaker, a surrogate for the Pankhursts themselves when they were in prison. Emmeline's letter concludes with the hope that Robins will 'shut out the opinions and doubts of your world and influence them rather than let them influence you' (ibid.). Robins did reluctantly take over a speaking tour for Emmeline Pankhurst in 1908, but she turned down many more speaking engagements than she accepted, preferring to work as a writer.

6. There is debate as to whether this was exclusively Mill's work or was developed collaboratively with his wife Harriet Taylor Mill. The major difference between her 'The Enfranchisement of Women' and his *The Subjection of Women* is that she advocates women working outside the home (H. Taylor Mill, 1998, pp. 60–61).

7. All men paying an annual rental of £10 or all those holding land valued at £10 were now able to vote, leaving 40 per cent of the male population and 100 per cent of the female population without a vote.

8. Almroth Wright was a pioneering immunologist who fiercely opposed women's suffrage and used his status as a scientist to refute women's claims to political, education and employment equality. In 1913 he published *The Unexpurgated Case Against Woman Suffrage* in which he argued that women's brains were so different from men's as to render them biologically incapable of dealing with social and political issues. Wright was parodied as Sir Colenso Ridgeon in Shaw's *The Doctor's Dilemma* (1906).

9. A former Yorkshire mill worker, Annie Kenney was the only working-class woman to become part of the senior leadership of the WSPU and was eventually put in charge of the organization when Christabel fled to Paris as a political refugee in 1912 (Elizabeth Robins was asked to witness Christabel's letter handing over control of the WSPU to Kenney). According to Martin Pugh's interpretation of the diary of Mary Blathwayt, Annie was Christabel's lover, though June Purvis disputes this.

10. Pankhurst was additionally charged with spitting at two police officers and striking one, presumably to ensure the arrest and imprisonment that she hoped would gain publicity for the cause.

11. See Katherine Cockin's book *Edith Craig and the Theatres of Art* (2017, pp. 100–01) on actresses' skills in assisting women with disguises that would help them gain access to spaces where they could lobby politicians or evade capture by the police.

12. Foreword to the 1948 reprint of *A Pageant of Great Women*.

13. The play was originally commissioned by actress-manager Gertrude Kingston, who, finding it more controversial that she would have liked, became reluctant to produce it. Kingston's hesitation cleared the way for the Vedrenne-Barker management to step in as producers at the Court, a turn of events Robins actively promoted.

14. In a letter to Mrs How-Martyn, Robins hopes that her financial contribution will encourage other women to contribute money or percentages of their earnings to the cause (9 April 1907. HRC: Robins Box 1, Folder 1).

15. Based on evidence from her correspondence, it is likely that Robins attended the first large public WSPU rally in Trafalgar Square on 19 May 1906. Robins wrote of the experience, 'on that Sunday afternoon, in front of Nelson's Monument, a new chapter was begun for me in the lesson of faith in the capacities of women' (WS, p. 39).

16. Flora Drummond addressing a mass-meeting in Trafalgar Square on 11 October 1908. A key speaker in the movement, Drummond earned the nickname 'General' for riding a horse at the head of WSPU processions dressed in epaulettes and a peaked cap. Her militant activity led to nine arrests.

17. In the original script Jean was called Beatrice after Beatrice D'Este. In the printed version Beatrice is changed to Jean for Jeanne D'Arc.

18. Robins drew from 'eye-witness' accounts by reformers like Mary Higgs, who wrote at length about sexual harassment in the tramp wards, from which she concluded, borrowing from Virgil, 'From such a life "*facilis descensus Averni*"' (the decent to hell is easy) (Higgs, 1906, p. 135).

19. Pankhurst wrote, 'I don't think she should be an actual member of the W.S.P.U., but a sympathiser and drawn to it by the insurgent work of its members. I think you treat her as a new comer, do you not? This could be emphasized by her in her speech. Don't think me squeamish but our work is so difficult as it is without paragraphs in the papers when the play appears suggesting that this person or that is the original of the heroine' (19 November 1906. HRC: Robins Box 2, Folder 2).

20. The Ladies' Gallery was created in 1834, a small chamber that only well-connected women could hope to gain access to. The windows of the Ladies' Gallery were covered with heavy metal grilles that made it difficult to see. Prior to 1834 women who wanted to observe the proceedings of parliament were obliged to listen from a ventilation shaft in the ceiling.

21. John takes an example of this delicate social straddling from Robins's diary: 'When a guest at Rounton began talking of *The Convert* she hushed him with the words, 'Nothing gained by discussion of that *here*' (1995, p. 154).

22. Elaine Showalter points out that the extensive brutality described by Robins in the corresponding scene in *The Convert* was suppressed in all other contemporary accounts (1982, p. 222).

23. Barker wrote much of the patter for the crowd used in the Court production as evidenced by his prompt book copy of the play in the Fales Collection, though Robins wrote the dialogue that appears in the published version of the play. See also Barker's letter to Robins (6 March 1907. HRC: Robins Box 1, Folder 7).

24. Desmond MacCarthy suggested that the stage-audience represented 'the Chorus in a Greek play more nearly than anything else in English drama since *The Knight of the Burning Pestle*, in as much as they gave vent to the gnomic and critical remarks of the ordinary spectator' (MacCarthy, 1907, p. 37).

25. Barker proposed extensive cuts to the first act, positing that it was not the 'vital' part of the play; Shaw also suggested extensive cuts in the first act (Barker to Robins, 6 March 1907. HRC: Robins Box 1, Folder 7; Shaw to Robins, 29 December 1906. HRC: Shaw Box 44, Folder 3; and Shaw to Robins, 8 March 1907. HRC: Shaw Box 44, Folder 3).

26. See Gates, 'Henry James's Dictation Letter to Elizabeth Robins: "The Suffragette Movement Hot from the Oven"' (2010).

27. All women between the ages of 25 and 40 years old.

28. The name Mitchener was presumed by contemporaries to be a play on Herbert Kitchener, Commander in Chief of the British Army in India 1902–09. Shaw maintained that the character was actually based on Prince George, Duke of Cambridge, head of the British Army from 1856 to 1895. The licence for this play was initially suspended due to the supposed allusions of Mitchner to Kitchener and Balsquith to Asquith and Balfour, though 'Bellachristina' was allowed to stand as the name of the fictional suffrage leader, despite obviously alluding to Christabel Pankhurst.

29. Balsquith is a conflation of Balfour and Asquith. Arthur Balfour served as Conservative Prime Minister from 1902 to 1905. H.H. Asquith served as Liberal Prime Minister from 1908 to 1916.

30. Emmeline Pethick-Lawrence was the treasurer of the WSPU and a brilliant fundraiser. With her husband Fredrick Pethick-Lawrence, she founded, ran and financed the suffrage paper *Votes for Women*.

31. Hamilton explained that every aspect of the dramaturgy was a joint affair with 'Edy'. See Hamilton in Adlard (1949, pp. 41–42).

32. Reports vary from 200 to 500 women, but 300 is the most commonly cited estimate.

33. Cecelia Haig (S. Pankhurst, 1931, p. 317).

34. Some male historians have allied themselves with the viewpoint of the police officer who declared, while wringing a woman's breast, 'You have been waiting for this for a long time, haven't you.' David Mitchell, for example, speculates

that the police might have been responding to the sexual wishes of the women: 'Wasn't this, they argued, what these women REALLY wanted? ... Perhaps in some cases, and in a deeply subconscious way it was' (Mitchell, 1977, p. 160).

35. A womanly touch was often employed by using a kitchen toffee hammer.

36. In the wake of this, Emmeline and Frederick Pethick-Lawrence were ousted by the Pankhursts over their disagreement with violent tactics. Robins was one of the governing WSPU Committee members unhappily caught in the middle of this conflict, and she ultimately resigned from the board. Preferring to collaborate rather than alienate, Robins managed to maintain ties with both the Pethick-Lawrences and the Pankhursts.

37. Contemporaries and historians have speculated that Emily Wilding Davison may have merely aimed to disrupt the race or attach a WSPU sash to the king's horse rather than die for the cause. In the Pathé footage her movements do look chillingly deliberate and doomed.

38. Kitty Marion was arrested multiple times for militant action, most famously for burning down the grandstand at Hurst Park Racecourse in retaliation for the death of Emily Wilding Davison in June of 1913. She served seven prison terms and endured nearly 200 forcible feedings.

39. See Leslie Hill, 'Suffragettes Invented Performance Art', 2000.

40. See Rebecca Cameron's article '"A somber passion strengthens her voice": The Stage as Public Platform in British Women's Suffrage Drama' for her exploration of how suffrage playwrights shrewdly 'exploited the connection between drama and political tract or speech to 'create a new, hybrid genre to authorize their political message' (2016, p. 295).

41. See Susan Carlson, 'Comic Militancy: The Politics of Suffrage Drama' (2000) for a wonderful account of journalistic theatre – plays published in suffrage newspapers. Carlson examines a number of plays and dialogues which, though they had endings too indeterminate to work at public rallies, created a unique thinking space for complex political opinions within the pages of newspapers that readers could digest privately.

BIBLIOGRAPHY

Achurch, Janet. *Mrs. Daintree's Daughter*, 1894. LCP, BL Add MS 53542 Q.

Acton, William. *The Functions and Disorders of the Reproductive Organs*. Philadelphia: Lindsay and Blakiston, 1883.

Adams, Jad. *Women and the Vote: A World History*. Oxford: Oxford University Press, 2014.

Adlard, Eleanor. *Edy: Recollections of Edith Craig*. London: Frederick Muller, 1949.

Allbutt, Henry Arthur. *The Wife's Handbook ... With Hints on the Management of the Baby, etc.* 2nd edition, revised. London: R. Forder, 1889.

Anderson, Elizabeth Garrett. 'Sex in Mind and Education: A Reply.' *Fortnightly Review* 15 (1874): 582–94.

Andes, Anna. 'The Evolution of Cicely Hamilton's Edwardian Marriage Discourse: Embracing Conversion Dramaturgy.' *English Literature in Transition, 1880–1920* 58(4) (2015): 503–22.

Archer, William. *Correspondence to Elizabeth Robins*. 1908–12. HRC: Robins Box 1, Folder 4.

Archer, William. *English Dramatists of Today*. London: Gilbert and Rivington, 1882.

Archer, William. Introduction. *Alan's Wife*. Ed. Elizabeth Robins and Florence Bell. London: Henry, 1893a. ix–lii.

Archer, William. 'The Mausoleum of Ibsen.' *Fortnightly Review* 60 (1893b): 77–91.

Archer, William. *The Old Drama and the New: An Essay in Re-valuation*. New York: Dodd, Mead & Co., 1923.

Archer, William. *Play-Making: A Manual of Craftsmanship*. 1912. New York: Dover, 1960.

Archer, William. *Study and Stage: A Year Book of Criticism*. London: Grant Richards, 1899.

Archer, William. *The Theatrical 'World' for 1893*. 1894. New York: Benjamin Blom, 1969.

Archer, William. *The Theatrical 'World' of 1894*. 1895. New York: Benjamin Blom, 1971.

Archer, William. *The Theatrical 'World' of 1896*. London: Walter Scott, 1897.

Archer, William. *The Theatrical 'World' of 1897*. 1898. New York: Benjamin Blom, 1969.

Ashwell, Lena. *Myself a Player*. London: Michael Joseph, 1936.

Aston, Elaine. *An Introduction to Feminism and Theatre*. London: Routledge, 1995.

Atkinson, Diane. *The Criminal Conversation of Mrs Norton*. London: Preface, 2012.

Auchmuty, Rosemary. *Victorian Spinsters*. Australian National U, doctoral thesis, 1975.

Bailey, Peter. '"Naughty but Nice"; Musical Comedy and the Rhetoric of the Girl, 1892–1914.' *The Edwardian Theatre: Essays on Performance and the Stage*. Eds. Michael R. Booth and Joel H. Kaplan. Cambridge: Cambridge University Press, 1996. 36–60.

Baker, Elizabeth. *Chains*. 1911. *Contemporary Plays*. Ed. Thomas H. Dickinson. Boston: Houghton Mifflin, 1925. 209–43.

Baker, Elizabeth. *Edith*. 1912. *Plays and Performance Texts by Women 1880–1930*. Eds. Maggie B. Gale and Gilli Bush-Bailey. Manchester: Manchester University Press, 2012. 278–91.

Baker, Elizabeth. *Miss Tassey*. London: Sidgwick & Jackson, 1913.

Bank, Clementina. *Married Women's Work: Being the Report of an Inquiry Undertaken by the Women's Industrial Council*. London: G. Bell & Sons, 1915.

Barker, Harley Granville. *Correspondence to Elizabeth Robins*. 1907. HRC: Robins Box 1, Folder 7.

Barker, Harley Granville. *The Madras House*. Author's copy printed version with handwritten revisions and inserts and extensive director's notes. London: Sidgwick & Jackson, 1909. HRC: Harley Granville-Barker Collection Box 1, Folder 4.

Barker, Harley Granville. *The Madras House*. 1909. Revised 1925. *Harley Granville Barker Plays: Two*. London: Methuen Drama, 1994. 93–236.

Barker, Harley Granville. *The Marrying of Ann Leete*. 1899. *Plays by Harley Granville Barker*. Ed. Dennis Kennedy. Cambridge: Cambridge University Press, 1987a. 33–82.

Barker, Harley Granville. *The Voysey Inheritance*. 1905. *Plays by Harley Granville Barker*. Ed. Dennis Kennedy. Cambridge: Cambridge University Press, 1987b. 83–159.

Barker, Harley Granville. *Waste*. 1907. *Plays by Harley Granville Barker*. Ed Dennis Kennedy. Cambridge: Cambridge University Press, 1987c. 161–239.

Barker, Harley Granville. *Waste*. London: Sidgwick and Jackson, 1919.

Barrie, J.M. *The Twelve-Pound Look*. 1921. *The Twelve-Pound Look and Other Plays*. Amsterdam: Fredonia, 2003. 3–40.

Barrie, J.M. *What Every Woman Knows*. TS with property plot, property of Charles Frohman. n.d. [c. 1908]. HRC: Playscripts and Promptbooks Collection, Box 1, Folder 6.

Beale, D. Chapter 1 reprint of *The Schools Inquiry Commission Report*. Vol 1 Chapter 6 (1867–68). *Reports Issued by the Schools' Inquiry Commission on the Education of Girls*. London: David Nutt, 1870.

Beckson, Karl. *London in the 1890s: A Cultural History*. New York: W.W. Norton, 1992.

Beerbohm, Max. *Around Theatres*. Vol II. New York: Alfred A. Knopf, 1930.

Bell, Florence. *At the Works: A Study of a Manufacturing Town*. London: Edward Arnold, 1907.

Bell, Florence. *The Way the Money Goes*. London: Sidgwick & Jackson, 1910.

Bellow Watson, Barbara. *A Shavian Guide to the Intelligent Woman*. London: Chatto & Windus, 1964.

Bennett, Hughes. 'Hygiene in the Higher Education of Women.' *Popular Science Monthly* 16 (1888): 519–30.

Bensusan, Inez. *The Apple*. 1909. *How the Vote Was Won and Other Suffragette Plays*. Eds. Dale Spender and Carole Hayman. London: Methuen, 1985. 143–54.

Bently, Eric. 'The Theatre.' *George Bernard Shaw's Man and Superman*. Ed. Harold Bloom. New York: Chelsea House, 1987. 15–19.

Besant, Annie. *The Law of the Population: Its Consequences and Its Bearing Upon Human Conduct and Morals*. New York: Asa K. Butts, 1879.

Besant, Annie. 'White Slavery in London', *The Link* 21 (23 June 1888): 2.

Billington-Greig, Theresa. *The Militant Suffrage Movement*. London: Frank Palmer, 1911.

Bird, Isabella. *The Hawaiian Archipelago, Six Months among the Palm Groves, Coral Reefs and Volcanoes of the Sandwich Islands*. New York: Putnam's Sons, 1894.

Birkett, Dea. *Spinsters Abroad: Victorian Lady Explorers*. London: Victor Gollancz, 1991.

Bissell, Mary T. 'Emotions Versus Health in Women.' *The Popular Science Monthly* 32 (February 1888).

Black, Clementina. 'Typewriting and Journalism for Women.' *Our Boys and Girls and What to do with Them*. Ed. John Watson. London: Ward Lock, 1892. 35–45.

Blackstone, William. *Commentaries on the Laws of England*, Volume 1, 1765. 442–45.

Blackwell, Elizabeth. *Essays in Medical Sociology*. London: Ernest Bell, 1902.

Blackwell, Elizabeth. *The Moral Education of the Young in Relation to Sex*. London: Hatchards, 1884.

Bland, Lucy. *Banishing the Beast: English Feminism and Sexual Morality 1885–1914*. London: Penguin, 1995.

Bloch, Iwan. *The Sexual Life of Our Time*. 1908. New York: Allied, 1926.

Bloom, Harold, ed. *George Bernard Shaw's Man and Superman*. New York: Chelsea House, 1987.

Bodichon, Barbara Leigh Smith. *A Brief Summary, in Plain Language, of the Most Important Laws Concerning Women*. London: John Chapman, 1854.

Bodichon, Barbara Leigh Smith. 'Women and Work.' 1857. *Barbara Leigh Smith Bodichon and the Langham Place Group*. Ed. Candida Ann Lacey. London: Routledge, 1986. 36–73.

Bolt, Christine. *Victorian Attitudes to Race*. London: Routledge & Kegan Paul, 1971.

Booth, Michael R., and Joel H. Kaplan, eds. *The Edwardian Theatre: Essays on Performance and the Stage*. Cambridge: Cambridge University Press, 1996.

Boucherett, Jessie. *Hints on Self Help: A Book for Young Women*. London: S.W. Partridge, 1863.

Boucherett, Jessie. 'How to Provide for Superfluous Women.' *Woman's Work and Woman's Culture: A Series of Essays*. Ed. Josephine Butler. London: Macmillan, 1869. Reel/Fiche Number: The Gerritsen collection of women's history; Number 434: 35.

Boyd-Kinnear, John. 'The Social Position of Women in the Present Age.' *Women's Work and Women's Culture: A Series of Essays*. Ed. Josephine Butler. London: Macmillan, 1869. 332–66.

Brandon, Ruth. *The New Women and the Old Men*. London: Harper Collins, 1990.

Bratton, J.S. 'Beating the Bounds: Gender Play and Role Reversal in the Edwardian Music Hall.' *The Edwardian Theatre: Essays on Performance and the Stage*. Eds. Michael R. Booth and Joel H. Kaplan. Cambridge: Cambridge University Press, 1996. 86–110.

Bratton, Jacky. *New Readings in Theatre History*. Cambridge: Cambridge University Press, 2003.

Bratton, Jacky. 'Reading the Intertheatrical, or, the Mysterious Disappearance of Susanna Centlivre.' *Women, Theatre and Performance: New Histories, New Historiographies*. Eds. Maggie B. Gale and Viv Gardner. Manchester and New York: Manchester University Press, 2000. 7–24.

Briggs, Asa. *Victorian People: A Reassessment of Persons and Themes 1851–67*. 1965. London: Penguin, 1990.

Bright, Florence. *A Girl Capitalist*. London: Chatto & Windus, 1902.

Bristow, Robert. *Vice and Vigilance: Purity Movements in Britain Since 1700*. London: Rowan & Littlefield, 1977.

Brooke, Emma. *A Superfluous Woman*. London: Heinemann, 1894.

Browne, Stella. 'The Sexual Variety and Variability among Women and Their Bearing upon Social Reconstruction.' 1917. *A New World for Women: Stella Browne – A Socialist Feminist.* Ed. Sheila Rowbothan. London: Pluto, 1977. 87–105.

Burke, Edmund, ed. *The Annual Register: A Review of Public Events at Home and Abroad for the Year 1894.* London: Longmans, Green, 1895.

Burney, Estelle. *An Idyll of the Closing Century.* London: Samuel French, 1896.

Bushnell, Horace. *Women's Suffrage: The Reform Against Nature.* New York: C. Scribner, 1869.

Butler, Josphine. 1913. 'The Voice of One Crying in the Wilderness.' *Josephine Butler and the Prostitution Campaigns: Diseases of the Body Politic.* Eds. Jane Jordan and Ingrid Sharp. London: Routledge, 2003.

Caine, Barbara. 'Feminism.' *Oscar Wilde in Context.* Eds. Kerry Powell and Peter Raby. Cambridge and New York: Cambridge University Press, 2013. 289–96.

Caine, Barbara. *Victorian Feminists.* Oxford: Oxford University Press, 1992.

Caird, Mona. *The Daughters of Danaus.* London: Bliss, Sands & Forster, 1894.

Caird, Mona. 'Marriage.' *Westminster Review* 130 (1888): 186–201.

Cameron, Rebecca. '"A Somber Passion Strengthens Her Voice": The Stage as Public Platform in British Women's Suffrage Drama.' *Comparative Drama* 50(4) (2016): 293–316.

Campbell, Harry. *Differences in the Nervous Organisation of Man and Woman.* London: H.L. Lewis, 1891.

Campbell, Mrs. Patrick. *My Life and Some Letters.* 2nd edition. London: Hutchinson, n.d. [c. 1925].

Carlson, Susan. 'Conflicted Politics and Circumspect Comedy: Women's Comic Playwrighting in the 1890s.' *Women and Playwriting in Nineteenth-Century Britain.* Eds. Tracy C. Davis and Ellen Donkin. Cambridge and New York: Cambridge University Press, 1999. 256–76.

Carlson, Susan. 'Comic Militancy: The Politics of Suffrage Drama.' *Women, Theatre and Performance: New Histories, New Historiographies.* Eds. Maggie B. Gale and Viv Gardner. Manchester and New York: Manchester University Press, 2000. 198–215.

Carpenter, Edward. *The Intermediate Sex: Study of Transitional Types of Men and Women.* Manchester: S. Sonnenschein, 1908.

Chew, A. Nield. 'The Problem of the Married Working Woman.' *Common Cause* 5 (1914): 909–10.

Cholmondeley, Mary. *Votes for Men.* 1909. *Literature of the Women's Suffrage Campaign in England.* Ed. Carolyn Christensen Nelson. Peterborough: Broadview, 2004. 201–08.

Christ, Carol. 'Victorian Masculinity and the Angel in the House.' *A Widening Sphere: Changing Roles of Victorian Women.* Ed. Martha Vicinus. Bloomington: Indiana University Press, 1977. 146–62.

Cima, Gay Gibson. 'Elizabeth Robins: The Genesis of an Independent Manageress.' *Theatre Survey* 21(2) (1980): 145–63.

Cima, Gay Gibson. '"To be Public as a Genius and Private as a Woman": The Critical Framing of Nineteenth-Century British Women Playwrights.' *Women and Playwriting in Nineteenth-Century Britain*. Eds. Tracy C. Davis and Ellen Donkin. Cambridge and New York: Cambridge University Press, 1999. 35–53.

Clarke, Edward. *Sex in Education: A Fair Chance for Girls*. 1873. Reproduction: Microfilm. New Haven: Research Publications, 1977. History of Women, Reel 374, Number 2596.

Clouston, T.S. *Clinical Lectures on Mental Diseases*. 6th edition. Edinburgh: Neill, 1904.

Cobbe, Frances Power. 'The Final Cause of Woman.' *Woman's Work and Woman's Culture*. Ed. Josephine Butler. London: Macmillan, 1869. 1–26.

Cobbe, Frances Power. 'The Little Health of Ladies.' *Contemporary Review* 31 (1878): 276–96.

Cockin, Katherine. *Edith Craig and the Theatres of Art*. London: Bloomsbury, 2017.

Cockin, Katherine. *Women and the Theatre in the Age of Suffrage: The Pioneer Players, 1911–1925*. Houndmills: Palgrave, 2001.

Cockroft, Irene and Susan Croft. *Art, Theatre and Women's Suffrage*. London: Aurora Metro, 2010.

Cocks, Harry. 'Wilde and the Law.' *Oscar Wilde in Context*. Eds. Kerry Powell and Peter Raby. Cambridge and New York: Cambridge University Press, 2013. 297–304.

Colemore, Gertrude. *Suffragette Sally*. 1911. Ed. Alison Lee. Peterborough: Broadview, 2008.

Collins, F. Howard. *An Epitome of the Synthetic Philosophy*. New York: D. Appleton, 1889.

Collins, Tracy J.R. 'Shaw's Athletic-Minded Women.' *Shaw and Feminisms: On Stage and Off*. Eds. D.A. Hadfield and Jean Reynolds. Gainesville: University Press of Florida, 2013. 19–36.

Conolly, L.W. Introduction. *The Philanderer*. Peterborough: Broadview Editions, 2015. 13–46.

Craigie, Pearl Marie [published under John Oliver Hobbes]. *The Ambassador*. New York: Frederick A. Stokes, 1898.

Croft, Susan, ed. *Votes for Women and Other Plays*. London: Aurora Metro, 2009.

Darwin, Charles. *The Descent of Man and Selection in Relation to Sex*. 1859. London: John Murray, 1901.

Davidoff, Leonore. 'Class and Gender in Victorian England.' *Sex and Class in Women's History*. Eds. Judith Newton, Mary Ryan and Judith Walkowitz. London: Routledge & Kegan Paul, 1983. 17–71.

Davies, Emily. 'The Influence of University Degrees on the Education of Women.' *Victoria Magazine* 1 (1863): 260–71.

Davis, Tracy C. *Actresses as Working Women: The Social Identity in Victorian Culture*. London: Routledge, 1991.

Davis, Tracy C. *The Broadview Anthology of Nineteenth Century British Performance*. Peterborough: Broadview, 2012.

Davis, Tracy C. *The Economics of the British Stage, 1800–1914*. Cambridge and New York: Cambridge University Press, 2000.

Davis, Tracy C. *George Bernard Shaw and the Socialist Theatre*. Westport: Greenwood, 1994.

Davis, Tracy C., and Ellen Donkin, eds. *Women and Playwriting in Nineteenth-Century Britain*. Cambridge and New York: Cambridge University Press, 1999.

Davis, Tracy C., and Thomas Postlewait, eds. *Theatricality*. Cambridge and New York: Cambridge University Press, 2003.

Diamond, Elin. *Unmaking Mimesis*. London: Routlege, 1997.

Dixey, Kate, and Lillian Feltheimer. *A Girl's Freak*. 1899. LCP, BL Add MS 53679 C.

Dixon, Ella Hepworth. *The Story of a Modern Woman*. 1894. Ed. Steve Farmer. Toronto: Broadview, 2004.

Dolgin, Ellen Ecker. *Shaw and the Actresses Franchise League*. Jefferson: McFarland, 2015.

Dorynne, Jess. *The Surprise of His Life*. Unpublished manuscript, Smallhythe Museum, 1912.

Drake, Barbara. *Women in Trade Unions*. 1920. London: Virago, 1984.

Dugdale, Joan. *10 Clowning Street. Innocent Flowers*. Ed. Julie Holledge. London: Virago, 1981. 173–88.

Dymkowski, Christine. 'Case Study: Cicely Hamilton's Diana of Dobson's, 1908.' *The Cambridge History of British Theatre*. Volume 3. Ed. Baz Kershaw. Cambridge: Cambridge University Press, 2004. 110–26.

Egan, Michael. *Ibsen: The Critical Heritage*. London and Boston: Routledge & Kegan Paul, 1972.

Ehnenn, Jill R. *Women's Literary Collaboration, Queerness, and Late-Victorian Culture*. Aldershot: Ashgate, 2008.

Elliott, Bridget and Jo-Ann Wallace. *Women Artists and Writers: Modernist (im)positionings*. London: Routledge, 1994.

Elliott, Dorice. *The Angel out of the House: Philanthropy and Gender in Nineteenth-Century England*. Charlottesville: University of Virginia Press, 2002.

Ellis, Havelock. *Man and Woman: A Study of Secondary and Tertiary Sexual Characteristics*. 1894. London: Heinemann, 1934.

Ellis, Havelock. *Studies in the Psychology of Sex, Volume II Sexual Inversion*. 1897. Philadelphia: F.A. Davis, 1906.

Ellis, Havelock. *Studies in the Psychology of Sex, Volume III Analysis of the Sexual Impulse; Love and Pain; The Sexual Impulse in Women*. 1903. New York: Random House, 1936.

Ellis, Havelock. *Studies in the Psychology of Sex, Volume VI Sex in Relation to Society.* 1910. Philadelphia: F.A. Davis, 1921.

Ellis, Sarah Stickney. *The Women of England.* London: Fisher & Son Co, 1872.

Elmy, Elizabeth C. Wolstenholme. *The Criminal Code in its Relation to Women.* Manchester: A. Ireland, 1880.

Eltis, Sos. *Acts of Desire: Women and Sex on Stage, 1800–1930.* Oxford: Oxford University Press, 2013a.

Eltis, Sos. 'The Fallen Woman in Edwardian Feminist Drama: Suffrage, Sex and the Single Girl.' *English Literature in Transition, 1880–1920* 50(1) (2007): 27–49.

Eltis, Sos. 'Reception and Performance History of Wilde's Society Plays.' *Oscar Wilde in Context.* Eds. Kerry Powell and Peter Raby. Cambridge and New York: Cambridge University Press, 2013b. 319–27.

Ervine, St. John. *The Magnanimous Lover.* London: Maunsel, 1912.

Ethelmer, Ellis [Elizabeth Wolstenholme Elmy and Ben Elmy]. *Life to Woman.* Congleton: Mrs Wolstenholme Elmy, 1896.

Etherington-Wright, Christine. *Gender, Professions and Discourse: Early Twentieth-Century Women's Autobiography.* Houndmills: Palgrave Macmillan, 2009.

Ewbank, Inga-Stina. "Ibsen and the Language of Women." *Women Writing and Writing about Women.* Ed. Mary Jacobs. London: Croom Helm, 1979. 114–32.

Faderman, Lilian. *Surpassing the Love of Men.* London: Women's Press, 1985.

Fagan, James Bernard. *The Earth.* New York: Duffield & Company, 1910.

Farfan, Penny. *Women, Modernism, and Performance.* Cambridge and New York: Cambridge University Press, 2004.

Fawcett, Millicent Garrett. *Correspondence to Elizabeth Robins.* 1907. HRC: Robins Box 1, Folder 3.

Fawcett, Millicent Garrett. *What I Remember.* 1925. Westport: Hyperion Press, 1975.

Fitzsimmons, Linda, and Viv Gardner, eds. *New Woman Plays.* London: Methuen Drama, 1991.

Fitzsimmons, Linda. 'Typewriters Enchained: The Work of Elizabeth Baker.' *The New Woman and Her Sisters 1850–1914.* Eds. Viv Gardner and Susan Rutherford. New York: Harvester Wheatsheaf, 1992. 189–204.

Fletcher, Constance [published under George Fleming]. *Mrs. Lessingham,* 1894. LCP, BL, Add MS 53546 A.

Fletcher, Sheila. *Feminists and Bureaucrats: A Study in the Development of Girls' Education in the Nineteenth Century.* Cambridge: Cambridge University Press, 1980.

Fordyce, James. *Sermons to Young Women.* London: D. Payne, 1766.

Forman, Ross. 'Race and Empire.' *Palgrave Advances in the Modern History of Sexuality.* Eds. H.G. Cocks and Matt Houlbrook. Houndmills: Palgrave Macmillan, 2006. 109–32.

Forster, Margaret. *Significant Sisters*. London: Penguin, 1986.

Forte, Jeanie. 'Focus on the Body: Pain, Praxis, and Pleasure in Feminist Performance.' *Critical Theory and Performance*. Eds. Janelle Reinelt and Joseph Roach. Ann Arbor: University of Michigan Press, 1992. 248–62.

Foucault, Michel. *The History of Sexuality, Volume I: An Introduction*. London: Allen Lane, 1979.

Franz, Nellie Alden. *English Women Enter the Professions*. New York: Columbia University Press, 1965.

Gainor, J. Ellen. *Shaw's Daughters: Dramatic and Narrative Constructions of Gender*. Ann Arbor: University of Michigan Press, 1991.

Gale, Maggie B., and Gilli Bush-Bailey, eds. *Plays and Performance Texts by Women 1880–1930*. Manchester: Manchester University Press, 2012.

Gale, Maggie B., and Viv Gardner, eds. *Women, Theatre and Performance: New Histories, New Historiographies*. Manchester and New York: Manchester University Press, 2000.

Gallichan, W. *Sexual Apathy and Coldness in Women*. London: T. Werner Laurie, 1927.

Galsworthy, John. *The Plays of John Galsworthy*. London: Duckworth, 1932.

Gamble, Eliza Burt. *The Evolution of Woman*. New York: G.P. Putnam's Sons, 1894.

Gardner, Viv, and Susan Rutherford, eds. *The New Woman and Her Sisters 1850–1914*. New York: Harvester Wheatsheaf, 1992.

Garnett, Edward. *The Breaking Point: A Censured Play*. London: Duckworth, 1907.

Gates, Joanne E. *Elizabeth Robins, 1862–1952: Actress, Novelist, Feminist*. Tuscaloosa: University of Alabama Press, 1994.

Gates, Joanne E. 'Henry James's Dictation Letter to Elizabeth Robins: "The Suffragette Movement Hot from the Oven."' *The Henry James Review* 31(3) (2010): 254–63.

Gates, Joanne E. Introduction. *Votes for Women. Modern Drama by Women 1880s–1930s*. Ed. Katherine E. Kelly. London: Routledge, 1996. 108–11.

Gissing, George. *The Odd Women*. Volumes 1–3. London: Lawrence & Bullen, 1893.

Glover, Evelyn. *A Chat with Mrs. Chicky*. 1912. *How the Vote Was Won and Other Suffragette Plays*. Eds. Dale Spender and Carole Hayman. London: Methuen, 1985. 103–13.

Glover, Evelyn. *Mrs. Appleyard's Awakening*. 1911. *How the Vote Was Won and Other Suffragette Plays*. Eds. Dale Spender and Carole Hayman. London: Methuen, 1985. 115–24.

Grand, Sarah. *The Heavenly Twins*. 1893. Ann Arbor: University of Michigan Press, 1992.

Grand, Sarah. 'The New Aspect of the Woman Question.' *North American Review* 158 (1894): 270–76.

Grand, Sarah. 'The New Woman and the Old.' *Lady's Realm* 4 (1898): 466–70.

Graves, Clotilde (Richard Dehan). *London Vendetta*. HRC: MS–1704, container 4.12–13, n.d.

Graves, Clotilde. *A Mother of Three*. London: Samuel French, 1909.

Graves, Clotilde. *The Wooing*, 1898. LCP, BL, Add. MS 53664.

Graves, Clotilde, and Gertrude Kingston. *A Matchmaker*, 1896. LCP, BL, Add MS 53601.J.

Green, Barbara. *Spectacular Confessions: Autobiography, Performative Activism, and the Sites of Suffrage 1905–1938*. New York: St. Martins, 1997.

Gregory, John. *A Father's Legacy to His Daughters*. London: Wood & Innes, 1808.

Grein, J.T. Editor's Preface. *Alan's Wife*. Eds. Elizabeth Robins and Florence Bell. London: Henry, 1893. v–viii.

Grundy, Sydney. *The New Woman*. 1894. *The New Woman and Other Emancipated Plays*. Ed. Jean Chothia. Oxford: Oxford University Press, 1998. 1–59.

Hadfield, D.A. 'Writing Women: Shaw and Feminism behind the Scenes.' *Shaw and Feminisms: On Stage and Off*. Eds. D.A. Hadfield and Jean Reynolds. Gainesville: University Press of Florida, 2013. 112–32.

Hadfield, D.A., and Jean Reynolds, eds. *Shaw and Feminisms: On Stage and Off*. Gainesville: University Press of Florida, 2013.

Hamilton, Cicely. *Correspondence to Elizabeth Robins*. 1909. HRC: Robins Box 1, Folder 7.

Hamilton, Cicely. *Diana of Dobson's, A Romantic Comedy in Four Acts*. London: Samuel French, 1925.

Hamilton, Cicely. Foreword. *A Pageant of Great Women*. London: Suffragette Fellowship, 1948.

Hamilton, Cicely. *Jack and Jill and a Friend*. London: Samuel French, 1911a.

Hamilton, Cicely. *Just to Get Married*. London: Chapman Hall, 1911b.

Hamilton, Cicely. *Life Errant*. London: J.M. Dent & Sons, 1935.

Hamilton, Cicely. *Marriage as a Trade*. London: Chapman and Hall, Ltd, 1909.

Hamilton, Cicely. *A Matter of Money*. London: Chapman and Hall, 1916.

Hamilton, Cicely. *A Pageant of Great Women*. 1909. *Literature of the Women's Suffrage Campaign in England*. Ed. Carolyn Christensen. Peterborough: Broadview, 2004. 221–32.

Hamilton, Cicely, and Christopher St. John. *How the Vote Was Won*. 1909. *How the Vote Was Won and Other Suffrage Plays*. Eds. Dale Spender and Carole Hayman. London: Methuen, 1985. 17–33.

Hankin, St. John. *The Charity that Began at Home*. *The Dramatic Works of St. John Hankin: Volume Two*. London: Martin Secker, 1912. 2–116.

Hankin, St. John. *The Last of the De Mullins*. *The Dramatic Works of St. John Hankin: Volume Three*. London: Martin Secker, 1912a. 1–87.

Hankin, St. John. *The Return of the Prodigal*. *The Dramatic Works of St. John Hankin: Volume One*. London: Martin Secker, 1912b. 115–213.

Harraden, Beatrice. *Lady Geraldine's Speech.* 1909. *How the Vote Was Won and Other Suffragette Plays.* Eds. Dale Spender and Carole Hayman. London: Methuen, 1985. 92–98.

Harris, Frank. *Bernard Shaw: An Unauthorized Biography Based on Firsthand Information. With a Postscript by Mr Shaw.* London: Gollancz, 1931.

Harris, Janice Hubbard. *Edwardian Stories of Divorce.* New Brunswnick: Rutgers University Press, 1996.

Hatton, Bessie. *Before Sunrise.* 1909. *Literature of the Women's Suffrage Campaign in England.* Ed. Carolyn Christensen Nelson. Peterborough: Broadview, 2004. 209–20.

Heilmann, Ann. *New Woman Fiction: Women Writing First Wave Feminism.* London: Macmillan, 2000.

Heilmann, Ann. *New Woman Strategies.* Manchester, New York: Manchester University Press, 2004.

Hellerstein, Erna Olafson, Leslie Parker Hume, and Karen M. Offen, eds. *Victorian Women: A Documentary Account of Women's Lives in the Nineteenth-Century England, France and the United States.* Brighton: Harvester, 1981.

Hill, Leslie. 'Suffragettes Invented Performance Art.' *The Routledge Performance Reader.* Ed. Lizbeth Goodman. London: Routledge, 2000. 150–56.

Higgs, Mary. *Glimpses into the Abyss.* London: P.S. King & Son, 1906.

Hirshfield, Claire. 'The Actresses' Franchise League and the Campaign for Women's Suffrage 1908–1914.' *Theatre Research International* 10(2) (1985): 129–53.

Hobbes, John Oliver. *The Ambassador.* London: T. Fisher Unwin, 1898.

Holbrook Gerzina, Gretchen, ed. *Black Victorians/Black Victoriana.* New Brunswick: Rutgers University Press, 2003.

Holcombe, Lee. *Victorian Ladies at Work: Middle-Class Working Women in England and Wales 1850–1914.* Hamden: Archon, 1973.

Holledge, Julie. *Innocent Flowers: Women in Edwardian Theatre.* London: Virago Press, 1981.

Hollis, Patricia, ed. *Women in Public 1850–1900: Documents of the Victorian Women's Movement.* London and Boston: Allen & Unwin, 1979.

Holloway, Gerry. *Women and Work in Britain since 1840.* London: Routledge, 2005.

Holroyd, Michael. *Bernard Shaw, Volume 1, 1865–1898: The Search for Love.* New York: Random House, 1988.

Holroyd, Michael. *Bernard Shaw, Volume 2, 1898–1918: The Pursuit of Power.* New York: Random House, 1989.

Horniman, Annie. MS. personal scrapbook: press cuttings. 1907. John Rylands Library, Manchester GB 133 AEH/2/1.

Houghton, Stanley. *Hindle Wakes.* 4th impression. Boston: John W. Luce, 1913.

Hughes, Annie. *A Husband's Humiliation.* 1896. LCP, BL, Add. MS 35605F.

Innes, Christopher, ed. *The Cambridge Companion to George Bernard Shaw*. Cambridge and New York: Cambridge University Press, 1998.

Irish, Annie. *Across Her Path*, 1890. LCP, BL, Add MS 53444 B.

Jalland, Pat. *Women, Marriage and Politics 1860–1914*. Oxford: Clarendon, 1986.

Jeffreys, Shelia. *The Spinster and Her Enemies, Feminism and Sexuality 1880–1930*. London: Pandora, 1985.

Jennings, Gertrude. *Acid Drops: A Play in One Act*. London: Samuel French, 1914a.

Jennings, Gertrude. 'The Rest Cure.' *Four One Act Plays*. London: Samuel French, 1914b. 11–36.

Jennings, Gertrude. *A Woman's Influence*. London: Actresses' Franchise League, 1913.

Jerome, J.K. *The Master of Mrs. Chilvers – An Improbable Comedy*. London: T. Fisher Unwin, 1911.

John, Angela V. *Elizabeth Robins: Staging a Life 1862–1952*. New York: Routledge, 1995.

Johnson, Katie N. *Sex for Sale: Six Progressive-Era Brothel Dramas*. Iowa City: University of Iowa Press, 2015.

Jones, Henry Arthur. *The Case of Rebellious Susan*. 1894. *Plays by Henry Arthur Jones*. Ed. Russell Jackson. Cambridge and New York: Cambridge University Press, 1982. 105–62.

Jones, Henry Arthur. *Mrs. Dane's Defence*. London: Samuel French, 1905.

Jones, Wilton, and Gertrude Warden. *Woman's Proper Place*. London: Samuel French, 1896.

Jordan, Jane, and Ingrid Sharp, eds. *Josephine Butler and the Prostitution Campaigns: Diseases of the Body Politic*. London: Routledge, 2003.

Jordanova, Ludmilla. 'Natural Facts: A Historical Perspective on Science and Sexuality.' *Nature, Culture and Gender*. Eds. Carol MacCormick and Marilyn Strathern. Cambridge and New York: Cambridge University Press, 1980. 42–69.

Jordanova, Ludmilla. *Sexual Visions: Images of Gender in Science and Medicine between the Eighteenth and Twentieth Centuries*. Madison: University of Wisconsin Press, 1989.

Kaplan, Joel H. 'Pineroticism and the Problem Play: Mrs Tanqueray, Mrs Ebbsmith and "Mrs Pat."' *British Theatre in the 1890s: Essays on Drama and the Stage*. Ed. Richard Foulkes. Cambridge: Cambridge University Press, 1992. 38–58.

Kaplan, Joel, and Sheila Stowell. *Theatre & Fashion: Oscar Wilde to the Suffragettes*. Cambridge and New York: Cambridge University Press, 1994.

Kennedy, Dennis. *Granville Barker and the Dream of Theatre*. Cambridge: Cambridge University Press, 1985.

Kennedy, Dennis, ed. *Plays by Granville Barker*. Cambridge: Cambridge University Press, 1987.

Kenney, Annie. *Memories of a Militant*. London: Edward Arnold, 1924.

Kent, Susan Kingsley. *Sex & Suffrage in Britain 1860–1914*. London: Routledge, 1990.

Kershaw, Baz, ed. *The Cambridge History of British Theatre*. Volume 3. Cambridge: Cambridge University Press, 2004.

Kiberd, Declan. *Men and Feminism in Modern Literature*. London: Palgrave Macmillan, 1985.

Krafft-Ebing, Richard von. *Psychopathia Sexualis*. First unexpurgated edition in English. Trans. Harry E. Wedeck. 1886. New York: G.P. Putnam's Sons, 1965.

Laite, Julia. *Common Prostitutes and Ordinary Citizens: Commercial Sex in London, 1885–1960*. Houndmills: Palgrave Macmillan, 2012.

Langer, William L. 'The Origins of the Birth Control Movement in England in the Early Nineteenth Century.' *The Journal of Interdisciplinary History* 5(4) (1975): 669–86.

Langland, Elizabeth. *Nobody's Angels: Middle-Class Women and Domestic Ideology in Victorian Culture*. Ithaca: Cornell University Press, 1995.

Laurence, Dan H., ed. *G.B. Shaw, Collected Letters 1874–1897*. London: Max Reinhardt, 1965.

Leask, Margaret. *Lena Ashwell: Actress, Patriot, Pioneer*. Hatfield: University of Hertfordshire Press, 2012.

Lecky, William Edward Hartpole. *History of European Morals from Augustus to Charlemagne*. Volume II. New York: D. Appleton, 1876.

Ledger, Sally. 'New Woman Drama.' *A Companion to Modern British and Irish Drama 1880–2005*. Ed. Mary Luckhurst. Oxford: Blackwell, 2006. 48–60.

Lee, Alison, ed. *Suffragette Sally*. Ed. Gertrude Colemore. Peterborough: Broadview, 2008.

Leighton, Dorothy. *Thyrza Fleming*, 1894. LCP, BL, Add MS 53565 F.

Lewis, Jane. *Women and Social Action in Victorian and Edwardian England*. Aldershot: Edward Elgar, 1991.

Littell. *The Living Age*. Fifth Series. Volume 63. Boston: Littell and Co. July–September 1888.

Linton, Elizabeth Lynn. *The Autobiography of Christopher Kirkland*. London: R. Bentley, 1885.

Lorimer, Douglas A. 'Race, Science and Culture: Historical Continuities and Discontinuities, 1850–1914.' *The Victorians and Race*. Ed. S. West. Brookfield: Scolar, 1996. 12–33.

Lorimer, Douglas A. 'Reconstructing Victorian Racial Discourse: Images of Race, the Language of Race Relations, and the Context of Black Resistance.' *Black Victorians/Black Victoriana*. Ed. Gretchen Holbrook Gerzina. New Brunswick: Rutgers University Press, 2003. 187–208.

Luckhurst, Mary, ed. *A Companion to Modern British and Irish Drama 1880–2005*. Oxford: Blackwell, 2006.

Lyttelton, Edith. *Warp and Woof.* 1908. *Plays and Performance Texts by Women 1880–1930*. Eds. Maggie B. Gale and Gilli Bush-Bailey. Manchester: Manchester University Press, 2012. 155–206.

Lytton, Constance. *Prisons & Prisoners: Some Personal Experience.* 1914. London: Virago, 1988.

MacCarthy, Desmond. *The Court Theatre 1904–1907.* London: A.H. Bullen, 1907.

Macnamara, (Mack) Margaret. *The Baby in the Ring.* London: William Heinemann, 1918.

Macnamara, (Mack) Margaret. *The Gates of the Morning*, 1908. LCP, BL, Add MS 65817 'O' 1908/2.

Malthus, Thomas. *An Essay on the Principle of Population and other writings.* 1798. London: Penguin Classic, 2015.

Marcus, Jane. Introduction. *The Convert.* London: The Women's Press, 1980. v–xvi.

Marshall, Gail. *Actresses on the Victorian Stage: Feminine Performance and the Galatea Myth.* Cambridge and New York: Cambridge University Press, 1998.

Martin, Jane. *Women and the Politics of Schooling in Victorian and Edwardian England.* London: Leicester University Press, 1999.

Martindale, Louisa. *Under the Surface.* 1900. Microfilm. New Haven: Research Publications, 1976. 1 reel. 35 mm. History of women, Reel 577, Number 4505.2.

Martindale, Louisa. *The Woman Doctor and Her Future.* London: Mills & Boon, 1922.

Mason, Michael. *The Making of Victorian Sexual Attitudes.* Oxford: Oxford University Press, 1994.

Maudsley, Henry. *Body and Mind.* New York: D. Appleton, 1874a.

Maudsley, Henry. 'Sex in Mind and Education.' *Fortnightly Review* 15 (1874b): 466–477.

Mazer, Cary M. 'Granville Barker and the Court Dramatists.' *A Companion to Modern British and Irish Drama 1880–2005.* Ed. Mary Luckhurst. Oxford: Blackwell, 2006. 75–86.

MacCarthy, Desmond. *Desmond MacCarthy's The Court Theatre 1904–1907: A Commentary and Criticism.* 1907. Ed. Stanley Weintraub. Coral Gables: University of Miami Press, 1966.

McCarthy, Lillah. *Myself and My Friends.* New York: E.P. Dutton, 1933.

McClintock, Anne. *Imperial Leather: Race, Gender and Sexuality in the Colonial Contest.* London: Routledge, 1995.

McCord, Norman. *British History 1815–1906.* Oxford: Oxford University Press, 1991.

McDonald, Jan. 'New Women in the New Drama.' *New Theatre Quarterly* 6(21) (1990): 31–42.

McDonald, Jan. '"The Second Act Was Glorious": The Staging of the Trafalgar Scene from *Votes for Women!* at the Court Theatre.' *Theatre History Studies* 15 (1995): 139–60.

Macmillan's Magazine. 'The Glorified Spinster.' *Macmillan's Magazine* 58 (1888): 371–76.

MacKay, Carol Hanbery. *Creative Negativity: Four Victorian Exemplars of the Female Quest.* Stanford: Stanford University Press, 2001.

Medd, Mabel S. *Imogen's New Cook.* London: Samuel French, 1898.

Mill, Harriet Taylor. *The Complete Works of Harriet Taylor Mill.* Eds. Jo Ellen Jacobs and Paula Harms. Bloomington: Indiana University Press, 1998.

Miller, Jane Eldridge. *Rebel Women: Feminism, Modernism and the Edwardian Novel.* London: Virago, 1994.

Mitchell, David. *Queen Christabel: A Biography of Christabel Pankhurst.* London: Macdonald & Jane's, 1977.

Mitchell, Sally. *The New Girl: Girls' Culture in England 1880–1915.* New York: Columbia University Press, 1995.

Mitchell, Sally, ed. *Victorian Britain: An Encyclopedia.* London: Routledge, 2011.

Morgan, Margery, ed. *Granville Barker Plays: Two.* London: Methuen, 1994.

Mukherjee, Sumita. 'Herabai Tata and Sophia Duleep Singh: Suffragette Resistances for India and Britain 1910–1920.' *South Asian Resistances in Britain, 1858–1947.* Eds. Rehana Ahmed, and Sumita Mukherjee. London: Continuum, 2012. 106–21.

Mukherjee, Sumita. 'A Short Sketch of Indian Women's Franchise Work.' *Women's Voices: Selections from Nineteenth and Early-Twentieth Century Indian Writing in English.* Eds. Eunice de Souza and Lindsay Pereira. Delhi: Oxford University Press, 2002. 127–34.

Murray, Jessie and H.N. Brailsford. 'The Treatment of the Women's Deputations by the Metropolitan Police. Copy of evidence collected by and forwarded to the Home Office by the Conciliation Committee for Women Suffrage', etc. [Sennett (M.A.) A collection of press cuttings, pamphlets, etc. vol 12.] London: Woman's Press, 1911.

Nelson, Alec. *My Niece*, 1890. LCP, BL, Add MS 53465 I.

Nelson, Carolyn Christensen, ed. *Literature of the Women's Suffrage Campagain in England.* Peterborough: Broadview, 2004.

Nesbit, E. 'The Girton Girl.' *Atalanta: The Victorian Magazine* 8 (1895): 755–59.

Nevinson, Wynne Margaret. *In the Workhouse.* London: International Suffrage Shop, 1911.

Newey, Katherine. 'Ibsen in the English Theatre in the *Fin de Siècle.*' *A Companion to Modern British and Irish Drama 1880–2005.* Ed. Mary Luckhurst. Oxford: Blackwell, 2006. 35–47.

Nietzsche, Friedrich. *Thus Spoke Zarathustra.* Trans. R. J. Hollingdale. New York: Harmonsworth, 1969.

Pankhurst, Christabel. *Correspondence to Elizabeth Robins.* 1906–13. HRC: Robins Box 1, Folder 12 and Box 2, Folder 1.

Pankhurst, Christabel. *The Great Scourge and How to End It.* London: E. Pankhurst, 1913.

Pankhurst, Emmeline. *Correspondence to Elizabeth Robins.* 1906–13. HRC: Robins Box 2, Folder 2.

Pankhurst, Sylvia E. *The Suffrage Movement: An Intimate Account of Persons and Ideals.* 1931. London: Virago, 1988.

Patmore, Coventry. *Poems, Vol. I: The Angel in the House & The Victories of Love.* London: George Bell and Son, 1890.

Paxton, Naomi. *The Methuen Drama Book of Suffrage Plays.* London: Bloomsbury Methuen Drama, 2013.

Peters, Sally. 'Shaw's Life: A Feminist in Spite of Himself.' *The Cambridge Companion to George Bernard Shaw.* Ed. Christopher Innes. Cambridge and New York: Cambridge University Press, 1998. 3–24.

Peters Vogt, Sally. 'Ann and Superman: Type and Archetype.' *George Bernard Shaw's Man and Superman.* Ed. Harold Bloom. New York: Chelsea House, 1987. 105–23.

Pethick-Lawrence, Emmeline. *The Meaning of the Women's Movement.* 1938. London: The Woman's Press, 1977.

Phibbs, L.S. *Jim's Leg.* 1911. *Votes for Women and Other Plays.* Ed. Susan Croft. London: Aurora Metro, 2009. 211–15.

Phillips, William H. *St. John Hankin: Edwardian Mephistopheles.* Cranbury: Associated University Press, 1979.

Pinero, Arthur W. *The Amazons.* Boston: Walter H. Baker, 1895.

Pinero, Arthur W. *Iris.* London: William Heinemann, 1900a.

Pinero, Arthur W. *The Notorious Mrs Ebbsmith.* 1895. London: Oberon Modern Plays, 2014.

Pinero, Arthur W. *The Profligate.* New York: United States Book Company, 1891.

Pinero, Arthur W. *The School Mistress.* Boston: Walter H. Baker, 1894.

Pinero, Arthur W. *The Second Mrs Tanqueray.* 1893. Peterborough: Broadview Editions, 2008.

Pinero, Arthur W. *Sweet Lavender.* Boston: Walter H. Baker, 1893.

Pinero, Arthur W. *The Times.* 1891. 2nd Impression. London: William Heinemann, 1900b.

Postgate, J.P. 'Shall Women Graduate at Cambridge.' *National Review* 10 (1887): 191–201.

Postlewait, Thomas. *Prophet of the New Drama: William Archer and the Ibsen Campaign.* Westport: Greenwood, 1986.

Powell, Kerry. *Acting Wilde: Victorian Sexuality, Theatre, and Oscar Wilde.* Cambridge: Cambridge University Press, 2009.

Powell, Kerry. *The Cambridge Companion to Victorian and Edwardian Theatre.* Cambridge and New York: Cambridge University Press, 2004.

Powell, Kerry. 'New Women, New Plays, and Shaw in the 1890s.' *The Cambridge Companion to George Bernard Shaw*. Ed. Christopher Innes. Cambridge and New York: Cambridge University Press, 1998. 76–100.

Powell, Kerry. *Oscar Wilde and the Theatre of the 1890s*. Cambridge: Cambridge University Press, 1990.

Powell, Kerry. 'Oscar Wilde, Elizabeth Robins, and the Theatre of the Future.' *Modern Drama* 37(1) (1994): 220–237.

Powell, Kerry. *Women and Victorian Theatre*. Cambridge and New York: Cambridge University Press, 1997.

Powell, Kerry, and Peter Raby, eds. *Oscar Wilde in Context*. Cambridge and New York: Cambridge University Press, 2013.

Pugh, Martin. *The Pankhursts*. London: Allen Lane, 2001.

Purvis, June. 'Pugh's book is full of errors.' *Times Higher Education*, 25 January 2002.

Pykett, Lyn. *Engendering Fictions: The English Novel in the Early Twentieth Century*. London: Edward Arnold, 1995.

Quilter, Harry. *Is Marriage A Failure?* 1888. London: Swan Sonnenschein, 1984.

Rainey, Lawrence. 'From the Fallen Woman to the Fallen Typist, 1908–1922.' *English Literature in Transition, 1880–1920* 52(3) (2009): 273–97.

Rappaport, Erika Diane. *Shopping for Pleasure: Women in the Making of London's West End*. Princeton: Princeton University Press, 2000.

Re-Bartlett, Lucy. *Sex and Sanctity*. London: Longmans, 1912.

Recchio, Thomas. 'Elizabeth Gaskell as "A Dramatic Common": Stanley Houghton's Appropriation of Mary Barton in Hindle Wakes.' *The Gaskell Journal* 26 (2012): 88–102.

Reeves, Amber. *Correspondence to Elizabeth Robins*. 1909–10. HRC: Robins Box 1, Folder 6.

Reinhardt, Nancy S. 'New Directions for Feminist Criticism in Theatre and the Related Arts.' *A Feminist Perspective in the Academy: The Difference It Makes*. Eds. Elizabeth Langland and Walter Gove. Chicago and London: University of Chicago Press, 1981. 25–51.

Richardson, Mary R. *Laugh a Defiance*. London: George Weidenfeld & Nicolson, 1953.

Robb, George. 'Eugenics, Spirituality, and Sex Differentiation in Edwardian England: The Case of Frances Swiney.' *Journal of Women's History* 10(3) (1998): 97–117.

Robins, Elizabeth [published anonymously]. *Ancilla's Share: An Indictment of Sex Antagonism*. London: Hutchison, 1924.

Robins, Elizabeth. *Both Sides of the Curtain*. London: William Heinemann, 1940.

Robins, Elizabeth. 'The Coming Woman.' Unpublished manuscript, 1893. Fales Library, NYU, Robins Series 7, Folder 15.

Robins, Elizabeth. *The Convert*. 1908. New York: Feminist Press, 1980.

Robins, Elizabeth. *Correspondence*. 1897–1938. HRC. 2 boxes. MS-3568.

Robins, Elizabeth. *Ibsen & the Actress*. London: Hogarth, 1928.

Robins, Elizabeth. *The Magnetic North*. New York: Frederick A. Stokes, 1904.

Robins, Elizabeth. *My Little Sister* [Novel]. New York: Mead, 1913.

Robins, Elizabeth. *My Little Sister*. 1913. *Sex for Sale: Six Progressive-Era Brothel Dramas*. Ed. Katie N. Johnson. Iowa City: University of Iowa Press, 2015. 107–75.

Robins, Elizabeth. *The Open Question*. London: William Heinemann, 1898.

Robins, Elizabeth. *Raymond and I*. London: Hogarth, 1956.

Robins, Elizabeth. *Theatre and Friendship: Some Henry James Letters*. New York: G.P. Putnam's Sons, 1932.

Robins, Elizabeth. *Votes for Women!*. 1907. *The New Woman and Other Emancipated Woman Plays*. Ed. Jean Chothia. Oxford: Oxford University Press, 1998. 135–210.

Robins, Elizabeth. *Way Stations*. New York: Hodder and Stoughton, 1913.

Robins, Elizabeth. 'Whither and How.' Unpublished manuscript. Fales Library, NYU, MSS 001Box: 143.5, Folder: 1b.

Robins, Elizabeth. *Why?* London: The Women Writer's Suffrage League, 1910.

Robins, Elizabeth. *Woman's Secret*. Letchworth: Garden City, 1907.

Robins, Elizabeth, and William Archer. 'The Mirkwater.' Unpublished manuscript, n.d. [early 1890s]. Fales Library, NYU, MSS 002, Box 43, Folder 2.

Robins, Elizabeth, and Florence Bell. *Alan's Wife*. 1893. *New Woman Plays*. Eds. Linda Fitzsimmons and Viv Gardner. London: Methuen Drama, 1991. 1–25.

Rogers, Maud M. *When the Wheels Run Down*. London: Samuel French, 1899.

Rover, Constance. *Love, Morals and the Feminists*. London: Routledge & Kegan Paul, 1970.

Rowbotham, Sheila. *A New World for Women: Stella Browne – A Socialist Feminist*. London: Pluto, 1977.

Rowold, Katharina. *The Educated Woman: Minds, Bodies and Women's Higher Education in Britain, Germany, and Spain 1865–1914*. London: Routledge, 2010.

Roydon, Maude. 'Votes and Wages: How Women's Suffrage Will Improve the Economic Position of Women.' *NUWSS*. 3rd edition, 1912.

Saleeby, C.W. *Woman and Womanhood: A Search for Principles*. London: Mitchell Kennerly, 1911.

Sanghani, Radhika. 'The Uncomfortable Truth about Racism and the Suffragettes.' *Daily Telegraph*, 6 October 2015.

Scarry, Elaine. *The Body in Pain: The Making and Unmaking of the World*. New York and Oxford: Oxford University Press, 1985.

Schaffer, Talia. *The Forgotten Female Aesthetes: Literary Culture in Late-Victorian England*. Charlottesville: University Press of Virginia, 2000.

Scharlieb, Mary. 'Adolescent Girlhood Under Modern Conditions, with Special Reference to Motherhood.' *The Eugenics Review* 1(3) (1909): 174–83.

Schneer, Jonathan. 'The Pan-African Conference of 1900.' *Black Victorians/ Black Victoriana*. Ed. Gretchen Holbrook Gerzina. New Brunswick: Rutgers University Press, 2003.

Schreiner, Olive. *The Story of an African Farm*. 1883. London: Virago, 1989.

Scullion, Adrienne. *Female Playwrights of the Nineteenth Century*. London: Everyman, 1996.

Sharp, Evelyn. *Correspondence to Elizabeth Robins*. 1907–13. HRC: Robins Box 2, Folder 4.

Sharp, Evelyn. *Rebel Women*. New Edition. London: United Suffragists, 1915.

Shaw, George Bernard. *Correspondence to Elizabeth Robins*. 1906–07. HRC: Shaw Box 44, Folder 3.

Shaw, George Bernard. *Correspondence to Harley Granville Barker*. 1900–08. HRC: Shaw Box 37, Folder 2.

Shaw, George Bernard. *Fanny's First Play*. 1911.

Shaw, George Bernard. *Fanny's First Play. 1911. Misalliance, The Dark Lady of the Sonnets and Fanny's First Play. With a Treatise on Parents and Children*. London: Constable and Company. 1914. 149–234.

Shaw, George Bernard. *Getting Married. 1908. Getting Married and Press Cuttings*. London: Penguin, 1986a. 10–222.

Shaw, George Bernard. *Heartbreak House* and *Misalliance. 1919.* 1910. New York: Bantam, 1995.

Shaw, George Bernard. *Man and Superman*. 1903. London: Penguin, 1946a.

Shaw, George Bernard. *Mrs Warren's Profession*. 1894. *Plays Unpleasant*. London: Penguin, 1946b.

Shaw, George Bernard. *The Philanderer*. Print proofs, 1898. HRC: Box 22 Folder 11.

Shaw, George Bernard. *The Philanderer*. Peterborough: Broadview Editions, 2015.

Shaw, George Bernard. *Prefaces by Bernard Shaw*. London: Constable, 1934.

Shaw, George Bernard. *Press Cuttings. 1909. Getting Married and Press Cuttings*. London: Penguin, 1986b. 223–69.

Shepherd-Barr, Kirsten. *Ibsen and Early Modernist Theatre, 1890–1900*. Westport: Greenwood, 1997.

Shepherd-Barr, Kirsten. *Theatre and Evolution from Ibsen to Beckett*. New York: Columbia University Press, 2015.

Showalter, Elaine. *The Female Malady: Women, Madness and English Culture, 1830–1980*. London: Virago, 1987.

Showalter, Elaine. *A Literature of Their Own: British Women Novelists from Brontë to Lessing*. London: Virago, 1982.

Showalter, Elaine. *Sexual Anarchy: Gender and Culture at the Fin de Siècle*. London: Virago, 1992.

Sidgwick, Eleanor Mildred. 'Health Statistics of Women Students of Cambridge and Oxford and of Their Sisters.' Printed at the University Press, 1890.

Sinclair, William. *On Gonorrhoeal Infection in Women.* London; Manchester: H. K. Lewis, 1888.

Smith-Rosenberg, Carroll. 'Discourses of Sexuality and Subjectivity: The New Woman, 1870–1936.' *Hidden from History.* Ed. Sheila Rowbotham. New York: NAL, 1989.

Snowdon, Ethel. *The Feminist Movement.* London: Collins, 1911.

Solnit, Rebecca. '"Hope is an Embrace of the Unknown": Rebecca Solnit on Living in Dark Times.' *The Guardian*, 15 July 2016.

Solnit, Rebecca. 'Protest and Persist: Why Giving Up Hope is Not an Option.' *The Guardian*, 13 March 2017.

Sowerby, Githa. *Rutherford and Son.* 1912. *New Woman Plays.* Eds. Linda Fitzsimmons and Viv Gardner. London: Methuen Drama, 1991. 133–89.

Spencer, Herbert. *An Epitome of the Synthetic Philosophy.* New York: Appleton, 1889.

Spencer, Herbert. *A System of Synthetic Philosophy Vol VI: The Principles of Sociology.* 3rd edition, Volume I. New York: D. Appleton, 1896.

Spencer, Herbert. *A System of Synthetic Philosophy Vol VIII: The Principles of Sociology.* Volume III. New York: D. Appleton, 1897.

Spender, Dale, and Carole Hayman, eds. *How the Vote Was Won and Other Suffrage Plays.* London: Methuen, 1985.

Sprague, Robert. 'Education and Race Suicide.' *The Journal of Heredity: A Monthly Publication Devoted to Plant Breeding, Animal Breeding and Eugenics.* I(4) (1915): 158–62.

Stead, W.T. *The Maiden Tribute of Modern Babylon.* Lambertville, New Jersey: True Bill, 1885.

Steinbach, Susie. *Women in England 1760–1914: A Social History.* London: Weidenfeld & Nicolson, 2004.

Stepan, Nancy. *The Idea of Race in Science: Great Britain 1800–1960.* Hamden: Archon Books, 1982.

Stephen, Barbara. *Emily Davies and Girton College.* London: Constable, 1927.

Stephens, Judith L. 'Gender Ideology and Dramatic Convention in Progressive Era Plays, 1890–1920.' *Performing Feminisms: Feminist Critical Theory and Theatre.* Ed. Sue-Ellen Case. Baltimore: Johns Hopkins University Press, 1990.

Stetz, Margaret D. 'Oscar Wilde and the New Woman.' *Oscar Wilde in Context.* Eds. Kerry Powell and Peter Raby. Cambridge and New York: Cambridge University Press, 2013. 230–41.

Stoler, Ann Laura. *Carnal Knowledge and Imperial Power: Race and the Intimate in Colonial Rule.* Berkeley: University of California Press, 2002.

Stopes, Marie. *Married Love.* New York: Eugenics Publishing, 1931.

Stowell, Sheila. 'Drama as a Trade: Cicely Hamilton's Diana of Dobsons.' *The New Woman and her Sisters 1850–1914.* Eds. Viv Gardner and Susan Rutherford. New York: Harvester Wheatsheaf, 1992a. 177–88.

Stowell, Sheila. *A Stage of Their Own: Feminist Playwrights of the Suffrage Era.* Manchester University Press, 1992b.

Stowell, Sheila. 'Suffrage Critics and Political Action.' *The Edwardian Theatre: Essays on Performance and the Stage.* Eds. Michael R. Booth and Joel H. Kaplan. Cambridge: Cambridge University Press, 1996. 166–84.

Strachey, Ray. *'The Cause': A Short History of the Women's Movement in Great Britain.* London: G. Bell and Sons, 1928.

Strachey, Ray. *Millicent Garrett Fawcett.* London: J. Murray, 1931.

Sutherland, Gillian. *In Search of the New Woman: Middle-Class Women and Work in Britain 1870–1914.* Cambridge: Cambridge University Press, 2015.

Swiney, Frances. *The Awakening of Women or Women's Part in Evolution.* 1899. London: William Reeves, 1908.

Swiney, Frances. *The Bar of Isis.* London: Open Road, 1907.

Swiney, Frances. 'The Evolution of the Male.' *Westminster Review* 163 (1905): 454.

Syrett, Netta. *The Finding of Nancy.* 1902. *The Broadview Anthology of Nineteenth-Century British Performance.* Ed. Tracy C. Davis. Peterborough: Broadview, 2012. 643–84.

Syrett, Netta. *Might is Right,* 1909. LCP, BL, Add MS 65869 N.

Syrett, Netta. *Portrait of a Rebel.* London: Geoffrey Bles, 1929.

Szreter, Simon. *Fertility, Class and Gender in Britain, 1860–1940.* Cambridge and New York: Cambridge University Press, 1996.

Thompson, F.M.L. *The Rise of Respectable Society: A Social History of Britain, 1830–1900.* London: Fontana, 1988.

Thompson, Tierl, ed. *Dear Girl: The Diaries and Letters of Two Working Women (1897–1917).* London: Women's Press, 1987.

Thorpe, Vanessa, and Alec Marsh. 'Diary Reveals Lesbian Love Trysts of Suffragette Leaders.' *The Guardian* 11 June 2000. www.theguardian.com/uk/2000/jun/11/vanessathorpe.theobserver. Accessed 6 April 2018.

Tickner, Lisa. *The Spectacle of Women: Imagery of the Suffrage Campaign 1907–14.* London: Chatto & Windus, 1987.

Tilghman, Carolyn. 'Staging Suffrage: Women, Politics, and the Edwardian Theater.' *Comparative Drama* 45(4) (2011): 339–60.

Tilly, Louise A., Joan W. Scott and Miriam Cohen. 'Women's Work and European Fertility Patterns.' *The Journal of Interdisciplinary History* 6(3) (1976): 447–76.

Townsend, Joanna. 'Elizabeth Robins: Hysteria, Politics and Performance.' *Women, Theatre and Performance: New Histories, New Historiographies.* Eds. Maggie B. Gale and Viv Gardner. Manchester and New York: Manchester University Press, 2000. 102–20.

Trudgill, Eric. *Madonnas and Magdalens: The Origins and Development of Victorian Sexual Attitudes.* London: Heinemann, 1976.

Van Laan, Thomas F. 'Ibsen and Nietzsche.' *Scandinavian Studies* 78(3) (2006): 255–302.

Vaughan, Gertrude. *The Woman with the Pack*. London: W. J. Ham-Smith, 1912.

Vicinus, Martha. 'Distance and Desire: English Boarding School Friendships, 1870–1920.' *Not a Passing Phase: Reclaiming Lesbians in History 1840–1985*. Eds. Martin Bauml Duberman, Martha Vicinus and George Chauncey Jr. London: Women's Press, 1989. 212–29.

Vicinus, Martha. *Independent Women: Work and Community for Single Women, 1850–1920*. Chicago and London: University of Chicago Press, 1985.

Vicinus, Martha. *Suffer and Be Still; Women in the Victorian Age*. Bloomington: Indiana University Press, 1972.

Vicinus, Martha. *A Widening Sphere: Changing Roles of Victorian Women*. Bloomington: Indiana University Press, 1977.

Vickery, Amanda. 'Golden Age to Separate Spheres? A Review of the Categories and Chronology of English Women's History.' *The Historical Journal* 36(2) (1993): 383–414.

Votieri, Adelene. *That Charming Mrs Spencer*, 1897. LCP, BL, Add MS 53645 E.

Walby, S. *Theorizing Patriarchy*. Oxford: Blackwell, 1990.

Walkowitz, Judith R. *City of Dreadful Delight: Narratives of Sexual Danger in Late-Victorian London*. Chicago: University of Chicago Press, 1992.

Walkowitz, Judith R. *Prostitution and Victorian Society: Women, Class and the State*. Cambridge and New York: Cambridge University Press, 1980.

Watson, Barbara Bellow. *A Shavian Guide to the Intelligent Woman*. London: Chatto & Windus, 1964.

Webb, Beatrice. *My Apprenticeship*. 1926. New York: Longmans, Green, 1950.

Weeks, Jeffrey. *Sex, Politics and Society: The Regulation of Sexuality Since 1800*. London: Longman, 1981.

Weintraub, Rodelle, ed. *Fabian Feminist: Bernard Shaw and Woman*. University Park: Pennsylvania State University Press, 1977.

Ward, Lester. *Pure Sociology*. New York: Macmillan, 1903.

Warden, Gertrude and Wilton Jones. *Woman's Proper Place*. London: Samuel French, 1896.

Wentworth, Vera. *An Allegory*. London: Actresses' Franchise League, 1913.

West, Shearer, ed. *The Victorians and Race*. Brookfield: Scolar, 1996.

Westermarck, Edward. *The History of Human Marriage*. New York: Macmillan, 1894.

Whitebrook, Peter. *William Archer*. London: Methuen, 1993.

Whitelaw, Liz. *The Life and Rebellious Times of Cicely Hamilton*. London: Women's Press, 1990.

Wilberforce, Octavia. *Backsettown & Elizabeth Robins*. Published for private circulation by Octavia Wilberforce, 1952.

Wilde, Oscar. *Lady Windermere's Fan: A Play about a Good Woman*. 1892. *The Importance of Being Earnest and Other Plays*. Ed. Peter Raby. Oxford and New York: Oxford University Press, 2008a. 1–59.

Wilde, Oscar. *A Woman of No Importance*. 1893. *The Importance of Being Earnest and Other Plays*. Ed. Peter Raby. Oxford and New York: Oxford University Press, 2008b. 93–157.

Wiley, Catherine. 'The Matter with Manners: The New Woman and the Problem Play.' *Women in Theatre*. Ed. James Redmond. Cambridge: Cambridge University Press, 1989.

Wiley, Catherine. 'Staging Infanticide: The Refusal of Representation in Elizabeth Robins's Alan's Wife.' *Theatre Journal* 42(4) (1990): 432–46.

Williams, A.R. *The Street. Three New Plays*. 2nd edition. London: T. Werner Laurie, n.d.

Wilson, A.E. *Edwardian Theatre*. London: Arthur Barker, 1951.

Wilson, Ann. 'Shutting Out Mother: Vivie Warren as the New Woman.' *Shaw and Feminisms: On Stage and Off*. Eds. D.A. Hadfield and Jean Reynolds. Gainesville: University Press of Florida, 2013. 56–72.

Wolff, Janet. 'The Culture of Separate Spheres: The Role of Culture in Nineteenth-Century Public and Private Life.' *The Culture of Capital: Art, Power and the Nineteenth-Century Middle Class*. Eds. Janet Wolff and John Seed. Manchester: Manchester University Press, 1988. 117–34.

Woodfield, James. *English Theatre in Transition 1881–1914*. London: Croom Helm, 1984.

Woodworth, Christine. 'Luggage, Lodgings, and Landladies: The Practicalities for Actresses on the British Provincial Circuits in the Late Nineteenth and Early Twentieth Centuries.' *Theatre Symposium* 22 (2014): 22–32.

Wright, Almroth. *The Unexpurgated Case Against Woman's Suffrage*. London: Constable, 1913.

Young, Margaret. *Honesty: A Cottage Flower*, 1897. LCP, BL, Add MS 53645 T.

Young, Margaret. *Self-Supporting: A Duologue for Two Female Characters*. London: Samuel French, 1914.

Zackodnik, Teresa, 'Ida B. Wells and "American Atrocities" in Britain.' *Women's Studies International Forum* 28(4) (2005): 259–73.

Zangwill, Israel. *The Old Maid's Club*. London: Heinemann, 1892.

Zangwill, Israel. *Six Persons*. London: Samuel French, 1893.

INDEX